AF557795

FAMILY
AND
DHANDA

'I applaud Srinath for having brought a key issue of corporate India front and centre. Despite clear empirical evidence that this is one of the main reasons why many of the old corporate houses have fallen by the wayside in the last half-century, it is surprising that this topic doesn't get more attention. Though family enterprises have been playing a crucial role, unlike the Western world, Indian business families have historically struggled with separating ownership from management, with the exception of a VERY few.

'There are some uniquely Asian (versus Anglo-Saxon) characteristics that drive this, including a belief that no one can quite replace the founder, respect for age, the founder is always right, the right combination of passion and skills is impossible to replicate, there's no hurry, etc. As a result, in recent years, there have been a number of situations where poor succession planning has precipitated families splitting, some amicably, most less so. This has repercussions across all stakeholders.

'Srinath has, in his usual eloquent way, captured the essence with the phrase "succession planning is a process, not an event".'

—Ajay Nanavati

Chairman, Alicon Castalloy Ltd; Former Managing Director, 3M India Ltd; Former Chairman, Syndicate Bank

'This book offers a deeply insightful exploration of this often overlooked, crucial topic, addressing the complexities and challenges that family businesses and boards usually fail to notice. With a sharp focus on the importance of proactive succession planning, Srinath brilliantly navigates the risks of intergenerational conflicts and provides a clear, practical roadmap with real-world examples showcased without their identities, guiding business families towards balancing family unity and modern-day governance, and driving sustainable future-focused business growth. A must-read for both established family businesses and aspiring young leaders looking to secure their legacy and future success. *Family and Dhanda* is a wake-up call for family businesses and boards on urgency and thoughts on succession planning.'

—Dr Anil K. Khandelwal

Former Chairman and Managing Director, Bank of Baroda; Author; Thought Leader

'This is a very important book on a very important issue that is coming to gain prominence in Indian business, particularly in the future-proofing and sustainability of corporations. Succession planning is more than just choosing the right biological inheritor for a family-run enterprise. In an increasingly complex environment, it calls for optimal triangulation of enlightened ownership, professional management, and the nurturing of institutions and individuals. This book deftly captures the challenges and opportunities of succession planning.'

—Ashok Malik

Partner, The Asia Group, and Chair of its India practice

'Succession planning is crucial for Indian business families as it ensures the seamless transition of leadership and ownership across generations. This process safeguards the legacy and continuity of the business while addressing complex family dynamics and governance issues. However, challenges such as managing family conflicts, ensuring fair successor selection and balancing interests can complicate the transition process. *Family and Dhanda* is a comprehensive guide on effective succession planning, which fosters stability, growth and long-term success in a family business, making it indispensable for the sustainability of family-owned enterprises.'

—Gopal Srinivasan

Chairman and Managing Director, TVS Capital Funds

'Family businesses are integral to India's socio-economic landscape, combining tradition with modern business practices. The changing market dynamics pose challenges to their success. With effective succession planning, these businesses can sustain growth and adapt to changes in the market. This book is a comprehensive guide on succession planning and family business, and would be a rich resource for the readers.'

—Harivansh Singh

Deputy Chairman, Rajya Sabha

'This topic was waiting to be written.'

—Harsh Mariwala

Founder & Chairman, Marico Limited

'Succession planning is a critical aspect of ensuring the longevity and sustainability of any organization. The goal is to ensure that the business not only survives but thrives. At Dabur, we were amongst the first business families in India to realize this. The promoter family—after successfully running the business for four generations—took the strategic decision to separate ownership from management, a move that has set us apart from many family-owned businesses in India and played a significant part in Dabur's success story. It is today the template on which the Burman family operates all its personal ventures, with the family providing a long-term vision for the company and a professional team managing the day-to-day show efficiently.

'By fostering a culture of trust and collaboration, family businesses can navigate the succession process successfully and continue to grow and prosper for generations to come, which Srinath commendably describes in his book.'

—Mohit Burman
Chairman, Dabur India, and
a fifth-generation member of the Burman family

'Many companies have failed for lack of succession planning and yet it remains more on paper and driven by emotions. Srinath has rightfully brought the focus on the most important aspect of creating a sustainable institution.'

—Nilesh Shah
Group President & Managing Director, Kotak Mahindra AMC

'Succession planning is one of the most important but challenging tasks for any business. It is an opportunity to either create or destroy value. This book highlights how a structured process, commitment to the founder's values, and vision and discussions amongst stakeholders can lead to superior outcomes. *Family and Dhanda* is a must-read for those who want to build enduring institutions in the volatile and unpredictable world of today. It provides invaluable insights for families to thrive across generations as they expand.'

—Puneet Yadu Dalmia
Managing Director, Dalmia Bharat Group

'A candid book on the challenges and complexities of passing the torch in family businesses. Covering every aspect from must-have family conversations, family differences, leadership transitions and grooming the successors to governance frameworks, this book is an invaluable resource for business families, executives and management students looking to balance legacy with innovation for their succession planning. A thoughtful and comprehensive guide to navigating succession planning with both respect for tradition and an eye on the future, *Family and Dhanda* is essential reading for business families at any stage of their journey.'

—Dr Rajiv Kumar
Chairman, Pahle India; Former Vice Chairman, NITI Aayog

'The founding figure defines an organization's legacy as Srinath Sridharan has rightly pointed out in this important read for family businesses. The younger family members must also understand the importance and long-term benefit of preserving core values. The emphasis on legacy, however, must go beyond the founding figure; the legacy must keep pace with the times, and this is only possible with the right levels of mentoring and succession planning. *Family and Dhanda* gives valuable lessons in this regard and this comprehensive view makes it an important read for all members of a family-owned business—whether they are a part of the business or not.'

—Sunil Kant Munjal
Chairman, Hero Enterprise

A to Z of
Succession Planning
for
Founders *and* Successors

Srinath Sridharan

RUPA

Published by
Rupa Publications India Pvt. Ltd 2025
7/16, Ansari Road, Daryaganj
New Delhi 110002

Sales centres:
Bengaluru Chennai Hyderabad
Jaipur Kathmandu Kolkata
Mumbai Prayagraj

The views and opinions expressed in this book are the author's own and the facts are as reported by him, which have been verified to the extent possible, and the publishers are not in any way liable for the same. The information contained in this book is not intended as a substitute for any rules, laws or regulations that govern the processes of estate or tax planning, or corporate governance norms, etc. Instead, readers should consult succession planning advisors on any matter relating to their businesses. The publisher has used its best endeavours to ensure that URLs for external websites referred to in this book are correct and active at the time of going to press. However, the publisher has no responsibility for the websites and can make no guarantee that a site will remain live or that the content is or will remain appropriate.

P-ISBN: 978-93-6156-687-5
E-ISBN: 978-93-6156-961-6

First impression 2025

10 9 8 7 6 5 4 3 2 1

Printed in India

To
millions of Indian businesses
and
business families
for making our economy and society thrive,
be it single-person nano business,
MSMEs, SMEs,
promoter-led conglomerates,
multi-generational business families,
or
new-age startups

and

to my existential pillars
Kalyani, Ninupta and Sannuta

CONTENTS

PREFACE

In writing this book, I was inspired by my own journey of becoming a relevant and worthy successor, even if as a non-business-family professional. Reflecting on my experiences, I have aimed to offer a comprehensive guide tailored to the unique challenges faced by Indian business families in succession planning.

Throughout my career, I continually improved my skill sets to be seen as a potential successor in a family business ecosystem. I embraced a digital-first mindset to lead businesses that require such an edge and employed reverse mentoring to equip myself to lead Gen Z and millennials. For example, I have not used a computer or laptop for the past 10 years and have moved to an entirely mobile-first, followed by mobile-only behaviour. These experiences and learnings are what I picked up from working with younger cohorts.

As a business leader, I have seen the effective leadership transition from an old-school command-hierarchy structure to the modern impact-influence leadership style. I realized that, in the corporate hierarchy, the one who is expected to work using their wisdom or knowledge ends up being assigned the fastest processor-computing device, and the one who works with large data to convert it into meaningful information gets the slowest, as they are lower in that organizational hierarchy. It is time to rethink human resources in view of this data, information, knowledge, wisdom or the DIKW pyramid and its importance in decision-making. I thank my reverse mentors for these nuggets.

Succession planning is a critical topic in the context of Indian business families and the sustainability of businesses over generations. Despite the prevalence of family-owned enterprises in India, fewer than one-fifth actively engage in succession planning until it is too late. This book addresses this gap by offering a resource specifically tailored to the nuances of Indian business families.

I realized the need for a comprehensive guide while noticing the lack of literature that addresses the unique aspects of succession planning in the Indian context. This realization, coupled with my extensive professional work, motivated me to write this book. One key thread often overlooked in Indian business families is the emphasis on legacy beyond the founding figure, which includes succession planning, grooming younger family members, and preserving core values.

Navigating succession planning requires facing uncomfortable discussions, especially with family principals at the helm. Many families find it easier to discuss succession with the younger generation rather than their older counterparts. However, these conversations cannot be perpetually deferred. In a rapidly evolving world, procrastination is a luxury we can no longer afford. While many business leaders advocate for corporate governance and professionalism, there's often a gap in planning for their own succession, revealing a significant incongruity between words and actions.

Drawing from my own experience, I have attempted to bridge the gap in this book by offering a meticulous roadmap that navigates through the cultural, familial and business dimensions unique to Indian business families. The book provides valuable perspectives and strategies relevant to businesses of all sizes, making it an essential resource for any business with promoters.

My aim is to present complex topics in a simple and accessible manner, using jargon only when necessary. At times, this book may be provocative and uncomfortable, but that is not its primary intent. Rather, it aims to pose critical questions for Indian business families, encouraging them to champion their family members and fulfil their aspirations.

I have seen numerous succession planning projects falter due to the misconception that they can be replicated from other families or executed with a cookie-cutter approach. Such shortcuts often lead to lost valuations and missed opportunities. Each family faces unique challenges, but the necessity to think differently and take bold strides forward is a common thread. Succession planning, therefore, is a complex and significant effort that requires careful consideration of each family's unique dynamics, values and aspirations.

This book aspires to be a valuable companion for families navigating the complexities of succession planning and fostering a legacy that withstands the test of time. In short, I would like you to be successful in your own family business journey—that is my aim.

OPEN LETTER TO THE HEAD OF THE BUSINESS FAMILY

Whether you are the head of your family business or a successor to one, whether your business is small-sized, medium or large, it does not matter. The reality is that running a family business is like dancing to a unique tune. Nowadays, it comes with a bunch of worries that are different from the past. The first big concern is about keeping up with all the new technology. Things change so fast that there is a constant fear of falling behind and losing relevance. Another worry is about the family sticking together. Sometimes, family members have different ideas about what they want, which can cause arguments or even split the family apart. It is like trying to balance everyone's goals and keep everyone happy, which is not easy.

Additionally, ideas about life and values can also cause issues. With the changing world, family members might have different opinions, which can lead to disagreements. Not only this, people in the family also have their own dreams and plans. Making sure the business grows while also helping each family member achieve their goals is tricky. It is like trying to balance what is good for the business with what each person wants. All in all, keeping the family united in the face of these concerns becomes a big challenge.

Looking into the future, there is also this big worry about the family name and what it represents. It is not just about money, it is about passing down values and a strong foundation. The fear is that something might happen, either from within the family or outside, that could damage the family's reputation.

Being in charge of a family business in today's world is not easy. You are dealing with a list of worries—from keeping up with technology to managing family differences and ensuring the family name stays strong and respected. It is a complex job that requires not just business skills but also an understanding of how the institution of 'family' and the world are changing. And accordingly, deciding who takes over is a mixture of honouring tradition and serious planning for the future.

Think about this—in a world that is always changing, is your plan ready for unexpected challenges? Is your plan just a tradition, or is it flexible enough for the changing business world? Look beyond family members and ask yourself—are you spotting and supporting talent within your company, creating a culture that goes beyond family connections?

As you look ahead, challenge the usual way of doing things. Choosing the next leader shouldn't just be a tradition; it should be based on merit and looking ahead. Is your successor picked for their ability to lead in a digital age, where being adaptable and knowing technology is crucial?

Reflect on your leadership impact. Does your successor represent your family business values, or is there room for a change that fits the evolving world? Succession is not only about passing the baton but also about a chance to introduce new ideas into the company.

Think about the future of your business beyond your time. Does your plan deal with risks? Have you made sure unexpected issues will not harm what you have built? Look at your plan as if you are an outsider, making sure it can handle the challenges of a changing world.

In choosing who comes after you, break away from what is usual. Question traditional expectations about age and gender roles. Having a mix of varied experiences and points of view can spark new ideas that push your family business into new territories.

As the keeper of your family business story, your job is to think about the future and not only the past. You need to create leaders who can adapt and guide the business through tough times.

In the planning for what comes next, forget about what is expected. Challenge yourself, think deeply and imagine a different future. Passing on the business isn't just a handover—it is a story that connects the past, present and future. The legacy you leave isn't set in stone; it is written in the choices you make today for the leaders of tomorrow.

This book should help you introspect on these and more. All within a safe private zone.

INTRODUCTION

This book explores the intricacies of succession planning within the context of Indian business families, shedding light on critical success factors, common challenges and the pervasive influence of family politics.

Family businesses play a crucial role in the Indian economy, contributing significantly to its growth and resilience. Their unique blend of risk appetite, bolstered by promoter capital, and their ability to raise growth capital positions them as key drivers of economic expansion. The intricate dynamics within business families, encompassing their risk-taking spirit, financial acumen and commitment to long-term sustainability, make them pivotal contributors to India's corporate landscape. Discussing family businesses is not just a conversation about corporate entities, it is an exploration of the finer nuances that weaves together risk, capital and legacy, shaping the very fabric of the Indian economy.

Family businesses hold a significant role in India, constituting two-thirds of publicly traded companies and over 80 per cent of private firms.[*] In parts, family businesses exhibit more innovation and higher performance than institutionally held professionally-run counterparts.[**] This stems from their unique strengths, allowing owners, who are also managers, to make quick decisions without bureaucratic layers. Additionally, they resist short-term profitability pressures, enabling long-term innovation investments.

In India, family companies establish most businesses. Financial modernization and industrial development offer growth opportunities,

---

*Bakhru, Pallavi, 'Challenges to Succession Planning in Indian Family Businesses', *Grant Thornton*, 16 March 2023, https://tinyurl.com/3t2stbj7. Accessed on 22 November 2024.

**Kammerlander, Nadine, and Marc van Essen, 'Research: Family Firms Are More Innovative than Other Companies', *Harvard Business Review*, 25 January 2017, https://tinyurl.com/5933pr28. Accessed on 22 November 2024.

leading some to conserve resources while others take an enterprising approach. Families play a crucial role in their success. Over the past three decades, especially after the economic liberalization of the early 1990s, India has seen numerous professionally run businesses surviving through management-style shifts, professional integrations and an effective blend of ownership and executive roles. Successful family businesses thrive by choosing the right sectors and focusing on quality products at affordable prices, irrespective of government connections.

Perceived as having traditional mindsets, some family businesses, however, embrace contemporary and forward thinking. Progressive family businesses empower non-family professionals, encourage innovation and contribute to societal issues beyond tax obligations. These families, due to their open and progressive approach, follow good governance practices, maintain transparency, and attract investors and corporate clients. Conversely, families with authoritarian cultures resist external perspectives, risking conflict and hindering succession planning, leading to challenges in scaling and surviving in a fast-changing economy.

Micro, small and medium enterprises, from local stores to sophisticated enterprises, dominate family-business narratives, requiring policy support and funding. In today's competitive landscape, family businesses face challenges not only from established entities but also from niche start-ups. The influence of millennial consumers, largely digital natives, prompts a constant need for adaptation and realignment to succeed in such an ecosystem.

A business family encompasses not only those engaged in traditional corporate enterprises but also families of professionals such as doctors, lawyers and chartered accountants who operate their independent practices or firms. In this broader definition, the term includes families where the enterprise value is derived from how these professional practices are managed, whether on an individual basis or as institutional entities. The dynamics of succession planning, governance and continuity are relevant not only to corporate businesses but also to these professional practices, emphasizing the broad landscape of family-led enterprises across various professions and sectors.

Succession planning, in essence, is the art of seamlessly passing the leadership baton while safeguarding the core values, ethos and prosperity of a family business. It is a delicate ballet between tradition and innovation, family bonds and professional acumen, where the intricate steps of preparation and foresight are crucial for a graceful transition.

Whether you are at the helm of a seasoned business empire, navigating the complexities of generational transitions, or a fledgling scion seeking to comprehend the responsibilities that come with a family legacy, this book is designed with you in mind. This book is not only for established business families but also for start-up founders navigating the dynamic landscape of entrepreneurship. As first-generation entrepreneurs, they are laying the foundation for their ventures, striving to scale their entities and make a mark in their respective industries.

FROM LIBERALIZATION TO DIGITAL START-UPS: JOURNEY OF THE INDIAN BUSINESS FAMILY

The winds of change that swept through India in 1991 with economic liberalization brought a seismic shift in the business landscape. For many venerable business families that had thrived under the protective umbrella of the License Raj, this period marked not just a transformation but a challenge to their very existence.

In the era of License Raj, businesses held sway over markets, and consumers had limited choices. The shift to a consumption-based economy, however, altered this dynamic. Suddenly, consumers were bestowed with the power of choice, and markets became fiercely competitive. This transition proved to be a litmus test for many business families that had built their fortunes on the foundations of a controlled market.

The harsh reality was that some families, once titans in their industries, were unable to adapt to the winds of change. Their erstwhile success in a regulated market didn't necessarily translate to survival in an open, competitive economy. The mantra of 'produce, and the market will accept' was replaced by a more daunting reality—innovate and cater to consumer preferences or risk obsolescence.

What are the lessons that emerge from this narrative of evolution or extinction? First, adaptability is paramount. The ability to pivot from a protected market to one where consumer choices reign supreme requires a nimble mindset. Business families need to embrace change, not resist it, and continually assess their relevance in an ever-evolving market.

Second, the importance of consumer-centricity cannot be overstated. The businesses that weathered the storm understood the pulse of the new-age consumer. They invested in understanding changing preferences, adapting product lines and embracing innovation to meet the demands of a more discerning audience.

Third, diversification emerged as a survival strategy. Families that expanded their portfolios, ventured into new sectors and explored untapped markets found a lifeline. Relying solely on past successes or a single business vertical proved to be a risky proposition.

Lastly, the shift brought to the forefront the significance of professional management. Many successful business families recognized that the transition required a blend of family legacy and professional expertise. Those who seamlessly integrated external talent with family values found a winning formula.

In essence, the post-liberalization era was a wake-up call for business families in India. It was a period of reckoning, forcing them to evolve or face extinction. The key takeaway is clear—in the ever-changing business landscape, survival demands not just resilience but a proactive approach to change. For those willing to learn, adapt and innovate, the story continues. For others, it stands as a poignant reminder that for running a successful business, evolution is not an option; it is a necessity.

The entrepreneurial landscape in India has undergone a radical transformation with the advent of start-ups. A new breed of promoters, often dubbed first-generation business families, has emerged, rewriting the rules of success and wealth creation. These trailblazers, hailing from diverse backgrounds, have not only built empires for themselves but have also become architects of prosperity for their employees and investors.

In the traditional narrative, business families were often associated with legacy, continuity and inherited wealth. However, the rise of start-ups has introduced a dynamic shift. These new-age promoters, driven by innovation, risk-taking and a relentless pursuit of their vision, are shaping a narrative where the concept of a business family is evolving rapidly.

One defining feature of these first-generation entrepreneurs is their ability to leverage technology and adapt swiftly to changing market dynamics. Their ventures, rooted in radical ideas, have not only created substantial wealth but have also become engines of job creation, fostering a sense of community and shared success.

The impact goes beyond individual wealth creation. The ecosystem has cultivated a culture of ownership and participation, turning employees into stakeholders through stock options and incentive programmes. This democratization of wealth distribution challenges the traditional hierarchical structures seen in conventional business families.

Moreover, the success of these start-ups has attracted a new breed of investors, both domestic and international, contributing to the financial ecosystem's diversification. It signifies a departure from the era where family wealth was primarily sustained through inherited businesses. Now, wealth creation is increasingly dynamic, with new opportunities and risks.

However, this paradigm shift does not diminish the relevance of traditional business families. Instead, it opens avenues for collaboration and coexistence. The learnings from culture—agility, adaptability and embracing change—can infuse vitality into established business families, ensuring they remain competitive in an ever-evolving marketplace. As these first-generation business families navigate the complexities of scaling their ventures, they lay the foundation for a transformed concept of family businesses. The emphasis is shifting from maintaining existing enterprises to creating new ones, fostering a culture of entrepreneurship within the family.

The coexistence of traditional business families and first-generation entrepreneurial founders is becoming increasingly crucial. Recognizing that fortunes don't guarantee continuity by default, but demand sustained effort and hard work, is a shared realization. As first-generation entrepreneurs carve their paths, business families are learning to embrace their innovative spirit, recognizing the potential for cross-pollination of ideas and methodologies. Simultaneously, the younger scions of established business families, inspired by the dynamic culture, may venture beyond the familiar confines of the family enterprise.

This convergence signifies not only a blending of old and new but also an acknowledgement that success stems from a continuous process of adaptation and learning. The future of business families lies in a harmonious synthesis of tradition and innovation, where the spirit of entrepreneurship bridges generational and conceptual divides.

Basically, the rise of new-age promoters through start-ups is reshaping the landscape of family businesses in India. The infusion of fresh ideas, technology-driven approaches and inclusive wealth creation are challenging the conventional notions of family businesses. It heralds an era where entrepreneurship is not just an individual endeavour but a shared journey, transforming the very essence of what it means to be a business family in the future.

In this book, we embark on a comprehensive journey through the intricate world of succession planning, tailored specifically for Indian business families. The structure of the book is meticulously designed to cover a wide array of topics and themes, each critical to understanding and effectively implementing succession planning in the unique cultural and business landscape of India.

We begin by setting the stage, exploring the fundamental importance of succession planning, and its critical role in ensuring the longevity and prosperity of family enterprises. This introductory section delves into the pressing need for Indian business families to prioritize succession planning, given the high prevalence of family-owned businesses and the alarming statistics that fewer than one-fifth of these businesses actively engage in succession planning until it is too late. Through this exploration, we underscore the urgency of this practice and the risks associated with procrastination.

The subsequent sections dive deep into the multifaceted challenges and considerations specific to Indian business families. We address the complex interplay of family politics, gender dynamics and generational differences that often complicate succession planning. By examining these dynamics, we provide readers with a nuanced understanding of the interpersonal and cultural factors that must be navigated to achieve a successful transition of leadership.

A significant part of the book is dedicated to practical strategies and best practices for grooming the next generation of leaders. This includes insights into how family members can prepare themselves to be worthy successors, much like my own journey of continuous skill enhancement and embracing a digital-first mindset. These strategies equip readers with actionable steps to cultivate leadership qualities within their families.

We explore the necessity of aligning succession plans with the overall strategic goals of the business and the core values of the family. This alignment ensures that the succession process supports long-term growth and sustainability while preserving the family's legacy and cultural ethos. Through real-world examples and case studies, albeit with maintained confidentiality to respect the privacy of the families involved, we illustrate how these principles have been successfully applied in various contexts.

Moreover, this book brings many nuances and practical examples not only for effective succession planning but also to address the critical skills needed for a successful transition by the scions of business families. We delve into essential competencies, such as strategic vision, leadership and adaptability, which are crucial for the next generation to lead effectively in a rapidly changing business environment.

Throughout the book, we tackle the often-overlooked aspects of succession planning, such as the emotional and psychological dimensions. We discuss how to facilitate open and honest conversations within the family, addressing fears, aspirations and potential conflicts. By fostering an environment of transparency and trust, families can navigate the succession process more smoothly and collaboratively.

We also delve into the practicalities of succession planning, including legal, financial and governance frameworks that support a seamless transition. This involves exploring different succession models, the role of external advisors and the importance of setting up robust governance structures to manage the succession process effectively. We provide detailed guidance on implementing these frameworks, ensuring that the technical aspects of succession planning are as robust as the interpersonal ones.

In essence, this book serves as a comprehensive guide for Indian business families, offering a detailed roadmap for navigating the complex terrain of succession planning. It combines theoretical insights with practical advice, real-world examples (with no names, and many times, the industry masked to avoid the identity of the families involved), and a deep understanding of the unique cultural context of India.

❧

To make the most of this book, it is essential to approach your family business succession planning with an open mind. The key is to start the process when it might not seem immediately necessary.

In my interactions with business families and boards, I frequently say, 'Lack of succession planning and stupidity is never felt by the person, but only by those around.' It is not a rude statement but serves as a practical reminder—albeit with shock value—of the critical importance of succession planning. It underscores the reality that the consequences of inadequate succession planning are not borne by the individual in question but by those surrounding them, be it family members, employees, the company shareholders or other stakeholders.

Create that initial plan and consistently update it. Consider working with an external advisor who brings a fresh perspective and can navigate tough questions. Keep these discussions private and confidential, allowing for honest introspection. This project is about your intent and commitment—the more sincere and proactive you are, the more likely your succession plan will lead to a smooth and successful transition for your family business.

❧

I want to acknowledge that this book aims to cover a comprehensive spectrum of relevant topics. However, given the nuanced nature of family dynamics and business intricacies, there may be a few aspects left untouched or warranting more profound discussion. Succession planning is not a one-size-fits-all venture and certain family-specific considerations might benefit from a more personalized, in-depth dialogue.

Therefore, I encourage families to view this book as a starting point—a guide to prompt valuable reflections. For those moments when specific situations or complexities arise, I recommend confidential discussions with a trusted succession planning advisor, ensuring a tailored approach that aligns seamlessly with the unique fabric of each family and their business.

This book can be an invaluable resource for a diverse audience, including members of Indian business families, board members, and senior leaders tasked with ensuring the longevity and prosperity of family enterprises. It is particularly beneficial for current and future family business leaders who seek practical strategies and insights to navigate the complexities of succession planning. Advisors, consultants and professionals who work closely with family-owned businesses will also find this book instrumental in understanding the unique challenges and dynamics that influence succession in the Indian context. Additionally, regulators, private investors and stakeholders in family businesses will gain crucial insights into the governance and sustainability of these enterprises. Educators, academicians and students of business management and family business studies too can derive a deeper appreciation of the nuanced interplay between family values and business imperatives. In essence, anyone involved in or concerned with the sustainability and growth of family enterprises will find this book an essential guide.

Every succession plan is like a human fingerprint—unique and distinct. Just as the ridges in the fingerprints of two individuals may appear similar, we know there are differences. The message is clear: although there's a lot to learn from the experiences of many business families, your position, situation and risk-taking ability shape a unique journey in succession planning.

Embarking on the journey of succession planning can indeed feel lonely and daunting. The weight of decisions that may shape the course for generations to come can be overwhelming. However, in this process, let honesty be your companion, candour your guide, introspection your ally, and your keen observations the North Star that steers you through. Remember, each step you take in this process is a profound investment in the legacy of your family business. With sincerity and care, the path may become clearer, and the decisions, though significant, can lead to a legacy that endures with strength and purpose.

Part One

The Importance of Succession Planning

This section highlights the usual obstacles encountered in succession planning, the mindset challenges that need to be overcome, and issues one must confront, debate and amicably resolve. Most of these are nuanced and different business families would have unique challenges.

SUCCESSION PLANNING IS A PROCESS, NOT AN EVENT

Family businesses, a prevalent form of ownership, constitute a substantial presence in various economies globally, ranging from countless local establishments to small- and mid-sized enterprises that form the backbone of economies. Indian ecosystem is no different.

As these Indian family businesses evolve beyond their entrepreneurial origins, they encounter distinctive challenges related to ownership, performance and governance. Notably, subsequent generations may either express a desire to lead the company, despite lacking suitability for the role, or they might not want anything to do with it.

Additionally, with an exponential increase in family shareholders across generations, many of whom are not actively involved in business operations, the commitment to sustained ownership becomes less assured. Statistics reveal that only around 10 per cent of family businesses survive till the third generation.*

Succession planning in Indian business families is a complex process, encompassing cultural, social and economic dimensions. It holds personal significance for Indian business families, transcending mere organizational transition to embody the essence of continuity, legacy and sustainable growth. At its core, it is a deliberate process that connects generations, representing their shared values and the enduring spirit of family entrepreneurship. Poorly managed successions can severely impact the legacy of family-owned enterprises, necessitating proactive frameworks within business families.

While navigating the intersection of tradition, modernity and generational risk appetite, maintaining financial equilibrium within family businesses is paramount. Often, failed transitions stem from a clash between the traditionalist mindset of one generation and the change-oriented outlook of another.

---

*Dhamija, Anshul, 'Family Businesses: Tripping at Three', *Forbes India*, 18 February 2019, https://tinyurl.com/bdhkyw78. Accessed on 25 November 2024.

It is commonplace in the Indian context to see that the founding and senior generations often prioritize family legacy, yet I observed that relevance in evolving markets is equally vital. While family business and associated pride come with it, embracing change is essential, as adaptability is an active component of the entrepreneurial success formula. Remaining stagnant amidst industry shifts jeopardizes sustained success. In India's family-centric economy, generational transitions are commonplace, aiming to preserve tradition while fostering adaptability. However, inadequate planning, lack of strategic foresight, and negligence towards resources can disrupt long-standing success.

Transitioning leadership and continued family involvement in decision-making across generations is complex, involving the preservation of core values, culture and legacy. Successful transitions necessitate meticulous planning and preparation well in advance, particularly when succession spans multiple generations. Early dialogue regarding roles, expectations and the business's future facilitates a seamless transition process.

Succession planning in business families often gets misconstrued as a mere act of making a legal will, but its scope extends far beyond this singular facet. It encompasses a comprehensive strategy for the seamless transition of leadership and ownership within the family business. True succession planning involves a nuanced understanding of the family dynamics, the capabilities of potential successors and the identification of a clear path for sustainable growth. It includes grooming the next generation, assessing their skills and aligning their aspirations with the strategic goals of the business. Moreover, it contemplates governance issues, addresses potential conflicts and ensures the continuity of the family legacy. Legal instruments, such as wills, play a part. However, they are just one element in the overall planning process, necessitating a holistic and forward-thinking approach to navigate the complexities inherent in family enterprises.

Succession planning in a business family is expected to facilitate the smooth transition of leadership and ownership from one generation to the next, ensuring the continued success and longevity of the family enterprise. This comprehensive endeavour involves several key components, including the intentional identification and development of future leaders based on competencies and skills rather than familial ties solely. Additionally, it encompasses the transfer of ownership stakes, the preservation of cultural values integral to the family business, and the professionalization of management practices to align with evolving business needs.

Furthermore, succession planning serves as a duty that families owe to themselves. Beyond the broader implications for the business, it is an investment in the family's legacy, unity and sustained prosperity. By engaging in deliberate planning, families mitigate the potential for internal conflicts, fostering an environment of open communication and collaboration. This duty also extends to preserving the family's cultural identity and values, ensuring that these enduring principles are not only passed down but adapted to navigate changing business landscapes. Thus, succession planning becomes a proactive measure to secure the family's collective interests and leave a lasting impact on both the business and the family legacy.

Having a succession strategy is not a one-time event but rather an ongoing process that requires continuous attention and proactive management. By treating it as a dynamic process rather than a one-off task, families can better prepare for the future and mitigate risks associated with unexpected changes in leadership.

For Indian business families, succession planning is a timeless investment in their own future—a legacy-building endeavour that goes beyond the confines of quarterly reports and profit margins. It is a conscious commitment to preserve the family's identity, ethos and collective wisdom, ensuring that the flame of entrepreneurial spirit burns brightly in the hands of successive custodians.

The need for succession planning is strong for the Indian family businesses, where profit and commerce are interwoven with the very threads of traditions and values. It is an acknowledgement that businesses are not just economic entities but living entities, linked to the destinies of the founding families that have nurtured and guided them. It thus becomes a vessel through which these destinies are navigated with purpose, ensuring a seamless transfer of wisdom, leadership and responsibility.

Beyond the practicalities of management transitions, planning for succession in Indian business families is an existential journey. It grapples with questions of identity, purpose and the need to balance tradition and adaptation. It is a rite of passage that demands introspection, foresight and a deep understanding of the family's collective aspirations.

Moreover, succession planning is a testament to the resilience of familial bonds. It acknowledges the impermanence of individual roles while celebrating the enduring strength of family ties. In the face of economic fluctuations, market uncertainties and global challenges, it stands as a beacon of stability—an anchor that allows the family to weather storms and navigate uncharted waters with unwavering unity.

A well-run succession plan is a pledge to the community, employees and stakeholders. It signals a commitment to responsible stewardship, ensuring the continued prosperity of the enterprise and the communities it serves. It reflects a sense of accountability that extends far beyond the boardroom, resonating with the collective consciousness of a nation that cherishes its familial business traditions.

THE HEART OF SUCCESSION PLANNING

Succession planning extends beyond the analytical aspects and is deeply intertwined with the heart of the families involved in the business. It hinges on shared values, a collective commitment to preserving the family legacy and fostering a sense of unity. The emotional dimensions, such as trust, open communication and a genuine desire to see the family enterprise thrive, play a pivotal role.

The heart of the family contributes to the resilience needed to navigate challenges and conflicts that may arise during the transition. A successful succession plan requires a balance between the strategic and financial considerations and the emotional well-being of the family members, making the art of succession planning a delicate dance that requires empathy, understanding and a shared passion for the family's success.

On another note, unless businesses and the fruits of their success continually grow, subsequent generations may find themselves squabbling over finances. Financial pressures and competition for a share of the business's prosperity can strain family relationships. As the business expands, diversifies or encounters challenges, economic interests become central, potentially leading to disputes over financial entitlements or control. Establishing sustainable growth strategies becomes crucial not only for the business's prosperity but also for maintaining harmony within the family. Adequate wealth management, strategic planning and a shared commitment to the ongoing success of the enterprise are essential to mitigate economic tensions and ensure the cohesion of subsequent generations involved in the family business.

Promoter families engaged in succession planning grapple with multiple concerns as they navigate the process of transitioning leadership to subsequent generations. A primary apprehension revolves around the competence and capability of the next generation, with families keen on ensuring that successors possess the requisite skills and experience to effectively manage the complexities of the business. Concurrently, the potential for conflicts among family members poses a significant worry, as succession planning can trigger disagreements over roles, responsibilities and decision-making authority, threatening familial harmony.

Promoter families are wary of any perception that leadership positions might be bestowed based on family ties rather than merit, cognizant of the adverse effects this could have on employee morale and the overall organizational culture. Striking a balance between family and business interests adds another layer of complexity, as decisions must align with the best interests of the business while considering familial relationships and dynamics.

Lastly, a paramount concern revolves around the resilience of the business under new leadership. Promoter families are acutely aware of the potential ramifications of the transition on the stability, growth trajectory and competitive positioning of the company. The challenge lies in ensuring that the next generation can adeptly navigate external challenges, industry dynamics and technological advancements while upholding the core values and organizational culture established by the founder. Addressing these multifaceted concerns necessitates a comprehensive and strategic approach to succession planning, emphasizing communication, professional development and a shared commitment to the business's enduring success.

In several supposedly modern-thinking Indian business families, a disconcerting challenge persists, where gender biases limit the inclusion of women in key business roles and board seats.* Despite adopting modern values, the traditional mindset often prevails, hindering the full realization of corporate governance principles. The exclusion of women from leadership roles not only undermines diversity but also poses a significant corporate governance issue, as it neglects a pool of talent that could bring fresh perspectives and contribute to the family business's growth. It creates an imbalance in decision-making and raises concerns about the fairness and transparency of governance practices within the family enterprise.

Gender injustice in succession planning within Indian business families is a pressing concern that reflects deep-seated societal norms and traditional gender roles. Despite advancements in various sectors, gender bias continues to permeate the decision-making processes related to the passing on of family businesses. Several concerns arise when examining this issue.

One of the primary concerns is the perpetuation of traditional gender stereotypes, where male heirs are often favoured over their female counterparts. This bias not only limits the opportunities available to competent and qualified female family members but also reinforces gender inequity within the family business. The assumption that certain roles or industries are better suited for men can unjustly restrict the potential contributions of women in leadership positions. Embedded cultural norms sometimes dictate that the continuity of the business should follow the genetic lineage of the male offspring. This bias extends further to resist the inclusion of sons-in-law into the family business, perpetuating a preference for bloodline over diverse qualifications or capabilities. Overcoming such cultural barriers requires a thoughtful reassessment of traditional norms to ensure that merit and competence take precedence over gender or lineage, fostering an environment where all capable individuals, regardless of gender or familial ties, are given equitable opportunities to contribute to the success of the family business.

---

*'Obstacles and Opportunities of India's Women in Family Businesses', *Women in Family Business*, 28 June 2022, https://tinyurl.com/rf4a6cut. Accessed on 25 November 2024.

The limited representation of women in leadership roles within family businesses is a direct outcome of gender injustice in succession planning. This not only hampers the professional growth of capable women but also deprives the business of diverse perspectives and talents that could contribute to innovation and sustainable growth. The trend of opening boutiques and random creative-pursuit-based businesses to keep daughters and wives 'busy' while men handle the family business has, at times, resembled a fashionable plot twist in many family narratives. While the intention may have been to provide entrepreneurial opportunities, it highlights a need for a shift in perspective. Embracing modern knowledge and moving away from traditional biases can pave the way for equal opportunities and recognition of skills and aspirations, ensuring that family members, regardless of gender, can contribute to the business based on merit rather than prescribed roles. The future is undoubtedly more couture than cliché.

Moreover, gender injustice in succession planning contributes to broader societal issues, reinforcing the notion that women are less suitable for leadership roles. This perpetuates a cycle where female family members may not be encouraged to pursue career aspirations or may face barriers to accessing the necessary resources and opportunities for professional development.

Several variables impact gender injustice in succession planning, including traditional beliefs, lack of awareness, and the absence of progressive policies. Societal expectations often dictate that male heirs are better equipped to handle the responsibilities of leadership, perpetuating gender bias within family structures. The absence of awareness about the importance of gender diversity and inclusion further compounds the problem, as family leaders may not recognize the value that female successors can bring to the business.

Ecosystem issues also play a role in sustaining gender injustice in succession planning. Prevailing societal norms and cultural expectations about gender roles can infiltrate family businesses, reinforcing stereotypes and hindering the implementation of more equitable succession plans. Additionally, the lack of legal frameworks or policies that actively promote gender equality may contribute to the persistence of gender injustice in succession planning.

Overcoming these concerns requires a concerted effort to challenge traditional gender norms and promote a culture of inclusivity within family businesses. Implementing transparent and merit-based succession planning processes, providing equal opportunities for skill development and fostering awareness about the benefits of gender diversity are essential steps towards addressing gender injustice in succession planning. Family businesses that embrace these changes not only contribute to a more equitable society but also position themselves for long-term success by harnessing the full potential of all family members, regardless of gender.

Often additional challenges emerge in the face of evolving social norms and individual behaviour. Adultery, interracial or inter-caste marriages, and global marriage laws can introduce complexities that impact shareholding structures. Some families may grapple with accepting spouses from different cultural backgrounds or adapting to the legal implications of cross-border unions. The citizenship of progeny or their spouses from other countries may affect inheritance laws and shareholding, requiring careful consideration in succession planning. Similarly, as attitudes towards same-sex marriages evolve, families may encounter challenges in accommodating diverse marital arrangements within the traditional framework of succession planning. Navigating these complexities demands a nuanced approach that aligns family values with the legal and societal shifts impacting marriage and family structures.

Self-destruction within successive generations of business families is a poignant phenomenon that highlights the challenges embedded in the continuity of family-owned enterprises. This destructive pattern often emerges as a complex interplay of psychological, interpersonal and business-related factors, leading to a gradual erosion of the family legacy. Several key aspects contribute to the manifestation of self-destruction across generations within business families.

One of the primary factors is the lack of effective succession planning. When there is a failure to establish clear and well-thought-out plans for passing on leadership and ownership, it can lead to internal conflicts, power struggles and a weakening of the family business. Inadequate preparation for the transition of responsibilities and authority can sow the seeds of discord among family members, contributing to the gradual decline of the business over successive generations.

Interpersonal dynamics and communication breakdowns also play a pivotal role in the self-destruction observed in many business families. Misunderstandings, unresolved conflicts and a lack of open communication can foster a toxic family environment. These relational challenges often extend beyond the business realm, affecting family unity and cohesion. As successive generations grapple with strained relationships, the overall fabric of the family and its business begins to unravel.

The impact of generational shifts further compounds the risk of self-destruction. Differing visions, values and priorities among family members from different generations can lead to a lack of alignment in the overarching goals of the business. Failure to reconcile these divergent perspectives may result in a loss of the family's original entrepreneurial spirit and a dilution of the core values that initially propelled the business to success.

Financial mismanagement and a lack of adaptability to changing market dynamics also contribute to self-destruction in successive generations of business families. The inability to innovate, diversify or address financial challenges can render a once-thriving enterprise obsolete. The absence of a strategic vision and an unwillingness to embrace change often accelerate the decline, particularly when younger generations are unable or unwilling to adapt to evolving business landscapes.

Ecosystem issues, including external economic factors and industry changes, can further exacerbate the self-destructive trajectory. Unforeseen challenges, such as economic downturns or shifts in consumer preferences, may expose vulnerabilities within the family business. Without a proactive and adaptive approach, the business may struggle to weather these external storms, leading to its gradual demise over successive generations.

Barriers to success in breaking this self-destructive cycle often include resistance to change, an unwillingness to seek external guidance, and the perpetuation of unhealthy family dynamics. Overcoming these barriers requires a fundamental shift in mindset, acknowledging the need for professional advice, adopting a culture of innovation, and fostering open communication within the family. Breaking the pattern of self-destruction in successive generations necessitates a holistic approach that addresses both the business and familial aspects. Establishing robust succession plans, prioritizing effective communication, fostering a culture of adaptability, and seeking external expertise are crucial steps in steering the family enterprise away from the self-destructive path. Ultimately, understanding the root causes and actively working to mitigate them can pave the way for a more resilient and sustainable legacy across generations.

Succession planning is a complex and challenging process that demands a significant commitment of time and patience due to its multifaceted nature. The intricacies arise from the need to balance family dynamics, individual aspirations and the strategic requirements of the business. Identifying and grooming potential successors, addressing varying skill levels among family members and navigating emotional attachments to the business are intricate tasks. Additionally, succession planning involves aligning the family's values and vision, which may require extensive communication and consensus-building. The long-term nature of succession planning requires a sustained commitment to adapt strategies as circumstances change and to account for unforeseen challenges. Developing the necessary skills and experiences in potential successors takes time, and the cultivation of trust and collaboration within the family necessitates patience. Furthermore, the process is often hindered by external factors like market volatility or industry shifts, which add layers of complexity. Successful succession planning, therefore, requires a steadfast commitment, a willingness to invest the necessary time, and the patience to navigate the intricate web of familial, financial and business dynamics.

The evolving landscape of Indian business families is gradually embracing the notion that scions should have the liberty to pursue diverse business interests or follow their individual career passions. Recognizing that each successor is a unique individual with distinct talents and ambitions, families are increasingly accepting the idea that not every scion needs to have a day-to-day role in the family business. This shift signifies a departure from traditional expectations, acknowledging that allowing scions to explore their own paths can lead to a more diversified and innovative family portfolio. Embracing varied interests and passions, whether they align with the core business or not, is seen as a positive approach. In this changing scenario, financial dividends from the family business can still provide substantial support, allowing scions to enjoy the benefits while contributing to the family's overall prosperity in their own distinctive ways. This broader perspective reflects a more contemporary and open-minded attitude within Indian business families, where success is measured not only by direct involvement in the business but also by the collective achievements of the family.

Integrating non-family professionals into the succession planning of business families is a strategic move that often brings fresh perspectives, expertise and a professional outlook to the leadership transition. To avoid conflicts, clear communication and transparency are paramount. Establishing well-defined roles and expectations for both family and non-family professionals helps mitigate potential tensions. Emphasizing merit-based selection and performance assessments ensures that professionals are valued for their contributions, fostering a culture of mutual respect. Creating a collaborative environment where ideas are openly discussed and decisions are made collectively contributes to harmonious integration. It is essential to address any pre-existing biases or concerns within the family and emphasize the shared goal of the business's success. Regular communication channels, such as family councils or advisory boards, can serve as platforms for resolving conflicts, aligning interests and facilitating a smooth transition that leverages the strengths of both family and non-family professionals.

THE BIG 'BUT'

Across Indian businesses of all sizes and generations, sensitive topics are like the proverbial elephants in the room—often swept under a metaphorical carpet, hidden from sight and ignored. These topics, whether they pertain to succession planning, familial disagreements or governance structures, are unanimously avoided until they become unavoidable or contentious. The reluctance to address these elephants in the room stems from various factors, including cultural norms that prioritize harmony and the preservation of family reputation. However, this avoidance can have detrimental consequences for businesses in the long run, as unresolved issues may fester and ultimately disrupt the harmony and continuity of the family enterprise.

Yet, amidst this reluctance to confront uncomfortable truths, there are exceptional family leaders who possess the courage and foresight to tackle these issues head-on. These leaders understand the importance of open communication, transparency and adherence to values in maintaining family unity and ensuring the long-term success of the business.

Moreover, these visionary leaders recognize the importance of succession planning in ensuring the continuity of the business across generations. They invest time and resources in grooming the next generation of leaders, imparting not only technical skills but also the ethos that defines the family's legacy. In doing so, these leaders break the cycle of intergenerational discord and fragmentation that plague many family businesses. Instead, they cultivate a culture of unity, purpose and shared vision, laying the foundation for a resilient and enduring enterprise.

Despite the abundance of intelligence, modern governance awareness and business acumen, the tendency among Indian promoters to underestimate the critical importance of succession planning has led to the unfortunate reality where many second- or third-generation scions find themselves entangled in business wrecks.

In Indian family businesses, a clear demonstration of publicly documented lapses in succession planning is available. From the stewardship issues of conglomerate giants to smaller enterprises, the toll of delays in the resolution of such disputes has been damaging. The cost, measured in terms of both fortunes and fortitude, is palpable. Families, irrespective of the scale of their empires, have grappled with heartburn, reputational setbacks and the burden of unnecessary worries. Reflecting on these instances underscores a clear learning—hope, while resilient, stands as an inadequate substitute for proactive succession planning. How many popular and once-successful business families have in a span of a few years simply disappeared into the abyss?

One contributing factor is often an over-reliance on individual brilliance or the founder's charisma. Promoters, buoyed by their own success, might assume that their innate business prowess alone is sufficient for the sustenance and growth of the enterprise. This overconfidence blinds them to the complexities surrounding leadership transition and cultivating the next generation of leaders. Additionally, there is a prevalent cultural trait of familial attachment and a sense of proprietorship that can impede the objective assessment of a successor's capabilities. The emotional ties to the business sometimes overshadow the need for merit-based decisions, resulting in the appointment of successors who might lack the requisite skills or experience.

In some cases, there is a misplaced belief that succession planning is a task to be undertaken later when the need is imminent. This procrastination overlooks the time required to groom successors adequately. Succession planning is not an event but a process that demands foresight, structured mentoring and a gradual transfer of responsibilities. Neglecting this process can leave successors ill-prepared and lead to turbulent transitions.

The usual politics and issues of family dynamics further compound the challenges. In hierarchical family structures, power struggles among siblings or cousins can ensue, each vying for control without a clear understanding of their individual strengths or the collective needs of the business. This internal strife erodes the business foundation, often resulting in setbacks that could have been avoided with a more thoughtful approach to succession.

A prevalent tendency is the assumption of immortality by the senior leader(s) or promoter(s). Despite the awareness of the necessity for succession planning, an unwarranted confidence persists that another year of delay in the inevitable preparations will not cause any harm. This delay often transforms a crucial responsibility into an urgent crisis upon the demise of the seniormost family member. The repercussions are visible in the form of familial disputes and struggles in the absence of a well-thought-out succession strategy.

Moreover, at times, a lack of awareness or unwillingness to embrace modern governance practices can hinder the establishment of robust succession plans. Inadequate governance structures, coupled with a dearth of transparent communication channels, contribute to an environment where critical discussions about the future of the business are often avoided or delayed. The consequences of taking succession planning lightly can be devastating. Business wrecks not only jeopardize the financial health of the enterprise but also tarnish the legacy painstakingly built by the founding generation. This highlights the importance of promoters recognizing succession planning as a strategic need rather than a distant concern and addressing such matters proactively rather than deferring them to an uncertain future.

The most formidable risk that business families face is the absence of a well-thought-out succession plan. This risk permeates every facet of the family enterprise, affecting not only the financial health of the business but also the harmony within the family unit. The repercussions of inadequate succession planning extend across all stakeholders, presenting a multifaceted challenge that can jeopardize the very foundation upon which the family's legacy is built. It is a common paradox: meticulous planning for the transfer of economic wealth through a will, yet a less defined roadmap for the transition of the family business. Many founders or promoters allocate considerable attention to securing their financial legacy but might leave the personal aspect of business succession inadequately addressed. This disjunction raises critical questions about the sustainability of the business and the potential challenges faced by the next generation. While a legal will—a subset in the entire succession planning—safeguards economic assets, the absence of a succession plan for the business itself can introduce uncertainties and complexities that transcend mere monetary considerations.

As we reflect on the challenges and losses brought about by the Covid-19 pandemic, we are reminded of the importance of proactive succession planning. The sudden and unexpected nature of the pandemic highlighted the vulnerability of businesses and families to unforeseen events. Many organizations, including prominent corporations, were caught off guard, facing leadership vacuums and uncertainty in the wake of key executives falling victim to the virus. Despite this stark wake-up call, the urgency of succession planning has not been fully registered across the board. The time to start succession planning is not tomorrow or next year—it is today. Delaying this critical process only increases the risk of being unprepared when the need arises.

One cannot simply bequeath a board seat or CEO position like an economic asset through a legal will, especially in listed or regulated entities. Regulatory frameworks impose stringent filters and guidelines on leadership appointments within organizations. Succession in key executive roles must adhere to transparent and meritocratic processes, ensuring that individuals are selected based on their qualifications, experience and capacity to lead. These regulations are designed to uphold principles of fairness, accountability and effective governance, emphasizing the importance of competence over familial ties in securing leadership positions.

For the business itself, the lack of a clear succession plan introduces uncertainty into leadership transitions. Without a designated successor who is adequately prepared and groomed for the role, the business faces the risk of a leadership vacuum. This vacuum can lead to a lack of strategic direction, decision-making delays and potential disruptions in day-to-day operations. Investors, both internal and external, are left in a state of unease, as the absence of a clear succession plan casts shadows over the business's long-term sustainability and growth prospects.

From the perspective of the employees, the absence of succession planning introduces ambiguity regarding the future direction of the company. Talented individuals may be hesitant to commit their careers to an organization that lacks a transparent and structured plan for leadership continuity. This can lead to a talent drain, with key employees seeking opportunities elsewhere, leaving the business with a depleted pool of skilled individuals.

Within the family, the risks are equally profound. Sibling rivalries, generational conflicts and uncertainties regarding the equitable distribution of wealth can emerge in the absence of a well defined succession plan. The lack of clarity can lead to disputes among family members, potentially fracturing familial bonds and eroding the very support system that should ideally underpin the family enterprise.

External stakeholders, such as joint venture partners, business associates, auditors, suppliers and clients, may also be apprehensive when faced with a business that lacks a succession plan. They rely on stability and dependability in their business relationships, and the uncertainty surrounding leadership transitions can create a sense of instability and impact the overall trust in the enterprise.

From a regulatory standpoint, the absence of a succession plan may lead to governance issues. Compliance with regulatory requirements often includes demonstrating sound governance practices, and the lack of a clear plan for leadership continuity can raise red flags.

Failure to develop a robust succession planning strategy can prove exorbitantly costly for all stakeholders, particularly the business families directly involved. At the core of this expense lies the potential erosion of accumulated wealth. Without a clear and intentional succession plan, the value of the family business becomes susceptible to fragmentation, disputes and mismanagement, resulting in financial losses that can have far-reaching consequences.

Trust, a critical currency in family businesses, is also on the line. The lack of a well-defined succession plan can breed mistrust among family members, leading to disputes and conflicts that tarnish relationships and jeopardize the familial unity crucial for sustained success. This erosion of trust extends beyond the family circle and can impact relationships with employees, partners and other stakeholders, further complicating business operations.

Reputation, a valuable asset, is not immune to the repercussions of inadequate succession planning. Businesses are closely scrutinized and any internal strife or mismanagement can tarnish the family's standing in the industry and the broader community. This can have lasting effects on the brand image, potentially deterring customers, clients and investors. Moreover, in today's corporate landscape, where shareholders and stakeholders expect higher levels of governance and transparency, the absence of a robust succession plan could significantly impact enterprise valuation. Shareholders are increasingly valuing businesses not just for their financial performance but also for the strength of their governance structures. The lack of a well-defined succession plan might signal governance weaknesses, leading to potential erosion of trust and confidence among investors. Consequently, a decline in enterprise valuation becomes not only a matter of internal family dynamics but a critical concern for those holding a stake in the business.

The leadership vacuum is another perilous consequence. Without a clear succession plan, the business may lack competent leaders to guide it through transitions. This leadership vacuum can stunt growth, hinder innovation and jeopardize the business's competitive edge. Additionally, the absence of a well-defined succession plan not only leads to internal strife but also poses risks to the talent pool within the enterprise. Key professionals might be hesitant to commit to an organization embroiled in prolonged succession battles, as uncertainty about the future leadership can drive them to explore opportunities elsewhere. Competitors may exploit this vulnerability by actively poaching talented individuals within the business, disrupting operations and siphoning away valuable expertise.

The long-term growth and sustainability of the business are also at stake. Succession planning ensures a seamless transition from one generation to the next, allowing for continuity in strategic decision-making and adaptability to market changes. Failure to plan for this transition risks leaving the business rudderless and unable to navigate the evolving business landscape effectively.

Perhaps the most intangible but profound risk is the erosion of the family's legacy and values. Succession planning is not just about transferring leadership; it is a vehicle for preserving the family's ethos, values and accumulated wisdom. Without a structured plan, there is a risk of losing the very essence that distinguishes the family business and gives it a unique identity.

WHY IS SUCCESSION PLANNING SO DIFFICULT?

Indian business families often grapple with the challenge of lacking proactive succession planning, which can lead to uncertainties and potential disruptions in their enterprises. A glaring example is when prominent business figures, buoyed by their financial success, neglect implementing a robust succession plan. The absence of a strategic roadmap for the post-founder era jeopardizes not only the business's longevity but also the livelihoods of countless employees and stakeholders dependent on its sustained success, its strategic positioning, the emotional well-being of family members, the preservation of legacy and overall continuity.

This usually happens for varied reasons. The cultural emphasis on family ties and traditional values sometimes results in a delay or neglect of structured succession strategies. Many families prioritize short-term financial gains over long-term sustainability, overlooking the broader implications of a smooth leadership transition. This delay often stems from concerns about potential conflicts, favouritism or a reluctance to discuss sensitive matters related to the transfer of power.

Subsequent generations often face a diminishing probability of continuing with the family business due to various factors. One significant challenge is the evolving interests and career aspirations of younger individuals, who may seek opportunities outside the established family enterprise. Changing economic landscapes and newly emerging industries can lure the younger generation towards career paths such as technology, finance or entrepreneurship, which may not align with the traditional family business. There are many creative pursuits that the younger generation can take up. At times, this causes a rift within the families, as this alternate career choice—misaligned with the family business—is seen as an affront.

Additionally, the lack of exposure and relevant skill development within the family can deter successors, as they may perceive the business as less appealing or competitive in comparison to other professional options. Interpersonal conflicts and divergent visions among family members regarding the future direction of the business can further contribute to a decreased likelihood of seamless succession. Without a deliberate effort to address these challenges and provide a compelling platform for the next generation, the probability of them continuing the family business diminishes over time.

FAILURE TO STEP BACK IS COMMON

Succession planning extends beyond the creation of legal or governance structures; it is a process that necessitates giving successors adequate time and space to assume leadership roles. In the context of many Indian business families, this crucial aspect is often overlooked. A common pitfall is the reluctance to step back.

The perpetuation of a mindset that considers the promoters indispensable can hinder the development of the next generation and impede the evolution of the business. One notable challenge to this purpose is the tendency among Indian promoters to immerse themselves fully in their businesses, often without cultivating personal hobbies or non-business passions to retire on. Many Indian promoters tend to define their identities primarily through their businesses. This absence of non-business passions contributes to a reluctance to retire or step back from active involvement in the business.

This oversight not only impacts the well-being of the promoters but also poses risks to the business and its governance. Creating a fulfilling post-business life is what promoters should focus their energy on. It will require cultivating hobbies, interests or social engagements beyond their business. This will make it easier to step back and provide successors with the necessary time and autonomy to gradually assume leadership responsibilities.

THE ILLUSION OF IMMORTALITY

The perception of immortality, wherein promoters continue to run businesses without a concrete succession plan, poses significant risks. Operating under the assumption that the current leadership will persist indefinitely can lead to a lack of preparedness for unforeseen events, disrupt governance structures and potentially jeopardize the long-term sustainability of the business. The human reality has to prevail that even the wealthiest and most influential owners are not immune to the inescapable fate of mortality.

The illusion of immortality that afflicts some business magnates can have dire consequences for the future of their enterprises. Ignoring the inevitability of life's end is a perilous oversight. It is like steering a ship into the deep sea without a navigation plan. The misguided belief that one's reign will last indefinitely perpetuates an air of invincibility, breeding complacency that could prove disastrous for the company's stability and continuity. This aspect is not just for business families, some of the larger-than-life professional CEOs have behaved similarly. Sadly, that is where the true test of board governance lies.

The analogy of succession planning as an insurance policy rings true. Just as prudent individuals secure insurance coverage to protect their families and assets in the event of unforeseen calamities, business owners must adopt a similarly diligent approach to safeguard the future of their enterprises. The lack of a comprehensive succession plan is tantamount to leaving one's fortune to chance, a reckless gamble that jeopardizes the legacy carefully crafted over years of hard work and dedication.

LIMITATIONS OF THE BOARD

One of the repeated suggestions to mitigate this issue is expecting the boards of family-owned enterprises to proactively engage in conversations with the promoters to instigate succession planning discussions. However, this undertaking is rife with challenges, particularly when board members owe their positions and other obligations to the promoter family. The existence of indebtedness, whether financial or relational, can create a culture of deference and reluctance to broach sensitive topics like succession planning.

Overcoming this challenge requires a delicate balancing act. Boards must cultivate an environment of trust and openness, emphasizing the long-term benefits of effective succession planning for the business's sustainability. Establishing independent governance structures within the board, with members free from indebtedness to the promoter family, can foster impartial discussions on succession without compromising the integrity of the process.

Boards can also leverage external expertise and engage consultants or advisors with experience in successful succession planning. This external perspective can offer impartial insights, guide discussions and ensure that the process remains focused on the strategic needs of the business rather than familial dynamics.

IMPACT ON GOVERNANCE

The absence of a well-thought-out succession plan not only affects the business's continuity but also places governance in a precarious position. Without a clear guide, governance structures may struggle to adapt, potentially leading to decision-making challenges, conflicts and a lack of strategic direction.

The absence of robust succession planning in many Indian business families, especially in the case of large unlisted or listed entities, represents a significant corporate governance lapse, posing profound risks to the stability and continuity of family-owned enterprises. This lapse is indicative of a systemic failure to align with fundamental principles of corporate governance, compromising transparency, accountability and the long-term interests of stakeholders.

The critique extends beyond the immediate impact on the business to encompass broader economic ramifications. Inadequate succession planning creates an environment of uncertainty that can erode shareholder value. Investors, unsure of the future leadership and strategic direction, may exhibit hesitancy, leading to diminished market confidence and, potentially, substantial financial losses for both the family and external investors. This lack of transparency contributes to a governance deficit, undermining the fundamental tenets that guide responsible business conduct.

Internal family dynamics further compound this lapse. The failure to establish a clear and inclusive succession plan intensifies the risk of familial conflicts, power struggles and a lack of cohesion among family members. Such discord not only disrupts the functioning of the family but also undermines the governance structures necessary for effective decision-making within the business.

ADDRESSING THE ISSUE

Internal family governance plays a pivotal role in the intricacies of succession planning within family-owned enterprises. Significant challenges arise from the intricate web of relationships, emotions and expectations inherent in family dynamics. Addressing these internal governance issues requires a nuanced approach beyond legal and structural considerations. The need for transparent communication emerges as a fundamental element of internal family governance. Establishing open channels facilitates the expression of individual aspirations, concerns and expectations. This transparency lays the groundwork for collaborative decision-making, fostering a shared understanding of the succession plan and mitigating potential conflicts.

Another critical aspect involves defining clear roles and responsibilities within the family. Ambiguity in expectations can lead to power struggles and resentment. Establishing a framework that outlines roles, decision-making processes and responsibilities helps create a structured environment where family members can contribute effectively, aligning their strengths with the needs of the business.

Equally important is cultivating a culture that values accountability and professionalism within the family. Professionalism instils discipline, encourages competence and fosters a commitment to the business's success. By emphasizing these values, family members contribute to a governance structure that prioritizes meritocracy over familial ties. Succession planning also necessitates the development of a shared vision for the family and the business. Aligning on core values, long-term goals and the legacy the family wishes to uphold provides a unifying framework for decision-making. This shared vision serves as a compass guiding the family through the complexities of succession planning.

Recognizing the importance of allowing successors time and space to assume leadership roles is another critical step. Indian business families should actively foster an environment that supports the development of the next generation, providing them with opportunities to learn and grow into their roles gradually.

Encouraging promoters to cultivate personal hobbies or passions outside the business is equally essential. This not only contributes to a more balanced and fulfilling life for the promoters but also facilitates a smoother transition as they gradually step back from day-to-day operations.

Internal governance challenges frequently arise when family members are unprepared or lack the skills needed to fulfil the demands of business ownership. Investing in family education programmes equips members with the knowledge and tools needed for effective governance, preparing them for the responsibilities that come with owning and managing a family business.

A crucial yet frequently overlooked aspect involves addressing conflicts directly. Unresolved disputes can escalate, jeopardizing the entire succession plan. Implementing conflict resolution mechanisms, perhaps with the assistance of external facilitators, provides a structured approach to addressing issues and maintaining family harmony. Furthermore, establishing regular family meetings contributes to ongoing dialogue and ensures that all members are informed and engaged in succession planning. These meetings serve as platforms for discussing challenges, celebrating achievements and reinforcing the familial bonds that underpin the business.

The urgency to establish clear succession plans cannot be overstated. Embracing the inevitability of change, acknowledging mortality and planning for the seamless transfer of leadership are imperative for ensuring the long-term success and resilience of Indian family businesses. This shift in mindset and approach not only benefits the current leaders but also lays a strong foundation for the sustained prosperity of the business across generations.

FORMAL CORPORATE GOVERNANCE

The evolution of formal corporate governance in Indian businesses has witnessed a transformative journey, marked by a shift towards transparency, accountability and professionalism. Regulatory bodies like the Securities and Exchange Board of India introduced codes and guidelines, following the recommendations of the Kotak Committee and the Committee on Corporate Governance, setting principles to protect minority shareholders. Stock exchanges mandated stricter disclosure norms, pushing listed companies to adhere to higher governance standards. Independent directors became a crucial aspect of corporate governance, aimed at reducing conflicts of interest within family-dominated boards.

Indian family businesses have made strides in adapting to formal corporate governance structures, with success stories exemplifying robust governance practices. However, challenges persist, particularly in achieving diversity within corporate boards, which can result in a narrow focus, overlooking critical issues and opportunities, ultimately impeding the organization's long-term growth and sustainability.

SUCCESSION AS AN ENTERPRISE RISK

Succession planning is not merely a strategic initiative but an integral component of comprehensive *risk management* for businesses. Beyond the conventional mapping of geographical, product or technological risks, the potential departure or retirement of key personnel poses a distinct category of risk that enterprises must navigate. In the regulatory landscape, particularly under 'listing regulations', the responsibility of the risk management committee extends to formulating a detailed risk management policy that explicitly incorporates a business continuity plan. This acknowledgement underscores the significance of succession planning as an essential subset of broader business continuity strategies.

Recognizing personnel transitions as a risk underscores the vulnerability that organizations face when key individuals, often holding critical knowledge and expertise, depart or retire. The seamless transition of leadership and responsibilities becomes imperative for maintaining operational continuity and mitigating potential disruptions. As businesses grapple with diverse risk scenarios, the people-centric aspect of succession planning becomes a linchpin in fortifying organizational resilience.

Succession planning, within the risk management framework, addresses the human capital element of risk. It goes beyond a reactive approach to personnel changes and adopts a proactive strategy, ensuring that a pool of qualified individuals is groomed to assume key roles seamlessly. This not only safeguards against knowledge gaps but also contributes to the sustained success of the business.

Criticism of poor governance in business families often revolves around instances where ethical lapses, conflicts of interest and implementation of inadequate governance structures have been observed. Such situations can significantly impact the business's reputation and, in many cases, result in failure in succession planning. One notable criticism is the prevalence of nepotism, where family members are favoured for key positions without due consideration for merit or expertise. This can lead to a lack of qualified leadership, hinder professional development and create resentment among non-family employees.

Another area of concern is the inadequate separation of family and business interests. When family members engage in related-party transactions without proper oversight, it can lead to financial impropriety and conflicts of interest. Poor governance and financial mismanagement impact the company's stakeholders and raises questions about oversight and accountability within the family-controlled boards.

Succession planning is of paramount importance in business families, particularly when there are aspirations for growth. This process becomes a strategic imperative as it involves meticulous preparation and transition of leadership from one generation to the next. In the context of aspiring for business expansion, effective succession planning ensures the continuity of the family legacy and business vision. It provides a framework for identifying, developing and nurturing the next generation of leaders, aligning their skills and aspirations with the evolving needs of the business.

INDIAN SCRIPTURES AND LEARNINGS FROM THE PAST

The underestimation of succession planning, even in the face of explicit guidance from ancient Indian scriptures, reveals a perplexing blind spot within the fabric of contemporary business cultures. Despite the wealth of wisdom embedded in these scriptures, which extol the virtues of foresight, preparedness and strategic thinking, the tendency to downplay the significance of succession planning persists.

One plausible explanation for this underestimation lies in a pervasive misconception fuelled by a relentless pursuit of immediate gains and a myopic focus on the present. Modern business landscapes, driven by the urgency of day-to-day operations and the pressure to deliver short-term results, often foster an environment that sidelines the importance of contemplating the future. The alluring illusion that the current leadership will remain at the helm indefinitely can overshadow the profound implications of failing to chart a course for the inevitable transitions that time imposes.

Another contributing factor to the underestimation of succession planning is the prevailing reluctance to confront uncomfortable truths, particularly those associated with mortality and the impermanence of leadership. This aversion to acknowledging the temporal nature of human existence can engender a false sense of invincibility, leading individuals and businesses to discount the necessity of preparing for an eventual changing of the guard.

The cultural resonance of familial bonds in the context of Indian business families may also contribute to the underestimation of succession planning. While the significance of family ties is paramount, the implicit assumption that these bonds alone can seamlessly guide the transition of leadership disregards the complexities inherent in business operations. The scriptures, which emphasize the importance of *dharma* (duty) and the righteous path, actually endorse the idea of meticulous planning to fulfil one's responsibilities effectively.

Furthermore, the prevailing optimism bias often clouds the judgement of business leaders, leading them to believe that challenges such as leadership transitions are distant concerns that can be addressed when the need arises. This unwarranted optimism fosters procrastination, with leaders postponing critical discussions and strategic decisions until they are forced to confront them hastily, often in the midst of unforeseen crises.

In contrast to this tendency, the ancient Indian scriptures advocate for the practice of 'Yajna'—the ritual of selfless service and duty. This ancient wisdom underscores the importance of preparing for future responsibilities with a sense of duty and selflessness, aligning with the essence of succession planning.

Indian history and Indic scriptures offer profound insights into the necessity of succession planning, emphasizing the continuity and stability of leadership for sustained societal and organizational well-being. The wisdom embedded in the Dharmic principles, as seen in the *Bhagavad Gita*, shapes succession planning not just as wealth transfer but as a sacred duty aligned with ethical values. The *gurukula* system's mentor–disciple relationships echo the importance of mentorship for passing on knowledge and values. Historical dynasties emphasize adaptability, innovation and inclusive governance, serving as cautionary tales for the complexities of changing times.

Indian joint family values underscore the strength of unity, advocating for collaborative decision-making and shared responsibilities in succession planning. *Karma yoga*, the philosophy of selfless action, guides leaders in family businesses to see their roles as stewards of a greater purpose who are responsible for the well-being of the family and society. The concept of *yuga*, representing cycles of time, teaches the impermanence of success and encourages family businesses to prepare for economic shifts, industry evolution and generational changes with resilience and foresight.

In Indian history, the Maurya Empire provides a notable example of the consequences of inadequate succession planning. After the demise of the great Mauryan emperor Ashoka, the empire faced internal strife due to unclear lines of succession. The ensuing power struggles weakened the empire, illustrating the historical imperative for a well-thought-out transition of leadership.

Indic scriptures, including the epics *Ramayana* and *Mahabharata*, delve into the intricacies of leadership transitions and the broader concept of dharma. The *Ramayana* narrates the importance of preparing the next generation for leadership roles through the character of Rama, who ensured that his sons were trained and educated for their future responsibilities. The *Mahabharata*, a narrative rich with moral dilemmas and strategic intricacies, underscores the significance of succession planning through its exploration of the Kuru dynasty's power struggles.

The ancient treatise *Arthashastra*, often attributed to Chanakya—the ancient Indian philosopher and advisor to Chandragupta Maurya—delves into statecraft and governance. It advocates for systematic approaches to succession planning, emphasizing the need for grooming capable successors, establishing clear rules of inheritance, and mitigating potential conflicts to ensure the stability of the state. The *Manusmriti*, an ancient legal text, addresses the family structure and succession planning. It emphasizes the importance of imparting education and responsibilities to the next generation, recognizing the role of each individual in maintaining the family's righteous path.

Another apparent cue is the concept of the Vedic *ashrama* system. *Vanaprastha*, one of the four ashramas in Vedic philosophy, traditionally signifies the stage of life where individuals transition from household duties to a more contemplative and retired life. In the context of business succession planning, vanaprastha can be seen as a metaphor for a leader stepping down from active executive roles, allowing the next generation to take charge. This intentional withdrawal is crucial for grooming successors and ensuring a gradual shift in leadership.

The timing of succession planning is as critical as the planning itself. Scriptures often highlight the importance of the right time for significant decisions. There is even an ancient Greek word for it—*kairos* or the right or critical moment. Hasty or delayed succession planning can lead to challenges. The *Mahabharata's* narrative on Karna's untimely revelation of his true identity serves as a cautionary tale—timing can alter the course of events.

These learnings collectively stress the timeless nature of succession planning in the Indian cultural and historical context. They highlight the holistic approach required, encompassing education, training, ethical considerations and a sense of duty towards the larger community. As India moves into a modern era, businesses and families can draw inspiration from these historical and scriptural insights to inform contemporary approaches to succession planning, aligning their practices with enduring principles of wisdom.

PLAN...BEFORE IT IS NEEDED

Proactive succession planning is the peg for future-proofing a family legacy, and the optimal time to embark on this strategic journey is when the need is not yet acutely felt or apparent. This forward-thinking approach transcends mere preparation; it is a commitment to the continuity of a family's legacy. By initiating succession planning before it becomes an immediate necessity, families position themselves to navigate transitions with foresight and grace. The absence of urgent pressures allows for a thoughtful, phased approach, providing ample time to identify and groom potential successors, foster their leadership capabilities and align them with the family's values and vision.

Engaging in succession planning when there is no immediate urgency provides several merits that can fortify the resilience and longevity of a family business. Firstly, it allows ample time for thorough assessment, deliberation and decision-making, enabling the identification and cultivation of potential successors well in advance. By initiating the process pre-emptively, families can navigate unforeseen emergencies, sudden changes in business circumstances, or unexpected loss of key family members with greater composure and preparedness.

Moreover, proactive succession planning fosters a culture of forward-thinking and strategic foresight within the family and the organization. By addressing succession needs before they become pressing concerns, families can align their long-term vision with actionable strategies, laying a robust foundation for sustained growth and adaptability in dynamic market environments. This proactive approach empowers families to anticipate and mitigate potential risks, capitalize on emerging opportunities and navigate transitions with agility and confidence.

Furthermore, initiating succession planning in calmer times allows families to engage in open and transparent dialogue. By facilitating constructive conversations around leadership roles and expectations, families can proactively address any concerns, laying the groundwork for smooth transitions.

Proactive succession planning is, at its essence, an investment in the future. It recognizes that the business landscape evolves, unforeseen challenges arise and leadership dynamics shift over time. By anticipating these changes, families can build a robust foundation that can withstand the test of time and adapt to the evolving needs of the business and the family.

∞

In the coming years, a positive transformation is poised to unfold within the landscape of Indian business families as the awareness and adoption of succession planning take centre stage. The increasing affluence and success of these families are paving the way for a strategic shift towards formalized structures that ensure the seamless transfer of wealth and leadership across generations. This paradigm shift is driven by a recognition of the need to protect and preserve the substantial wealth accumulated by Indian business families.

As the stakes become higher, the wisdom of strategic planning for the future is gaining prominence. Families are embracing a more professional, forward-thinking approach, leveraging the expertise of financial advisors, legal professionals and wealth managers to navigate the complexities of wealth preservation.

Legal structures, such as trusts and family constitutions, are gaining prominence as integral components of wealth preservation. These instruments provide a robust framework for governance, delineating the rights, responsibilities and expectations of family members and stakeholders. Trusts, in particular, offer a means to protect assets, provide for future generations and facilitate a seamless transition of wealth without the complexities associated with traditional inheritance.

A particularly encouraging aspect of this evolution is the growing emphasis on succession planning as an essential component of responsible wealth management. Families are proactively engaging in crafting comprehensive succession strategies that go beyond immediate concerns, considering the aspirations and needs of future generations. This long-term perspective not only safeguards the family's financial legacy but also fosters a sense of continuity and shared purpose.

Importantly, a cultural shift is underway, marked by a commitment to transparency and open communication within family businesses. This cultural evolution is instrumental in aligning family values, mitigating potential conflicts and fostering a collaborative environment where all stakeholders are informed and engaged in the succession planning process.

Technology too is playing a pivotal role in modernizing these efforts. Wealth management platforms, digital tools and financial analytics are empowering families to make informed decisions in real time. This technological integration enhances the agility and responsiveness of families in managing their financial portfolios, contributing to a more dynamic and proactive approach.

As families recognize the importance of education in preparing the next generation, investments in financial literacy programmes are on the rise as well. Equipping younger family members with the knowledge and skills necessary to navigate the complexities of wealth management ensures a continuum of responsible stewardship.

EVERY SUCCESSION PLANNING IS UNIQUE

Every succession planning journey is as unique as the family it pertains to. While we can draw inspiration and insights from the experiences of other families, it is essential to recognize that each family dynamic, circumstance and aspiration is distinct, akin to the intricacies of human DNA. Just as no two individuals are exactly alike, no two families or businesses share identical traits, challenges or goals. Therefore, attempting to replicate a succession plan from another family may not only overlook crucial nuances but also fail to address the specific needs and dynamics of the family at hand.

We can understand this by looking at the example of a large Indian textile manufacturing family business—a household name in its industry—known for its rich heritage and traditional values. The family patriarch, revered for his vision and leadership, decided to step down and pave the way for the next generation. The family initially looked to a prominent business family in the automotive sector for guidance, admiring their smooth succession transition. However, they soon realized that their own family structure, with its distinct values and operational style, required a different approach. The patriarch had always emphasized the importance of innovation and modernity in their business, which was initially deeply rooted in tradition. As a result, the family opted for a blended succession model that combined elements of the admired automotive family's plan with tailored strategies to foster innovation, ultimately ensuring that the succession process respected their unique heritage while embracing the future.

Succession planning should be approached with a deep understanding of the multifaceted factors that influence family members and businesses alike. From interpersonal relationships and individual aspirations to financial considerations and market dynamics, every aspect plays a pivotal role in shaping the succession journey. By embracing the uniqueness of each family and tailoring succession plans to suit their distinctive circumstances, values and objectives, families can navigate the complexities of succession with authenticity, adaptability and respect for their legacy. Instead of seeking ready-made solutions, families should embark on a journey of self-discovery and collaboration, leveraging their collective wisdom and strengths to craft a succession plan that honours their past, enriches their present and secures their future.

One cannot simply copy–paste a succession plan from other business families. Stick to your own core values and develop a succession plan to suit your business and family circumstances. Each family and its business are as unique as the fingerprints of its members, with distinct values, dynamics and goals that shape their journey. While it is tempting to look at successful succession stories of other family businesses and consider them as blueprints, this approach often overlooks the nuances that make your family and business distinct.

Sticking to your core values is paramount in developing a succession plan that truly resonates with your family and business. Core values serve as the guiding principles that have driven your family business to its current success. They encapsulate the legacy, vision and ethical foundation upon which your enterprise is built. When succession planning is rooted in these core values, it ensures continuity and stability, aligning the future leadership with the ethos that has long defined your business.

The nuances of family dynamics, business nature, market conditions and individual aspirations all play critical roles in shaping a successful succession plan. For instance, a family-owned construction firm, witnessing a smooth transition in a similar business, might be tempted to mirror their approach. However, recognizing their unique operational challenges and the importance of technical expertise, they might instead focus on integrating external advisors and professional managers alongside family successors to ensure a well-rounded leadership team.

Family dynamics play a pivotal role in sculpting the contours of succession planning. The relationships, power structures and communication styles within a family are inherently unique, influencing how decisions are made and leadership transitions are perceived. For instance, a family where siblings share an egalitarian bond may approach succession collaboratively, fostering a sense of unity. In contrast, a family marked by historical power struggles might necessitate more intricate negotiations.

Individual aspirations of family members inject another layer of distinctiveness into succession planning. The ambitions, skill sets and interests of potential successors vary, demanding a tailored approach. For example, a family member with a passion for innovation may require a different grooming process than one inclined towards maintaining traditional business practices. Recognizing and aligning with these individual nuances ensures a succession plan that resonates with the aspirations of each family member.

Additionally, the nature and culture of the business itself contribute to the uniqueness of succession planning. A legacy business deeply rooted in tradition may opt for a gradual transition to preserve core values, while a more agile and entrepreneurial venture might favour rapid changes to adapt to evolving market landscapes. The industry, market conditions and competitive landscape further influence the strategic considerations that shape the succession plan.

External circumstances, such as economic conditions or industry disruptions, introduce yet another element of unpredictability. An unexpected economic downturn might accelerate the need for succession, requiring agile decision-making and prompt transitions. Conversely, a thriving market might afford the luxury of a more phased and deliberate succession process.

While these factors contribute to the uniqueness of each succession plan, it is also essential to acknowledge reasons why some aspects may be similar across businesses. The adherence to best practices of governance, regulatory requirements and the pursuit of sustainable business practices are common threads that weave through succession planning across diverse family enterprises. The emphasis on transparency, communication and strategic alignment remains universal, underlining the foundational principles that guide successful transitions.

In essence, the idiosyncrasies of family dynamics, individual aspirations, business culture and external variables converge to craft the distinct aspect of each succession plan. Recognizing and embracing this uniqueness ensures that succession planning is not merely a template but a tailored strategy that resonates with the specific ethos and ambitions of each business family.

OWNERSHIP VS LEADERSHIP

Ownership in a family business does not inherently confer leadership rights or capabilities. While owning shares may entitle individuals to certain privileges within the company, effective leadership requires a distinct set of skills and qualities. In the context of succession planning, it is essential to recognize that the ability to lead and inspire extends beyond mere ownership status. Therefore, competency mapping of all stakeholders, including family members and non-family professionals, is crucial to identify individuals who possess the requisite leadership qualities that align with the cultural values of the business. By prioritizing competence and cultural fit over ownership alone, family businesses can ensure that leadership transitions are based on meritocracy and contribute to the long-term success and sustainability of the enterprise.

Equating ownership with leadership as an inherent birthright poses a significant governance issue in modern enterprises. In today's dynamic business landscape, leadership effectiveness is determined by factors such as skills, experience and merit, rather than solely by ownership status or familial lineage. Relying solely on ownership as a qualification for leadership roles can lead to nepotism, favouritism and a lack of accountability within the organization. Moreover, it undermines the principles of meritocracy and fair competition, stifling innovation and growth.

Furthermore, perpetuating the notion that ownership automatically confers leadership can result in the overlooking of talented individuals who may not possess significant shares in the company but possess the skills and vision necessary to drive the business forward. By prioritizing ownership over merit and talent, organizations risk entrusting leadership positions to individuals who may lack the requisite expertise or commitment, ultimately jeopardizing the company's performance and long-term success. Embracing a more inclusive and merit-based approach to leadership selection ensures that the most qualified individuals are empowered to lead, fostering innovation, diversity and sustainable growth within the enterprise.

In the complex landscape of family businesses, a crucial understanding that needs to be embraced is the distinction between ownership and executive management. While family members may hold significant ownership stakes, it does not automatically translate into an inherent right to assume executive management roles. Modern-day corporate governance emphasizes the separation of ownership and management functions, recognizing that effective governance and operational leadership require distinct skill sets and perspectives.

Critics argue that failing to acknowledge this separation can lead to several challenges. For instance, if family members are appointed to leadership positions solely based on their ownership status rather than their qualifications, it can result in suboptimal decision-making and hinder the company's competitiveness.

A prevalent criticism involves instances where family-owned businesses prioritize familial ties over meritocracy, leading to a lack of diversity and inclusivity in leadership. This approach can stifle innovation and hinder the business's ability to adapt to dynamic market conditions. A prime example is a family business where the leadership team primarily comprises family members without considering external talent with valuable industry experience.

Moreover, critics highlight the potential for conflicts of interest when family members serve both as executives and board members. This dual role can create challenges in ensuring unbiased decision-making, as executives may prioritize family interests over the broader company's welfare. Cases where family-controlled boards rubber-stamp decisions without rigorous scrutiny exemplify this concern, potentially impacting strategic direction and long-term sustainability.

To address these criticisms and promote effective governance, family businesses should establish robust board structures that include independent directors with relevant industry expertise. This ensures that decisions are subjected to objective evaluation and align with the company's overall strategic goals. Emphasizing professional development and qualifications for executive roles, regardless of familial connections, helps mitigate concerns about competence and meritocracy.

Another notable criticism surrounds succession planning, where the assumption that ownership automatically qualifies an individual for executive leadership can impede the development of a robust succession strategy. If family businesses prioritize lineage over competency, they risk entrusting crucial roles to successors who may not possess the requisite qualifications or experience, jeopardizing the company's future.

Moreover, critics often point to cases where the absence of independent voices on boards hampers effective decision-making. In family-controlled businesses with insular boards, there's a risk of overlooking diverse perspectives, strategic insights and industry expertise that independent directors could provide. This oversight can lead to missed opportunities, inadequate risk management and insufficient scrutiny of executive actions.

It is important to not allow familial bonds to outweigh the importance of objective decision-making, so that companies may effectively adapt to industry changes, technological advancements and shifting consumer preferences.

DISAGREEMENT IS OKAY

Recognizing that disagreement is not synonymous with opposition holds deep positive implications for members of family-owned enterprises. But then, most families take disagreement, especially from the younger generation, as a lack of respect. It is not so.

In Indian culture, where respect for elders is deeply ingrained, it can be challenging to separate disagreement from disrespect. This is due to long-standing traditions of deference to elders and hierarchical family structures. For instance, in a prominent Indian textile family business, a younger member's suggestion to modernize the production process was initially dismissed by the older generation as disrespectful, despite its potential benefits. Similarly, in a family-owned spice company, a son's proposal to expand into international markets was perceived by his father as a challenge to his authority rather than a strategic growth opportunity. While there are many examples across the Indian market, these are sufficient to illustrate how the cultural expectation of *unquestioning* respect for elders can stifle innovative ideas and necessary debates, ultimately hindering the business's progress.

Encouraging differing views within the family is a cornerstone for fostering open, transparent communication, which is essential for both family cohesion and business success. The difficulty in distinguishing between disagreement and disrespect can prevent open dialogue, leading to suppressed opinions and missed opportunities for growth and adaptation in the fast-evolving business landscape.

To illustrate, let us consider a hypothetical scenario within an Indian family business where the patriarch or matriarch holds traditional views on marketing strategies. Despite the changing consumer demographics and preferences, they insist on sticking to conventional methods that have served the business well in the past. When younger family members propose innovative digital marketing approaches or advocate for a more customer-centric approach, their suggestions are often dismissed as naive or disrespectful. This reluctance to embrace change not only hampers the business's ability to adapt to market dynamics but also alienates the younger generation, who are eager to contribute their insights and skills.

The need for a shift in mindset is paramount for modern-day enterprises to remain contemporary and competitive. Embracing diverse perspectives, especially from the younger generation, brings a myriad of benefits. Firstly, it fosters innovation by encouraging the exploration of new ideas and approaches. By leveraging the unique insights and experiences of younger family members, businesses can stay ahead of emerging trends and capitalize on untapped opportunities.

Moreover, promoting a culture of openness and inclusivity enhances employee engagement and retention, particularly among the younger workforce. When individuals feel valued and heard, they are more likely to be invested in the success of the business and contribute their best efforts. This, in turn, leads to greater creativity, productivity and ultimately, business growth.

Furthermore, acknowledging and incorporating generational perspectives fosters intergenerational learning and collaboration, bridging the gap between tradition and innovation. The senior generation can impart invaluable wisdom and experience, while the younger generation brings fresh ideas and technological savvy to the table. By embracing this synergy, family businesses can leverage the best of both worlds to drive sustainable growth and success.

Embracing diverse perspectives is crucial. Each family member brings unique experiences, insights and approaches to the table, and recognizing this diversity can lead to a richer blend of ideas. For instance, in a well-known Indian food processing family business, a younger family member's disagreement over traditional manufacturing methods led to the incorporation of innovative technology, significantly boosting productivity and profits.

Encouraging differing views also helps maintain the integrity of familial relationships. By viewing disagreements as a natural and healthy part of the decision-making process, families can avoid internal rifts that often arise from suppressing dissenting opinions. This approach fosters an atmosphere of mutual respect, where family members feel heard and valued, even when their views differ. For example, the patriarch of a leading Indian conglomerate in the automotive sector, known for his open-mindedness, encouraged each member to open up during family meetings. This inclusive approach allowed younger family members to suggest new technologies and market strategies, which eventually led to the company pioneering electric vehicles in India. The patriarch's willingness to listen and incorporate diverse viewpoints not only strengthened family bonds but also positioned the company as an industry leader in innovation.

A culture that appreciates differing views also enhances the overall governance of the family business. The behaviour of the patriarch and matriarch typically sets the tone for this cultural aspect. In many Indian families, the patriarch or matriarch's willingness to entertain and consider different viewpoints can significantly influence how the rest of the family perceives and engages in discussions. One Indian real estate family business, for instance, saw significant growth and innovation when the patriarch began to actively seek and incorporate the younger generation's consumer outreach and digital marketing strategies.

In another example, in a major Indian FMCG company, the matriarch played a pivotal role in fostering a culture of open dialogue. She instituted a policy where family members and key executives could propose ideas anonymously, ensuring that even the most junior members felt their voices were valued. This practice led to the adoption of a sustainable packaging initiative, which not only boosted the company's eco-friendly image but also opened new market segments. Her approach demonstrated that constructive debate and diverse perspectives could lead to significant business advantages.

The case of a renowned family-owned pharmaceutical company in India illustrates how a patriarch's behaviour can promote informed decision-making. The head of this business, known for his scholarly demeanour, encouraged family members to back their suggestions with data and research. This method of decision-making was evident when the family debated entering the biotechnology sector. Through rigorous discussions and data-driven debates, they collectively decided to invest in this area, which later became a major growth driver for the company. The patriarch's insistence on informed debate ensured that decisions were made based on sound evidence, enhancing the company's strategic direction.

In contrast, the absence of such leadership can stifle a family business's growth. In a well-known Indian real estate family business, the patriarch's autocratic style led to a culture where dissenting views were discouraged. This lack of open dialogue resulted in missed opportunities and outdated business practices, causing the company to fall behind its more progressive competitors. The patriarch's refusal to entertain differing viewpoints ultimately hampered the business's ability to adapt to market changes and innovate.

The behaviour of the patriarch or matriarch in promoting a culture of open dialogue is essential not only for the business's success but also for the harmony and unity of the family. When family leaders model respect for diverse opinions and encourage constructive debate, it sets a precedent for the entire organization. This culture trickles down to professional teams, fostering an environment where employees feel empowered to contribute ideas and challenge the status quo. It allows for the fostering of a sense of shared ownership and commitment to the business's success. An Indian agribusiness company experienced tremendous growth after implementing a policy where both family members and professional managers could openly discuss and debate strategies, leading to more innovative and effective business solutions.

In practice, promoting a culture where disagreement is viewed as constructive involves creating forums for open discussions, actively listening to different viewpoints and valuing the contributions of each family member and professional team member. Establishing clear communication channels and mechanisms for conflict resolution further supports this approach.

Seeing disagreement as a dialogue, not defiance, is vital for family businesses. By fostering an environment where differing views are seen as opportunities rather than threats, family businesses can navigate the complexities of succession and leadership transitions more effectively, ensuring long-term success and continuity. After all, when the younger generation questions the old ways, it is not about disrespect—it is about keeping the legacy lively and evolving.

AVOIDING MERITOCRACY IN INDIAN BUSINESSES

One notable failure in Indian businesses lies in its tendency to avoid meritocracy, where leadership positions are often not filled based on individual capabilities and achievements. Many family-controlled businesses continue to face challenges in implementing transparent and merit-based systems for appointing leaders. This failure often results in instances of nepotism and favouritism and leadership decisions influenced more by familial ties than by professional competence.

Despite the evolution of the corporate landscape in India, there are instances where family connections take precedence over merit. This can lead to a lack of motivation among non-family employees, hinder organizational innovation and compromise the overall efficiency and competitiveness of the business. On the other hand, companies that prioritize meritocracy tend to foster a culture of healthy competition, employee engagement and long-term sustainability.

Meritocracy, which is the principle of promoting and rewarding individuals based on their abilities and performance rather than factors like nepotism or seniority, is crucial for fostering a culture of excellence and driving business success. However, in many Indian businesses, entrenched cultural norms, traditional hierarchical structures and familial ties often hinder the establishment of a truly meritocratic environment.

One of the primary consequences of inadequate meritocracy is the stifling of talent and innovation within the organization. When promotions, opportunities and rewards are based more on familial connections or tenure rather than merit, it discourages high-performing employees from striving for excellence. Instead of focusing on enhancing their skills and delivering results, employees may become disillusioned and disengaged, leading to a decline in productivity and morale.

Moreover, the absence of meritocracy can result in a lack of diversity and inclusivity within the workforce. When individuals are not selected or promoted based on their qualifications and capabilities, it perpetuates a homogenous environment where only those with certain backgrounds or affiliations thrive. This not only limits the pool of talent available to the organization but also inhibits creativity and innovation, as diverse perspectives and ideas are overlooked or marginalized.

In addition, inadequate meritocracy can erode trust and morale among employees, leading to increased turnover and talent attrition. When individuals perceive that their hard work and contributions are not recognized or rewarded fairly, they may seek opportunities elsewhere. This turnover not only disrupts the continuity of business operations but also incurs significant costs in terms of recruitment, onboarding and training.

Furthermore, the failure to establish meritocracy can perpetuate a culture of mediocrity and complacency within the organization. When individuals believe that advancement is based more on who they know rather than what they know, it diminishes their incentive to strive for excellence and innovate. This can have far-reaching implications for the organization's competitiveness and ability to adapt to changing market dynamics.

To address these challenges, Indian businesses must prioritize the establishment of a robust meritocracy rooted in fairness, transparency and accountability. This requires implementing clear and objective criteria for performance evaluation, promotion and reward allocation, ensuring that decisions are based on merit rather than personal biases or preferences. Moreover, organizations must actively promote diversity and inclusivity, recognizing and celebrating the unique talents and perspectives of all employees.

Leadership plays a critical role in driving the cultural shift towards meritocracy within the organization. Leaders must lead by example, demonstrating a commitment to fairness, integrity and excellence in all aspects of decision-making and behaviour. They must also foster a culture of continuous learning and development, providing employees with opportunities to enhance their skills and grow professionally based on merit. A retail chain with a loyal customer base struggled to adapt to changing market trends and competition. Recognizing the need for professionalism, the promoters revamped their management practices to prioritize merit and competence. They invested in employee training and development programmes, empowering staff to deliver exceptional customer service and innovative solutions. This focus on professionalism not only improved customer satisfaction but also drove business growth and expansion.

LEADERSHIP IS NOT GENETIC

The notion that leadership traits are *not* genetic challenges the traditional notion of succession planning solely based on family lineage. While family businesses often prioritize continuity through blood ties, the assumption that leadership qualities are hereditary oversimplifies the complex nature of effective leadership. A more nuanced approach to succession planning acknowledges that leadership traits are cultivated through a combination of experiences, education, mentorship and individual effort.

In one of India's largest manufacturing conglomerates, the founder had built a formidable business from scratch. As he contemplated inducting his children into the succession fold, he faced the challenge of choosing a successor among his three children. Traditionally, as was his family custom, the eldest son was expected to take over. However, the founder realized that relying solely on familial hierarchy might not be in the best interests of the business. Recognizing the diverse skills and potential of his children, the founder implemented a comprehensive development programme. Each child was given an opportunity to work in different departments, ranging from operations and finance to marketing and international business. They were also encouraged to pursue higher education and specialized professional training outside the family business, gaining exposure to global best practices and diverse work cultures.

The youngest son, initially overlooked due to traditional biases, emerged as a strong contender. His innovative approach to organizational development and ability to lead diverse teams set him apart. The founder, valuing merit over tradition, appointed him as the successor. This decision was met with initial resistance within the family but proved to be a masterstroke. Under his leadership, the company navigated the challenges of a shift in consumer behaviour, how enterprises are designed to be contemporary, and digital disruption, and expanded its global footprint, showcasing that effective leadership emerges from a well-rounded development journey rather than mere familial ties.

Leadership is a dynamic and multifaceted skill set that evolves over time. Individuals develop these skills through a diverse range of experiences, including education, work environments and exposure to various leadership styles. Assuming that these qualities are automatically passed down within a family disregards the potential for external influences to shape and enhance leadership capabilities. Succession planning should reflect that effective leaders emerge not solely from familial ties but from a holistic and diverse development journey.

An illustrative example lies in the tech industry, where numerous successful leaders have emerged from diverse backgrounds, often without a direct familial connection to the industry. The tech industry in India has seen an impressive surge of growth, innovation and global recognition over the past few decades. What is particularly remarkable about this sector is the emergence of successful non-family professionals who have taken the reins of family-owned businesses, demonstrating that leadership is not confined to genetic inheritance. Almost all leaders running India's largest tech firms are non-promoter family professionals. These leaders, coming from diverse backgrounds, have steered family businesses to new heights with their expertise, vision and innovative strategies.

Furthermore, the digital era has transformed the way business operates, emphasizing the importance of tech-savvy leaders. The assumption that only promoter family members inherently possess the technological acumen required for modern business is actually silly. Succession plans should actively seek individuals with the relevant digital skills, irrespective of familial connections, to ensure the organization remains competitive in an increasingly technology-driven world.

The rejection of the genetic inheritance of leadership traits also highlights the need for continuous learning and development. Leaders who actively seek knowledge, adapt to emerging trends and embrace ongoing education contribute significantly to a company's resilience. Succession planning should focus on individuals who demonstrate a commitment to personal growth and are open to evolving leadership practices, regardless of whether they have familial ties to the business.

Ultimately, by embracing meritocracy as a guiding principle, Indian businesses can unlock the full potential of their workforce, drive innovation and competitiveness, and position themselves for long-term success in an increasingly complex and dynamic business environment.

I am often asked, 'I am a medium-sized enterprise, and all my clients know me personally. Why should I change into meritocracy?'

Transitioning to a meritocracy-based organization offers numerous benefits beyond the immediate familiarity and personal connections enjoyed in a small or medium-sized enterprise. While personal relationships with clients are undoubtedly valuable, embracing meritocracy can enhance organizational resilience, drive sustainable growth, and strengthen governance structures in several ways.

Firstly, it fosters a culture of excellence and performance-driven behaviour within the organization. By rewarding individuals based on their skills, capabilities and contributions rather than personal relationships or favouritism, you create a level playing field where everyone has an equal opportunity to succeed. This, in turn, motivates employees to strive for excellence, innovate and continuously improve their performance, ultimately enhancing the quality of products and services offered to clients.

Secondly, meritocracy promotes fairness and transparency in decision-making processes, which is crucial for building trust and credibility with clients. When clients see that your organization operates based on objective criteria and merit-based principles, they are more likely to perceive you as reliable, trustworthy and committed to delivering results. This can strengthen client relationships, improve customer satisfaction and ultimately drive business growth through positive word-of-mouth referrals and repeat business.

Furthermore, it can help mitigate risks associated with over-reliance on personal relationships. While personal connections may initially provide a competitive advantage, they can also create vulnerabilities such as nepotism, favouritism and potential conflicts of interest. By prioritizing meritocracy, you mitigate these risks and create a more robust governance framework that ensures decisions are made in the best interests of the organization and its stakeholders.

Moreover, embracing meritocracy can attract top talent to your organization and foster a culture of innovation and collaboration.

Talented individuals are more likely to be drawn to organizations that offer opportunities for growth, recognition and advancement based on their merits rather than external factors. By creating a merit-based environment, you position your organization as an attractive destination for high-performing professionals seeking opportunities for personal and professional development.

Overall, transitioning to a meritocracy-based organization is not about abandoning personal relationships with clients but rather complementing them with a strong foundation of fairness, transparency and accountability. By embracing meritocracy, you can drive organizational excellence, enhance client relationships, mitigate risks, attract top talent and foster a culture of innovation and collaboration, ultimately positioning your medium-sized enterprise for long-term success and sustainability in today's competitive business landscape.

It is understandable that promoters may fear that emphasizing professionalism could erode the employees' personal loyalty to them. However, this fear is often unfounded, as professionalism and personal loyalty are not mutually exclusive. In fact, prioritizing professionalism can strengthen the bond between promoters and employees by encouraging an environment of mutual respect, trust and integrity.

Promoters should recognize that personal loyalty based solely on emotional ties or favouritism may not always align with the best interests of the organization. While loyalty is undoubtedly important, it should ideally be rooted in shared values, professional ethics and a commitment to organizational success. Emphasizing professionalism encourages employees to uphold these principles, ensuring that their loyalty is based on a genuine dedication to excellence and integrity rather than personal allegiances.

By expecting employees to demonstrate personal integrity alongside professionalism, promoters set a positive example for their workforce and cultivate a culture of trust and transparency. Employees who feel valued and respected are more likely to exhibit loyalty and dedication to the organization, not because of personal allegiance to the promoters, but because they genuinely believe in the organization's mission and values.

A case in point here is a family-owned service sector company that faced challenges in retaining top talent due to its informal approach to management. By embracing professionalism and meritocracy, the company implemented transparent performance evaluation systems and offered opportunities for career advancement based on skills and contributions rather than personal connections. This shift not only boosted employee morale but also attracted new talent, enhancing the company's competitiveness in the market.

To bring meritocracy to their enterprises, business families can take several proactive steps:

1. **Lead by example:** Family leaders must lead by example and demonstrate a commitment to meritocracy in all aspects of decision-making and behaviour. They should prioritize hiring, promotion and reward allocation based on merit rather than familial ties or personal biases.
2. **Establish clear criteria:** Define clear and objective criteria for evaluating performance, promoting employees and allocating rewards. Ensure that these criteria are transparent, consistently applied and aligned with the organization's strategic objectives.
3. **Promote diversity and inclusion:** Foster a culture of diversity and inclusion where individuals from diverse backgrounds and perspectives are valued and respected. Encourage open dialogue and collaboration to leverage the full spectrum of talent within the organization.
4. **Invest in talent development:** Provide employees with opportunities for continuous learning and development to enhance their skills and capabilities. Offer training programmes, mentorship initiatives and career development opportunities to support professional growth based on merit.
5. **Encourage feedback and accountability:** Create a culture of open feedback and accountability where employees are encouraged to provide constructive feedback and hold themselves and others accountable for their actions and performance.
6. **Reward excellence:** Recognize and reward employees who demonstrate excellence, innovation and outstanding performance. Ensure that rewards are commensurate with achievements and contribute to a culture of meritocracy.

7. **Promote collaboration and teamwork:** Foster collaboration and teamwork across departments and functions to leverage collective expertise and drive organizational success. Encourage cross-functional projects and initiatives that promote merit-based decision-making and problem-solving.
8. **Embrace change and adaptability:** Encourage a culture of change and adaptability where employees are empowered to challenge the status quo, experiment with new ideas and adapt to changing market dynamics. Emphasize agility and resilience as key drivers of organizational success.
9. **Communicate transparently:** Maintain open and transparent communication channels to keep employees informed about organizational goals, priorities and performance expectations. Ensure that decision-making processes are transparent and accessible to all stakeholders.
10. **Evaluate and adjust:** Continuously monitor and evaluate the effectiveness of meritocracy initiatives within the organization. Solicit feedback from employees and stakeholders to identify areas for improvement and make necessary adjustments to policies and practices.

BLOOD AND SWEAT

In Indian business families, the adage 'blood is thicker than water' poses significant challenges to fostering a fair and transparent business environment and has implications for potential corporate governance concerns.

The prioritization of family ties over meritocracy can lead to nepotism, where key positions are reserved for family members irrespective of their qualifications or capabilities. In such cases, meritocracy—which should ideally be the driving force behind leadership appointments—takes a back seat, and decisions become influenced by familial connections rather than professional competence.

From a corporate governance perspective, the dominance of family relationships raises concerns about impartial decision-making and accountability. Boards that are predominantly composed of family members may lack the independence and diversity needed to ensure checks and balances within the organization. The potential for conflicts of interest, insider dealings and biased decision-making becomes more pronounced when familial bonds consistently take precedence over objective evaluation of skills and qualifications.

This can also affect the effective functioning of audit committees and other governance structures, as family members may be less likely to question or challenge decisions made by their relatives. The absence of an independent voice in governance discussions may result in a lack of transparency and accountability, raising doubts about the integrity of the decision-making processes.

To address these concerns, it is essential for Indian business families to strike a balance between family values and professional meritocracy. Encouraging fair competition, establishing transparent recruitment and promotion processes, and incorporating independent voices into governance structures are crucial steps towards mitigating the impact of the 'blood is thicker than water' phenomenon.

WOMEN'S PARTICIPATION IN BUSINESS ROLES

Another significant challenge in the Indian business landscape is the failure to fully open up governance and executive roles for women, particularly within family businesses. Despite increasing number of women entering higher education and industrial exposure, cultural and community precedents often limit women's progression to these leadership positions.

In many traditional business families, societal expectations and deeply ingrained cultural norms may perpetuate gender bias, hindering women from taking on business roles. While women are contributing significantly to various fields, their representation in top-level decision-making positions remains disproportionately low. This failure not only restricts the potential for diverse perspectives and innovation but also deprives businesses of the valuable skills and talents that women bring to the table.

Efforts to address these failures involve challenging gender stereotypes, promoting diversity and inclusion, and creating a supportive work environment that encourages women's professional growth. Recognizing that meritocracy knows no gender and that women can play pivotal roles in steering businesses towards success is essential for fostering a more equitable and progressive business landscape in India. The many examples of successful women entrepreneurs and leaders across second or subsequent generations in business families support this.*

---

*'Nisa Godrej to Yashasvini Jindal: 10 Lesser-known Daughters of Indian Billionaires Making Waves in the Business World', *Financial Express*, 13 May 2024, https://tinyurl.com/ywebkbsw; Lidhoo, Prerna, and Smita Tripathi, 'Women at Work: How Daughters Have Taken on Lead Roles in Family Businesses', *Business Today*, 18 September 2022, https://tinyurl.com/5n8rum7v. Both accessed on 31 December 2024.

WHY IGNORING WOMEN FOR LEADERSHIP ROLES IS DETRIMENTAL

Ignoring women, particularly those who may not be directly involved in their family's business, is detrimental to the succession planning process in Indian business families. This bias not only perpetuates gender inequity but also overlooks the valuable perspectives, skills and potential contributions that women can bring to the table. Overcoming this bias is essential for creating inclusive and effective succession plans that leverage the diverse talents within the family. Here's why ignoring women for leadership roles is detrimental.

Missed Perspectives and Skills

Neglecting women excludes a pool of diverse perspectives and skills that can be instrumental in shaping strategic decisions for the family business. It limits the innovation and adaptability of the succession plan, potentially overlooking valuable insights that could contribute to the business's long-term success. Furthermore, the absence of women in key decision-making roles within a family business may impede its ability to connect with a broader customer base.

As consumers become increasingly diverse, having a leadership team that mirrors this diversity can enhance the business's understanding of varied market segments. Women leaders can provide valuable insights into consumer preferences and trends, fostering a competitive edge and promoting a more inclusive brand image. Incorporating women into pivotal roles, thus, is not just a matter of equality but a strategic imperative for sustained growth and relevance in a rapidly evolving business landscape.

Undermines Talent Potential

Disregarding women irrespective of their involvement in the family business can result in the underutilization of talent and potential within the family. It hampers the ability of the family business to tap into a broader range of skills and capabilities, hindering its overall competitiveness and agility.

This short-sighted approach not only undermines the capabilities of women but also limits the overall prowess of the business. Talent is a crucial driver of innovation and adaptability, and excluding a significant portion of the family members based on gender perpetuates a missed opportunity for dynamic problem-solving and strategic thinking.

Embracing the full spectrum of talent within the family, regardless of gender, not only strengthens the business's internal capabilities but also positions it to thrive in an ever-evolving marketplace where versatility and agility are paramount.

Impact on Family Dynamics

The exclusion of women from succession planning discussions not only has professional repercussions but also significantly impacts family dynamics. Family businesses are unique in that they intertwine personal relationships with professional responsibilities, and neglecting the input of women in succession planning can disrupt the delicate balance. This lack of inclusivity may lead to power struggles, strained relationships and internal conflicts that have the potential to spill over into the business operations. It can create internal tensions and lead to a lack of cohesion. As a result, it can create resentment, a lack of trust and a divisive atmosphere within the family unit, potentially causing conflicts that can spill over into the business, jeopardizing the smooth execution of the succession plan.

WHAT CAN INDIAN BUSINESS FAMILIES DO?

Recognizing the value of diverse perspectives and talents, forward-thinking business families are increasingly prioritizing initiatives to promote a culture of inclusion and equity within their organizations. To embark on this transformative journey, families must first introspect into topics such as cultural norms, leadership development, succession planning and recruitment practices. They can thus identify areas for improvement and develop strategies to create a more inclusive and equitable environment. This introspective process lays the foundation for meaningful change and sets the stage for building a family business that thrives on the principles of diversity, equality and opportunity. Here are a few key areas for improvement; under each of these, pointed questions can be asked.

Promote Inclusive Mindsets

How can we actively foster an inclusive mindset within our family that not only acknowledges but also celebrates the diverse perspectives and potential contributions of all family members, regardless of gender?

Provide Equal Educational Opportunities

Are we taking proactive measures to ensure that women within the family have equitable access to quality education and professional development opportunities that can empower them to take on leadership roles within the business?

Establish Mentorship Programmes

In what ways can we establish mentorship programmes specifically tailored to support and nurture the talents and aspirations of women family members who may not currently be directly involved in the business but exhibit potential for future contributions?

Create Open Channels of Communication

Are we creating and maintaining open, transparent channels of communication that encourage and empower women within the family to voice their aspirations, concerns and innovative ideas related to the family business and succession planning?

Review and Update Governance Policies

How can we proactively review and update our governance policies to ensure they are not only gender-neutral but also actively promote equal opportunities for all family members to engage and participate meaningfully in succession planning discussions?

Cultural Norms and Traditions

How do cultural norms and traditions influence gender roles and expectations within our family business?

Are there any outdated customs or practices that may inadvertently hinder the participation of women or other marginalized groups?

Leadership Development

What initiatives do we have in place to cultivate leadership skills among women family members?

How can we provide mentorship and leadership development opportunities to individuals from underrepresented groups within our family?

Succession Planning

How can we ensure that succession planning processes are inclusive and equitable, taking into account the aspirations and capabilities of all family members?

Are there any biases or assumptions that may impact succession decisions, and how can we address them?

Work-Life Balance

How do we support work–life balance for all family members, especially women who may have additional caregiving responsibilities?

What policies or initiatives can we implement to promote flexibility and accommodate diverse family needs?

Recruitment and Hiring Practices

Are our recruitment and hiring practices designed to attract and retain diverse talent?

How can we ensure that our hiring processes are fair and unbiased, providing equal opportunities for all applicants?

Training and Development

How do we prioritize training and development opportunities for women and other underrepresented groups within our organization?

Are there specific skills or competencies that we need to focus on to support the advancement of diverse talent?

Promotion and Advancement

How do we ensure that promotions and career advancement opportunities are based on merit rather than gender or other factors?

What steps can we take to create a more transparent and merit-based promotion process?

Family Council Dynamics

How inclusive is our family council in terms of representation and decision-making authority?

Are there mechanisms in place to ensure that diverse voices are heard and respected within the family council?

External Partnerships and Networks

How can we leverage external partnerships and networks to promote diversity and inclusion within our industry and community?

Are there opportunities to collaborate with organizations or initiatives that focus on gender equality and equal opportunity?

Continuous Evaluation and Improvement

How do we measure progress towards greater inclusivity and equality within our family business?

What mechanisms do we have in place for feedback and continuous improvement in our diversity and inclusion efforts?

UNDERSTANDING AND WORKING WITH GEMZ CHALLENGES

With the emergence of the gig economy, millennials and Gen Z (GEMZ), the world has been undergoing a transformation that is making it younger and more complex than ever before. This demographic shift brings new challenges and opportunities for businesses across all sectors. The rise of gig workers, the influx of digital natives into the workforce, and the changing consumer preferences driven by younger generations are reshaping markets and industries. Businesses must adapt to the evolving needs and expectations of GEMZ to stay competitive and relevant.

The world is becoming increasingly interconnected and diverse, requiring businesses to navigate a complex web of technological advancements, cultural shifts and demographic changes to succeed in the modern era. These elements are reshaping the business landscape, consumption patterns and organizational dynamics. Ignoring them could render traditional family businesses obsolete in a rapidly changing world.

Markets and consumption are undergoing significant transformations due to the rise of millennials and Gen Z. These generations, characterized by their digital nativity and different value systems, are not only consumers but also key drivers of economic activity. They prioritize experiences over possessions, demand transparency and are socially conscious. For instance, a well-known Indian apparel brand had to completely revamp its product line and marketing strategies to cater to the eco-conscious preferences of millennials and Gen Z, emphasizing sustainable and ethical production practices.

This shift in consumption patterns necessitates that family businesses adapt their offerings and marketing strategies to remain relevant. Traditional marketing methods, heavily reliant on print media and word-of-mouth, are being replaced by digital marketing campaigns, influencer collaborations and social media engagement. An Indian

FMCG company, for example, significantly increased its market share by launching a digital-first brand targeted at millennials, leveraging influencer marketing and social media platforms to reach its audience effectively.

The gig economy is another transformative force that Indian family businesses need to understand and integrate into their operations. With the rise of freelance and contractual work, the traditional employment model is being challenged. This new economy offers businesses the flexibility to tap into a diverse pool of talent for short-term projects without the long-term commitments associated with traditional employment. An Indian technology firm, for instance, has successfully utilized gig workers to handle seasonal spikes in workload, accessing a broader talent pool without incurring significant long-term costs.

Embracing the gig economy also allows family businesses to be more agile and responsive to market demands. It fosters innovation by bringing in fresh perspectives from diverse freelancers and consultants. A well-established Indian media house tapped into the gig economy to revitalize its content strategy, hiring freelance writers and designers who brought innovative ideas and approaches, resulting in a substantial increase in readership and engagement.

The organizational needs and leadership styles required to manage millennials and Gen Z are different from those suited to older generations. Younger employees value autonomy, flexibility and a sense of purpose in their work. They are less inclined to accept hierarchical structures and rigid corporate cultures. A renowned Indian conglomerate realized this and restructured its corporate culture to be more inclusive and flexible. It implemented policies that promoted work–life balance, remote working options and opportunities for continuous learning and development.

Gen Z is anticipated to be the most significant disruptor globally, with their unique preferences, digital fluency, and distinct outlook on work and consumption. Businesses must deeply consider how to engage this generation, as they will not only comprise a significant portion of the workforce but also influence stakeholders, investors and customers alike. Their digital-first mindset, coupled with a penchant for innovation and social responsibility, demands that businesses tailor their strategies to resonate with Gen Z values and preferences. Adapting to this generational shift is imperative for businesses to thrive in the evolving marketplace and maintain relevance in the eyes of the increasingly influential Gen Z demographic.

Family business successors need to embrace these changes to attract and retain young talent. This involves creating an environment that values diversity, inclusivity and continuous innovation. Leadership must be empathetic, transparent and adaptable. For example, an Indian pharmaceutical company established a mentorship programme that paired seasoned executives with younger employees. This initiative not only facilitated knowledge transfer but also helped bridge the generational gap, fostering mutual respect and collaboration.

Furthermore, conventional distribution models are being disrupted by technology, making the understanding and integration of GEMZ even more critical across all sectors. The advent of the Internet of things (IoT) and other emerging digital technologies necessitates that businesses become more agile and proactive in implementing changes. Plain legacy will not suffice for modern consumers, who expect cutting-edge products or solutions.

For instance, an Indian retail chain had to overhaul its distribution model to incorporate IoT-enabled inventory management systems. This allowed for real-time tracking of stock levels and demand forecasting, significantly reducing wastage and improving supply chain efficiency. By adopting these technologies, the company not only met the expectations of tech-savvy consumers but also enhanced its operational efficiency.

The infusion of digital technologies and the adoption of agile practices are vital for staying relevant in a marketplace driven by millennials and Gen Z. These generations are accustomed to rapid technological advancements and expect businesses to keep pace with their evolving preferences. Legacy systems and traditional ways of doing business are often seen as outdated and inefficient.

By proactively embracing GEMZ, family businesses can ensure their longevity and relevance in an increasingly competitive market. Moreover, integrating GEMZ principles can lead to better business outcomes. By understanding and leveraging the consumption habits of millennials and Gen Z, businesses can develop products and services that resonate with these generations.

Succession planning in family businesses must incorporate these elements to ensure future leaders are equipped to navigate the complexities of the modern business environment. Successors should be trained to appreciate the dynamics of the gig economy, understand the motivations and expectations of millennials and Gen Z, and develop leadership styles that are inclusive and adaptive. An Indian automotive company, for instance, established a comprehensive leadership development programme that included modules on digital transformation, customer-centric innovation and managing a multi-generational workforce. This programme was instrumental in preparing the next generation of leaders to drive the company forward.

In today's rapidly evolving consumer landscape, I observe a significantly increasing trend, which I call the 'ME' economy as it captures memories and experiences. This concept encapsulates the shifting consumer behaviour towards prioritizing memories and experiences over material possessions. With the rise of the selfie generation and the prevalence of social media platforms, individuals are increasingly seeking out experiences that they can share and cherish, rather than accumulating tangible assets. This trend marks a significant departure from the frugality practised by previous generations, such as the baby boomers, who placed greater emphasis on saving and investing in traditional assets.

The ME economy presents a plethora of opportunities for businesses across various industries. From travel and hospitality to entertainment and dining, businesses that offer unique and memorable experiences stand to thrive in this new economy. For example, luxury resorts are now focusing on curating personalized experiences for guests, while adventure tourism companies are catering to the growing demand for adrenaline-fuelled escapades. Similarly, restaurants are not just selling food, they are selling an immersive dining experience complete with Instagram-worthy decor and innovative culinary creations.

In the context of Indian business families, the ME economy poses both challenges and opportunities for scions who may be inheriting family wealth and businesses. On the one hand, the desire to indulge in personal experiences and create lasting memories may lead them to pursue alternative paths outside the family business. This could include investing in passion projects, travelling the world or exploring entrepreneurial ventures unrelated to the family legacy. On the other hand, it also presents an opportunity for family businesses to adapt and innovate to cater to the evolving preferences of the younger generation. By leveraging technology and creativity, they can create experiential offerings that resonate with the ME economy mindset while still staying true to their core values and heritage.

Furthermore, the ME economy underscores the importance of authenticity and emotional connection in brand–consumer relationships. Businesses that prioritize transparency, sustainability and genuine human connection are more likely to resonate with consumers in the ME economy era. This is particularly relevant for family-owned businesses, which often have a rich history and legacy that can be leveraged to create compelling narratives and experiences. For Indian business family scions, GEMZ offers a unique opportunity to reimagine their roles and contributions within their family enterprises while also embracing their individual passions and aspirations.

IT IS OKAY TO DO SOMETHING ELSE

Many business families take it personally when a member of the younger generation expresses disinterest in involvement with the family business. Emotions run high, and anger is often common. This reaction usually stems from deep-rooted sentiments tied to the family legacy, personal sacrifices made by previous generations for the business, and a sense of continuity and tradition. The family business, for many, is not merely a commercial venture but a symbol of identity and pride. When a successor chooses a different path, it can be perceived as a deviation from a shared vision of the future that generations have collectively aspired for. The perceived rejection of the family business may evoke disappointment and concern about the legacy's preservation, making it challenging for family members to separate the personal and emotional investments from the practical decision at hand.

In the modern world, however, there are abundant opportunities for family members to pursue diverse paths beyond the family business. The expanding landscape of careers, entrepreneurial ventures outside of the family business, and educational and creative or artistic pursuits offer avenues for individuals to explore their passions and contribute to society in various ways. The shift towards recognizing and respecting individual aspirations is a hallmark of contemporary values, emphasizing personal fulfilment and diverse experiences. Acknowledging these alternative paths not only aligns with the principles of autonomy and self-discovery but also contributes to the holistic development of family members, fostering a more inclusive and adaptable family dynamic in the context of evolving societal norms and opportunities.

In the context of amassed wealth and expanded global exposure provided by preceding generations, successors may opt for distinct life paths outside their family businesses. This divergence represents a form of diversity, and concerns about safeguarding family wealth within the enterprise can be addressed through strategic exits or by introducing non-family business leaders. Successful instances of such transitions exist across various business scales in India, highlighting the adaptability and dynamism that can accompany family business transformations.

Encouraging a successor to explore opportunities outside the family business can be a positive and proactive approach to succession planning. It acknowledges the value of diverse skill sets and perspectives, recognizing that exposure to different industries and experiences enriches an individual's capabilities. This support for personal growth and development allows successors the freedom to explore their passions and interests, contributing to a well-rounded perspective that can prove beneficial when they choose to re-engage with the family business or contribute to it in an advisory or governance capacity.

Furthermore, providing the space for any exploration outside the established family business tree should not only be allowed but is in fact essential. In the current era of free-thinking, compelling scions to assume roles in the family business does not guarantee their genuine commitment or focused attention to executive responsibilities. This lack of intrinsic motivation can pose potential risks to the enterprise. Recognizing and respecting the individual choices of scions becomes imperative for fostering a more meaningful and effective engagement with the family business. Allowing successors to pursue independent ventures fosters a spirit of innovation and risk-taking, which can contribute to the family's legacy. Respecting and supporting a successor's decision to step outside the family business also mitigates potential conflicts that may arise from a sense of obligation, fostering open communication and maintaining family harmony, both crucial factors in the long-term success of familial relationships and the business.

Embracing the idea of tailored career paths for each family member acknowledges their uniqueness and individual goals. While some successors may thrive within the family business, others may find fulfilment in ventures beyond its confines. This approach promotes the satisfaction and happiness of family members, contributing to a supportive family environment.

Moreover, encouraging successors to explore alternative paths proactively involves creating an open dialogue about their aspirations and interests. This communication allows family leaders to understand the motivations behind such decisions, enabling them to provide the necessary support and resources. By embracing and celebrating the diverse journeys of family members, a family business can cultivate an environment where each individual feels empowered to pursue their distinct path. This forward-thinking approach not only supports personal growth but also positions the family business to benefit from the enriched perspectives, experiences and skills that returning successors may bring to the table.

FAMILY POLITICS

No matter how carefully the points mentioned earlier in this book have been considered, not all succession planning efforts succeed. So, why *do* they fail?

Succession planning within Indian business families is a complex endeavour, riddled with challenges stemming from the web of family politics. Managing succession planning in a family business is like playing a complex video game, with unexpected challenges and characters emerging continuously. The process's true stability becomes evident only after assessing outcomes patiently for a year or two of the executed succession plan.

Family politics is a nuanced and dynamic aspect that is present all across familial relationships, impacting decision-making processes and power dynamics. Whether unfolding within a modest household or a sprawling business empire, it defines relationships, influences power distribution and significantly shapes outcomes. The struggle for influence and control is a common theme, manifesting in decisions about finances, education, careers and major life events. Family structures evolve across generations, resulting in shifting power dynamics, with older and younger generations negotiating their roles. The emotional dimensions of family politics can both strengthen and complicate matters; they contribute positively through love and support, or negatively through jealousy, unresolved conflicts and emotional baggage. The impact extends to relationships between family members, necessitating the use of emotional intelligence and effective conflict resolution. Recognizing that the term 'politics' encompasses the everyday dynamics of decision-making and power negotiation adds depth to understanding its role in family affairs.

Succession planning often becomes a focal point *for* and *in* family politics, triggering negotiations and conflicts over inheritance and leadership roles. That is when all pent-up emotions and historic grouses appear in various forms of discussions and behaviour. Politics, whether the dining-room conversations or the kitchen kind, can manifest across negotiations.

In every business family, effective paternal or maternal leadership serves as a strong pillar, guiding the values that are deeply embedded within the family and the business itself. They act as the custodian of the family's values and traditions. Their influence is significant in shaping the ethos of the business, instilling a sense of identity, purpose and continuity. This leadership style not only shapes the core principles of the family enterprise but also plays a pivotal role in influencing the trajectories of succession planning. It provides a compass for decision-making, emphasizing long-term sustainability, ethical practices and a commitment to the community.

The values embedded by effective parental leadership act as a cultural glue, binding family members and business associates. This shared sense of purpose creates a foundation upon which succession plans can be built. When the values are clear and deeply ingrained, they serve as guiding principles for selecting successors, determining leadership styles and navigating the complexities of generational transitions.

JOINT FAMILY POLITICS

Joint family politics can significantly influence the dynamics of succession planning within a business family. In a joint family setup, where multiple generations and branches coexist, power struggles and complex relationships often come to the forefront. The distribution of authority, decision-making roles and control over family assets become subjects of negotiation and contention. The challenge lies in balancing the interests and aspirations of different family members, each with their own unique perspectives and ambitions.

On the one hand, joint family politics can foster a sense of unity and collaboration, pooling together diverse skills and experiences. This collaborative spirit may lead to well-rounded decision-making and the ability to navigate challenges collectively. However, on the flip side, it can also give rise to conflicts, as individual egos, personal differences and conflicting agendas may clash within the intricate web of family relationships.

Moreover, the influence of elder family members in a joint family can be both a stabilizing force and a potential source of resistance to change. The traditional hierarchical structure may resist the integration of fresh ideas and innovative approaches that younger generations may bring to the table. Striking a balance between respecting the wisdom of elders and embracing the dynamism of the youth becomes a delicate task.

In essence, joint family politics adds layers of complexity to succession planning, requiring a nuanced understanding of interpersonal dynamics, effective communication and the establishment of clear governance structures. Succession plans need to navigate the intricate web of relationships, ensuring that the chosen successors have the necessary support and cooperation from all family members for a smooth transition.

POWER STRUGGLES

The inherent power struggles among family members stand out as a pervasive challenge for succession planning. Decision-making processes can become convoluted, as conflicting interests and individual ambitions vie for dominance. The primary concern here is the potential disruption to the establishment of a clear succession plan, jeopardizing the long-term stability and growth of the family business.

Successful navigation of power struggles can result in a well-defined succession plan that aligns with the strategic interests of the business. Unresolved power struggles may lead to fragmentation or division within the family, resulting in the splintering of the business empire. Open and transparent communication channels can mitigate power struggles by fostering understanding among family members. Well-defined governance structures delineating roles and responsibilities help reduce ambiguity and power conflicts. Business decisions influenced by external factors such as market trends or economic conditions may exacerbate internal power struggles. Deep-rooted traditions and resistance to change can impede the adoption of progressive succession plans, exacerbating power struggles.

EMOTIONAL DYNAMICS

Emotional attachments and family relationships introduce a layer of subjectivity that can cloud objective decision-making during succession planning. The concern lies in the potential for emotional biases to compromise the merit-based selection of successors and strategic decision-making. A structured approach to emotional dynamics can lead to informed decisions that balance familial relationships with the strategic needs of the business.

Unmanaged emotional biases may escalate conflicts, negatively impacting both family bonds and business outcomes. The prevailing family culture significantly influences how emotions are managed within the succession planning process. The leadership style of the current patriarch or matriarch sets the tone for emotional dynamics within the family business. The absence of professional counselling resources can hinder the resolution of emotional conflicts, prolonging decision-making processes. Insufficient emotional intelligence among family members and leaders can impede the effective management of emotional dynamics.

The health and harmony of the family's 'hearth' or core are closely intertwined with the successful transition of leadership and ownership across generations. Hearth-related matters, or matters that encompass the emotional and well-being aspects within a family, are indeed integral to effective succession planning. Addressing these matters contributes to a more resilient family foundation and, consequently, a smoother succession planning process.

NAVIGATING THE CHALLENGES OF FAMILY POLITICS

Barriers to the success of succession planning often include communication breakdowns, stemming from misunderstandings or a lack of transparency. Additionally, resistance to change within the family unit poses a significant challenge, requiring a willingness to adapt to new traditions, roles and external perspectives. In essence, successfully navigating family politics to maintain the health and harmony of the family unit involves fostering open communication, embracing change and recognizing the need for adjustments to personal styles and expectations. Here are some areas in which concrete steps can be taken to allow for better handling of family politics.

Emotional Well-being

Maintaining the emotional well-being of family members is crucial for a successful succession plan. Open communication, active listening and fostering a supportive environment help address concerns, build trust and create a sense of unity. Emotional intelligence within the family facilitates a smoother transition by acknowledging the diverse perspectives and emotions that arise during succession discussions.

Intra-family Relationships

The dynamics of family relationships significantly impact succession planning. Strained relationships can hinder effective decision-making and collaboration. Proactively addressing conflicts, nurturing healthy communication and promoting understanding among family members contribute to a stronger family core. This, in turn, facilitates a more cooperative approach to succession planning, fostering shared goals and a collective commitment to the family's future.

Individual Well-being

Considering the well-being of individual family members is paramount. Succession planning involves recognizing each member's aspirations, capabilities and personal development goals. Providing support for individual growth, both within and outside the business, contributes to a more fulfilled family, minimizing potential sources of tension during the succession process.

Cultures and Traditions

Preserving and respecting cultural traditions is another dimension of hearth-related matters. Acknowledging cultural values and traditions ensures a sense of continuity, contributing to the family's identity. Simple family habits and routines, such as dining together and family get-togethers for events and festivals, add to a ritualistic behaviour that strengthens familial bonds, contributing to the overall coherence of the family unit. Integrating these elements into the succession plan helps align business decisions with the family's cultural heritage, fostering a strong connection between past, present and future.

Health and Work-Life Balance

Considering the health and work–life balance of family members is vital. Long-term success relies on the physical and mental well-being of those involved. Implementing policies that prioritize a healthy work–life balance and encouraging well-being practices contribute to a family culture that supports sustained success over generations.

Non-business Members

Engaging non-business members of the family in succession planning discussions is crucial, even if they are not directly involved in day-to-day business operations. Non-business members often wield significant influence within the family and can impact the decision-making process. Their perspectives on family dynamics, relationships and overall family well-being can provide valuable insights into developing a more comprehensive succession plan.

Kitchen Politics

Addressing issues between spouses of siblings within a business family, often referred to as kitchen politics, before delving into succession planning conversations is vital as spouses often play pivotal roles in supporting family members involved in the business. A unified spousal front fosters stability and provides a conducive environment for effective succession planning discussions. The dynamics within spousal relationships can significantly impact the family's cohesiveness and, consequently, the success of any succession plan. Conversely, unresolved kitchen politics can introduce additional complexities, potentially leading to disagreements, rifts and disruptions during the succession process.

Joint Family Politics

Joint family politics, characterized by relationships and power dynamics among extended family members, also require careful consideration. Clarity on roles, responsibilities and expectations within the extended family is essential for preventing conflicts that may spill over into the business realm. Establishing open channels of communication and addressing any latent issues within the joint family structure contribute to a more harmonious succession planning process.

A delicate balance is required between individual interests and the greater family good, which is crucial for maintaining harmony. Family politics doesn't exist in isolation; external factors such as societal norms, economic conditions and cultural expectations continuously influence it. Families must navigate the evolving socio-economic landscape, adapting to changes that may challenge traditional dynamics.

GURUJIS, SWAMIJIS AND BUSINESS FAMILIES

Family gurus, irrespective of their legacy being rooted in religion, spirituality or personal wisdom, often hold a profound influence in family businesses. These trusted advisors are frequently behind the scenes, providing guidance that extends beyond the confines of public visibility. Their role, while deeply personal, can transcend spiritual matters and seep into critical business decisions.

It is essential to recognize and integrate the role of these gurus in the succession planning process. Their intangible insights contribute to the family's collective wisdom and commitment to the entire succession journey.

The inclusion of spiritual gurus in the succession planning process carries significance. Beyond the business arena, these revered figures, deeply embedded in cultural traditions, hold a pivotal role as moral compasses. Acknowledging their wisdom and seeking their guidance becomes a way of respecting and preserving the ethical values that underpin family decisions. The influence of spiritual gurus extends into the realm of decision-making within the business family. Their considerable sway in familial matters, including those related to the business, makes their involvement in succession planning paramount. Their endorsement or disapproval can significantly shape the family's commitment to the chosen successors and the overarching succession strategy.

One of the key roles of these gurus lies in ensuring cultural harmony within the family. By fostering unity and upholding shared values, they contribute to the overall cohesion of the family unit. In the context of succession planning, their participation becomes crucial in aligning decisions with the family's cultural and spiritual ethos, preventing potential conflicts arising from differing perspectives.

Preserving the legacy and values of the family is another facet of the guru's role. Their guidance helps families navigate the intricate journey of succession, ensuring that chosen successors remain steadfast in upholding the principles and values passed down through generations.

Excluding gurus from pivotal decisions, especially those concerning succession, could be perceived as disrespectful and might give rise to familial discomfort. Their inclusion in the process not only aligns with cultural norms but also secures their commitment to the chosen succession plan. This approach mitigates the risk of family discord and, in extreme cases, ensures that the entire succession process continues without facing potential abandonment by one's guiding light. Involving these trusted advisors becomes a delicate yet essential aspect of effective succession planning in family businesses while balancing the spiritual and the practical.

However, there are certain challenges. While it is important to acknowledge that their counsel holds personal value, formal governance regulations typically do not recognize external individuals' sway in the operational and governance aspects of the business.*

Their contribution may not always align with modern governance rules or legal frameworks. The challenge lies in navigating this nuanced relationship and reconciling these cultural practices with the formalities required by contemporary governance standards. Respecting personal beliefs while aligning with the structured frameworks of business governance and striking a balance that acknowledges the cultural context without compromising legal compliance becomes essential in the integration of spiritual guidance into succession planning.

QUESTIONS FOR CONSIDERATION

1. Are spiritual gurus recognized in your family business governance structures, and is there a formalized mechanism for their inclusion in succession planning?
2. Is open communication about the role of spiritual gurus in decision-making, including succession planning, established within the family?

---

*Asi, Aiza, Michela Floris, and Giuseppe Argiolas, 'The Intersection of Spirituality and Succession in Family Firms: A Systematic Literature Review and Research Agenda', *Sinergie Italian Journal of Management*, Vol. 40, No. 2, 2022, 109–146, https://doi.org/10.7433/s118.2022.06. Accessed on 3 January 2025.

3. Have legal experts been consulted to ensure that cultural practices, such as involving gurus, align with legal frameworks governing business decisions?
4. What mechanisms are in place to address potential conflicts arising from the integration of spiritual guidance into the succession planning process?
5. Have potential successors been educated about the cultural significance of involving spiritual gurus in business decisions, particularly in the context of succession planning?
6. How do you address differences in perspectives among family members regarding the role of spiritual gurus in succession planning?
7. Is there a framcwork to respect individual beliefs within the family, especially when some members might not share the same level of reverence for spiritual gurus?
8. In what ways can potential successors express their views or concerns if they feel uncomfortable with the involvement of spiritual gurus in succession planning?
9. Have discussions been facilitated to understand and address any apprehensions or reservations family members might have regarding spiritual guidance in business decisions, including succession planning?
10. What steps have been taken to ensure inclusivity and consideration of diverse opinions regarding the influence of spiritual gurus in business matters?

SCEPTICISM AND LACK OF EFFORT

Scepticism about succession planning is a prevalent sentiment within Indian business families, reflecting a mix of cultural, traditional and practical considerations. This scepticism is rooted in various factors that contribute to a cautious approach towards the formalized transition of leadership and ownership within family-owned enterprises.

One of the primary sources of scepticism is the deeply ingrained cultural preference for familial relationships over formal structures. In many Indian households, familial bonds are considered sacrosanct, and the introduction of formal succession plans can be viewed as a departure from the traditional, relationship-driven approach to decision-making.

The fear often centres around the perceived imposition of corporate governance norms on familial dynamics, leading to concerns about potential discord within the family unit. The lack of clarity and openness about financial matters within the family exacerbates scepticism. Succession planning inherently involves discussions about wealth distribution, asset allocation and decision-making authority. The traditionally private nature of financial matters in many Indian families can give rise to scepticism about the transparency of these processes, leading family members to question the fairness and equitability of the succession plan.

Entrenched expectations regarding hierarchical structures also contribute to scepticism. In many cases, the patriarch or matriarch is considered the ultimate decision-maker, and the idea of deviating from this norm can be met with resistance. Younger generations, despite being qualified and capable, may encounter mistrust when assuming leadership roles, facing the challenge of proving their competence in the eyes of sceptical family elders.

The cautious nature of many Indian business families stems from a deep-rooted respect for tradition and a desire to maintain the legacy built by preceding generations. However, this attachment to established practices can impede the ability to adapt to evolving market landscapes, technological advancements, and changing consumer preferences. Striking a balance between preserving core values and fostering innovation is crucial to ensure relevance in dynamic business environments.

There is an adherence to such legacy practices and family rules; this creates in business families a reluctance to innovate. It also poses a significant challenge to the sustained growth and relevance of family-owned enterprises. In the context of Indian business families, where tradition and familial norms hold considerable influence, it becomes imperative to navigate the delicate balance between preserving heritage and embracing innovation. Awareness of the risks associated with stagnation and a proactive approach to change are essential for the long-term success of these businesses.

Furthermore, the historical lack of formal education on succession planning exacerbates scepticism. Many Indian business families have traditionally relied on informal, experiential learning within the family business. The introduction of structured succession planning processes may be met with scepticism due to a lack of understanding about the potential benefits and long-term advantages of adopting such approaches.

Economic and political uncertainties in the country also play a role in fostering scepticism. The ever-changing business landscape, coupled with unpredictable industry policy shifts, can make families hesitant to commit to long-term plans. The fear of unforeseen challenges and the potential need for flexibility can lead to a reluctance to embrace succession planning as a strategic necessity.

Barriers to success in overcoming scepticism about succession planning often include resistance to change, fear of disrupting family harmony, and concerns about the practical implementation of formalized processes. Additionally, the absence of external guidance and the reliance on traditional methods of decision-making can impede progress.

To avoid the pitfalls of stagnation, Indian business families should carefully consider the following:

Evaluate Cultural and Market Shifts

Are we regularly assessing how cultural and market shifts impact our industry, and are we prepared to adapt our practices accordingly?

Encourage a Culture of Innovation

Do we actively foster a culture that encourages new ideas, embraces experimentation and values continuous improvement within our family business?

Review Governance Structures

Have we critically assessed our governance structures to ensure they facilitate innovation and allow for agile decision-making?

Promote Professional Development

Are we investing in the professional development of family members and key personnel to equip them with the skills needed to navigate modern business challenges?

Seek External Expertise

Are we open to seeking external expertise and diverse perspectives to challenge our established norms and bring fresh insights to the family business?

Foster Inclusivity and Diversity

How are we promoting inclusivity and diversity within our family business to harness a variety of perspectives, experiences and talents?

Embrace Technology Integration

To what extent are we embracing technological advancements and integrating them into our operations to enhance efficiency, stay competitive, and adapt to the evolving business landscape?

By asking these questions, business families can initiate a reflective process that encourages a shift from rigid adherence to legacies to a more adaptive and forward-thinking approach. Embracing change and fostering a culture of innovation can position Indian business families for sustained success, allowing them to preserve their heritage while staying relevant in an ever-evolving business landscape.

Addressing scepticism requires a gradual shift in mindset and a commitment to education and awareness about the benefits of succession planning. Open and transparent communication within the family, coupled with professional guidance, can help dispel fears and build confidence in the efficacy of structured succession plans. Creating a culture that values both familial relationships and strategic planning is essential for navigating the scepticism that surrounds succession planning in Indian business families.

LOYALTY AND ITS CHALLENGES

In the context of Indian business families, loyalty is frequently regarded as a crucial competence, often valued even more highly than specific skills or qualifications. This emphasis on loyalty is rooted in cultural and familial values that prioritize unity, trust and commitment. The perceived advantages and concerns associated with placing such a premium on loyalty within family businesses are notable.

Take, for example, a prominent Indian family-owned manufacturing business that has been passed down through several generations. The current patriarch, having inherited the business from his father, places immense importance on family loyalty. He believes that unwavering dedication to the family's legacy and values is critical for the business's long-term success. As a result, key managerial roles are predominantly held by family members who have demonstrated steadfast loyalty over the years, regardless of their formal qualifications or professional experience.

Loyalty is considered a cornerstone competence for several reasons. First and foremost, it fosters a deep sense of trust and reliability within the family unit, creating a cohesive and supportive environment. In the context of business, this loyalty extends to the commitment of family members towards the collective success and longevity of the enterprise. This commitment often translates into a long-term perspective, where family members are willing to weather challenges and contribute to the business's sustained growth over generations. Additionally, loyalty helps maintain a harmonious family dynamic, reducing the likelihood of internal conflicts and fostering a collaborative atmosphere where decisions are made with the family's collective interests in mind.

However, while loyalty is a commendable trait, its overemphasis can pose certain challenges. In the aforementioned manufacturing business, for instance, there have been situations where critical managerial positions were filled based on loyalty rather than competence. This approach, at times, led to inefficiencies and missed opportunities for innovation and growth. The lack of merit-based promotions resulted in talented non-family employees feeling undervalued and seeking opportunities elsewhere, depriving the business of fresh perspectives and specialized skills.

Balancing loyalty and competence within a family business is a delicate equilibrium that requires a nuanced understanding of each component's value. In another example, a large Indian retail chain recognized the limitations of prioritizing loyalty over competence. The family decided to bring in a non-family CEO with extensive industry experience to inject new strategies and drive growth. While the family retained significant control and continued to value loyalty, the introduction of a competent professional brought a new dimension to their business, leading to remarkable expansion and modernization.

It is crucial not to conflate the distinct contributions of loyalty and competence. Loyalty ensures a shared commitment to the family's values and legacy, fostering a cohesive and supportive work environment. Competence, however, provides the necessary expertise and capability to navigate the complexities of the business landscape. By valuing both loyalty and competence, Indian business families can create a resilient and dynamic organization capable of sustaining success across generations.

The key lies in finding the right balance, where trust becomes the fulcrum. Trust allows family members to rely on each other's competence while upholding the shared values that loyalty brings. Striking this equilibrium requires open communication, a clear delineation of roles and a mutual understanding of how each member's strengths contribute to the overall success of the enterprise. Ultimately, it is the synergy between loyalty and competence, anchored in trust, that propels the family business towards sustainable growth and success.

The significance placed on loyalty within Indian business families is deeply rooted in cultural values, promoting trust, unity and long-term commitment. While this emphasis contributes to a harmonious family and business environment, there are concerns associated with potential limitations on diversity and individual growth. Striking a balance that values loyalty while recognizing and fostering a range of competencies is crucial for the sustained success of family businesses in a dynamic and competitive landscape.

BIAS IN FAMILIES

Bias, inherent in many facets of decision-making, weaves its subtle threads through the fabric of Indian business families. These biases, diverse and multifaceted, can manifest in various forms, influencing critical aspects such as succession planning. We have already discussed gender bias, often seen in favouring male heirs, which may hinder the recognition of female family members' leadership potential. Age bias, tied to traditional hierarchies, can impede the infusion of fresh perspectives from the younger generation. Experiential biases may limit opportunities for family members without extensive experience. Traditional biases can resist change and innovation, potentially constraining the family business's adaptability. Biases can also take any of the following forms:

Educational Bias

Some families exhibit bias based on educational qualifications, favouring successors with specific degrees or educational backgrounds. This bias can limit the potential of individuals who may bring unique skills or perspectives but lack the preferred educational credentials.

Marital Bias

It can be seen in preferences for individuals based on their marital status. For example, a bias favouring married family members over unmarried ones, assuming that marriage brings stability and responsibility.

Caste or Community Bias

It can influence decisions related to succession and key appointments, limiting opportunities for family members from different castes or communities. This bias may restrict diversity within the family business.

Appearance Bias

It involves favouring family members based on physical appearance, which may be linked to societal standards of beauty or conformity. This bias can lead to overlooking qualified individuals who don't fit certain aesthetic expectations.

Sibling Bias

Sibling bias occurs when certain family members receive preferential treatment over others based on sibling relationships. This bias may impact decision-making, leading to perceptions of favouritism and potential conflicts among siblings.

Financial Bias

It arises when family members with greater personal wealth or financial contributions are given more influence in business decisions. This bias may sideline individuals who contribute non-financial assets or skills.

Political Bias

In cases where family businesses have political affiliations, political bias may influence decision-making, favouring family members aligned with specific political ideologies or parties over others.

Religious Bias

This bias can impact decisions related to succession, favouring family members who adhere strictly to certain religious practices or beliefs. This bias may exclude individuals who don't conform to religious norms.

It is crucial to note that these biases are not mutually exclusive and often intersect, creating complicated situations within Indian business families. Acknowledging and addressing these biases are pivotal steps towards fostering inclusivity, embracing diversity and ensuring equitable opportunities within the intricate ecosystems of Indian business families. Overcoming biases requires open communication and a holistic understanding of individual capabilities beyond preconceived notions. It needs one influential member of the family to pick it up for an honest debate and to work with others to make any change possible.

Part Two

The A to Z of Succession Planning

This section is a comprehensive exploration of concepts associated with succession planning and business families. Each concept, carefully selected for its relevance, will be examined in the context of succession planning, offering a detailed and insightful perspective on its significance. For each of these concepts, there is also a set of questions at the end that will allow readers to introspect on its relevance in their journey.

A FOR ASPIRATION

Succession planning for promoter families commences with a shared vision for the future, encompassing the definition of long-term goals and the alignment of values with current leaders. These aspirations serve as guiding principles, influencing strategic decisions and shaping the preparation of the next generation.

Unrealistic or poorly communicated aspirations pose pitfalls, leading to a lack of direction and motivation. Setting overly ambitious goals without a practical roadmap may result in frustration and failure to meet expectations. Failing to ground aspirations in practicality can lead to unattainable goals, causing frustration and demotivation within the family. Poor communication of aspirations can result in a lack of clarity, misunderstanding and divergence in the family's vision for the business. Additionally, a lack of flexibility, stemming from an inability to adapt aspirations to changing market dynamics and industry trends, can hinder the family business's ability to navigate evolving challenges.

Recognizing and understanding the aspirations of every stakeholder is integral to the success of a succession plan. Each stakeholder—whether family members, key executives or external partners—brings a unique set of ambitions, values and expectations to the table, which are critical factors that shape the journey and outcomes of the succession process. Family members, as primary stakeholders, often harbour personal aspirations tied to the legacy and identity of the business. However, if some members have aspirations away from the family legacy, then the respect should still be there. Understanding whether a family member aspires to preserve tradition, innovate or pursue philanthropy within the business provides a roadmap for crafting a succession plan that resonates with their individual values. Acknowledging these aspirations becomes a starting point for alignment and unity amongst the family, providing a roadmap for crafting a succession plan that resonates with individual values.

Even in the case of non-family key executives within a family business, whose roles may undergo transformations during succession—

they harbour aspirations linked to career trajectories and organizational direction. Recognizing these aspirations is pivotal for ensuring a smooth transition and retaining valuable talent. Whether an executive aspires to lead a specific division, or work with a specific family member, or contribute to strategic decision-making, or seek new challenges outside the organization, addressing these aspirations proactively fosters a collaborative and supportive transition environment.

External partners, including investors or business collaborators, too have aspirations tied to the continuity and growth of the enterprise. Understanding their expectations and aspirations contributes to the strategic planning of the succession process. It ensures that the transition aligns with the broader business ecosystem, maintaining stability and confidence among external stakeholders.

Moreover, the intertwining of these diverse aspirations is where the complexity lies. Successful succession planning necessitates a delicate balance, weaving together individual aspirations to create a cohesive and forward-looking strategy. Aligning family, executive and external aspirations not only mitigates potential conflicts but also fosters a sense of shared purpose, which is essential for the sustained success of the business.

Failure to consider and incorporate these aspirations can lead to discord, resistance and a misalignment of interests. It jeopardizes the unity necessary for effective decision-making and can result in a succession plan that falls short of addressing the multifaceted needs of the stakeholders.

An example to learn from is the failure of a renowned family business that occurred when the next generation had aspirations that conflicted with the traditional values of the company. The lack of a shared vision led to internal conflicts and a decline in the overall success of the business. Instead, if the family had discussed how to bridge their differences, realistically and pragmatically, they could have sold their enterprise and monetized their legacy, and also allowed for members of the successive generations to pursue their professional interests.

QUESTIONS TO ASK YOURSELF

1. What are the long-term aspirations and goals of the current leadership in the family business?
2. How well are the aspirations of the current leadership communicated and understood by the next generation?
3. Are the aspirations aligned with the evolving dynamics of the industry and market trends?
4. Have we identified specific milestones and key performance indicators to measure the success of our aspirations?
5. In what ways can we ensure that the aspirations of the family align with the strategic vision for the business?

B FOR BRANDING

Establishing and preserving the family brand is a critical aspect of succession planning, extending beyond the business's external image to encapsulate the values, reputation and identity associated with the family. A strong family brand enhances trust, loyalty and continuity across generations.

Neglecting the family brand can result in a loss of reputation and identity, with inconsistencies in branding messages or a failure to adapt to changing market perceptions eroding the family's legacy. Inconsistent messaging, or neglecting consistency in putting out branding messages across family members and business ventures, can lead to confusion and a weakened family brand.

A prominent family business faced a decline in market trust due to inconsistent branding messages from family members. Each member had a different personality—some were inveterate party-goers while other's identities were rooted in the past. With changing times, and having listed entities within their family fold, they were expected to show a better public persona—that of individuals who took their work seriously and understood the updated business environment. As we can see, the lack of a cohesive family brand strategy, with poor choices being made by some of the family members while leading a life in the public eye, negatively impacted stakeholder perception.

There are other factors too. Brands have to stay relevant in changing markets and newer stakeholder cohorts. Resistance to change, which in this context means failing to adapt the family brand to changing market perceptions and consumer expectations, can result in a loss of relevance. Overemphasizing traditional branding without considering modern marketing practices can hinder the family business's competitiveness. Modern-day stakeholders will not pay much attention to a vintage family brand.

Importantly, brands don't have permanence either. The intertwining dynamics of family brand and individual personal brand stand as crucial decision variables in succession planning, forming the basis upon which the future of a family-owned business is built. The family brand, often an amalgamation of reputation, values and legacy, represents a legacy that spans generations. Preserving and enhancing this brand is not merely a matter of pride but an important decision point for most families.

For them, the family brand serves as a beacon, signalling stability, trustworthiness and a commitment to enduring values. Any decline in its value could have cascading effects on the business, influencing customer loyalty, investor confidence and overall market perception. Simultaneously, the personal brands of individuals within the family hold significant weight—shaped by accomplishments, expertise and ethical conduct. These personal brands contribute to the overall existence of the family brand, with potential successors' emerging brands becoming pivotal decision variables. Succession planning involves identifying individuals with the right skills and personal brands aligned with the values and aspirations of the family and business.

Families cannot afford to let these brands decline in value or recognition. A dilution of the family brand jeopardizes the trust accumulated over the years, potentially eroding customer loyalty and damaging relationships with stakeholders. Similarly, a decline in the personal brands of potential successors can compromise the strategic direction of the business and impact its competitive edge.

The symbiotic relationship between family brand and individual personal brand is evident in how stakeholders perceive the business. Customers often associate the family name with the quality of products or services, and investors gauge the commitment and competence of successors based on their personal brands. The decline of either element can lead to a loss of credibility, making it essential for succession planning to carefully consider and nurture both.

Moreover, in an era where transparency and authenticity are paramount, the family brand and individual personal brands become integral components of the business narrative. Successors who embody and enhance these brands contribute to a seamless transition, assuring stakeholders that the legacy and values they associate with the family business remain intact.

QUESTIONS TO ASK YOURSELF

1. How well-defined is our family brand, and what values does it represent?
2. Have we assessed the perception of our family brand both internally and externally?
3. Are there consistent branding strategies across different business ventures within the family portfolio?
4. How can the family brand evolve to stay relevant in changing markets and demographics?
5. What steps are in place to manage and enhance the reputation of the family brand?

C FOR COMPETENCIES

Succession planning is intricately linked with the identification and cultivation of competencies essential for effective leadership within a family business. Competencies cover a broad spectrum of skills, knowledge and leadership qualities that successors must possess to navigate the complexities of running the business successfully. This assumes that successors for certain roles would come from within the family. Neglecting competency assessments can lead to unprepared successors, resulting in operational inefficiencies and potential business challenges.

At the same time, focusing solely on technical competencies without considering leadership qualities can produce leaders ill-equipped to navigate complex business decisions.

Take this example: a family business faced operational challenges when the chosen successor lacked the necessary competencies in financial management. His ability to accept operational leadership from professionals within the entity was low, and it created a sense of distrust all around. The oversight in assessing core competencies led to financial setbacks for the family business until they changed the leadership and brought on board an external professional. But this hurt them in terms of reputation, time and expensive equity capital.

Basically, the failure to address competency gaps through ongoing training and development can impede the family business's ability to adapt to changing circumstances.

Succession planning is a forward-looking strategy that requires a meticulous assessment of competencies crucial for leadership roles within the family business. It goes beyond technical skills, exploring the aspects of emotional intelligence, strategic thinking, adaptability and interpersonal dynamics to ensure a comprehensive approach to leadership development.

Technical competencies form the foundational layer, encompassing the specific skills and expertise needed to execute the operational aspects of the business. Whether it's industry-specific knowledge, financial acumen or technological proficiency, successors must demonstrate a mastery of these technical competencies to steer the business with competence and foresight.

However, succession planning demands a more holistic view of competencies. Leadership qualities take precedence, with an emphasis on strategic thinking, decision-making and the ability to inspire and guide teams. Successors must be adept at navigating uncertainty, fostering innovation and aligning the business with evolving market landscapes.

Emotional intelligence too becomes a critical competency, as effective leadership within a family business often involves navigating complex interpersonal relationships. Successors need the capacity to understand and manage their emotions and those of others, fostering cohesion and resilience within the family and the broader business ecosystem. The discernment between individual emotional intelligence (also referred to as the emotional quotient or EQ) and not solely relying on intellectual intelligence or the intelligence quotient (IQ) emerges as a pivotal consideration. While IQ signifies cognitive abilities and problem-solving skills, EQ delves into the realm of emotions, interpersonal dynamics and the ability to navigate complex human interactions.* Recognizing the significance of both dimensions becomes integral to identifying successors who can not only excel in their roles but also foster a harmonious and resilient business environment.

Individuals with high emotional intelligence bring a nuanced set of competencies to leadership roles within family businesses. The ability to understand and manage one's emotions and those of others cultivate a conducive atmosphere for effective communication, collaboration and conflict resolution. These leaders exhibit empathy, a crucial component of EQ, allowing them to connect with team members, family members and external stakeholders on a deeper, more meaningful level.

---

*Goleman, Daniel, and Richard E. Boyatzis, 'Emotional Intelligence Has 12 Elements. Which Do You Need to Work On?', *Harvard Business Review*, 6 February 2017, https://tinyurl.com/2fkju6ab. Accessed on 7 January 2025.

While technical skills and intellectual prowess remain crucial, the ability to navigate the complex landscape of family dynamics, interpersonal relationships and emotional nuances is equally, if not more, significant. Successors who possess high EQ contribute to a positive workplace culture, fostering a sense of belonging and commitment within the family and the broader business community. Because of the above reasons, in the context of succession planning, the elevation of EQ beyond a secondary consideration is needed.

What leaders with elevated EQ also excel in is building and sustaining relationships, a facet particularly pertinent in family businesses where personal and professional lines often intertwine. The capacity to manage conflicts with tact, provide constructive feedback and inspire loyalty is deeply rooted in emotional intelligence. These leaders not only guide the business strategically but also serve as unifying forces within the family, ensuring a cohesive approach to decision-making and goal attainment.

Moreover, the dynamic nature of family businesses, characterized by unique challenges and opportunities, demands leaders who can navigate uncertainty with resilience and adaptability. High EQ individuals demonstrate a keen awareness of their own emotions and those of others, facilitating the agile decision-making and adept problem-solving required for sustained success.

Other competencies that distinguish successful successors are adaptability and a forward-looking mindset. The business landscape evolves and leaders must possess the agility to respond to change, seize opportunities and navigate challenges with resilience. This forward-looking approach aligns the business with long-term sustainability, ensuring that the chosen successors are equipped to guide the family business through dynamic and unpredictable scenarios.

Succession planning also extends beyond individual competencies to consider the collective competencies of the leadership team. Ensuring a diverse set of skills and perspectives within the leadership structure contributes to a robust and resilient business model.

QUESTIONS TO ASK YOURSELF

1. What are the core competencies required for leadership roles within the family business?
2. How are we identifying and nurturing competencies among potential successors?
3. Are there competency gaps that need to be addressed through training or external hires?
4. What mechanisms are in place for ongoing competency assessments and development?
5. How can we ensure a balance between technical competencies and leadership qualities in potential successors?

D FOR (PERSONAL) DESIRE

Let us begin with an example. In a prominent business family, the succession was decided by the founding generation, without any discussions with the potential successors. It was treated as if it was the only way to go about it and that family dignity was involved in the journey ahead. Such emotional decision-making is quite commonplace. The lack of personal desire among potential successors resulted in disengaged and chaotic leadership, leading to a decline in business performance. The family had to eventually sell the business at a valuation that barely covered the cost of staying in the business for decades.

In succession planning, individual desire to take on leadership roles is crucial. Family members must genuinely express interest in contributing to the business's success and be ready to invest the necessary time and effort for personal growth within the family enterprise.

A lack of enthusiasm or commitment among family members can lead to disengagement and disrupt the smooth execution of the succession plan. Ignoring personal desires and motivations may result in dissatisfaction and conflicts within the family. Additionally, the failure to harmonize personal aspirations with business goals can lead to internal conflicts and challenges in aligning individual and collective objectives.

Basically, the success of succession planning relies heavily on the genuine desire and commitment of family members to embrace leadership roles. How this motivation is expressed, its importance, potential challenges and the embodiment of this commitment collectively shape a robust succession plan.

Expressing a genuine interest in contributing to the business's success is a cornerstone of effective succession planning. This involves family members proactively conveying their passion for the enterprise and showcasing a deep understanding of its operations, values and long-term goals. This expression of interest serves as a clear signal to both the family and the broader business community that the individual is invested not just in familial obligations but in actively steering the business towards prosperity.

The 'how' of this process involves transparent communication and engagement. Family members must openly communicate their aspirations, aligning personal goals with the strategic objectives of the business. This involves active participation in family discussions, sharing insights and showcasing a willingness to collaborate and learn. It also extends to the demonstration of competencies and a continuous commitment to personal and professional growth, positioning the individual as a viable candidate for a leadership role.

The 'why', on the other hand, revolves around the intrinsic motivation that propels individuals to seek leadership roles. This motivation often stems from a deep sense of responsibility towards preserving the family legacy, contributing to the community or realizing personal aspirations within the business context. Understanding this 'why' becomes essential for succession planners to gauge the authenticity and sustainability of the individual's commitment. However, the pathway to leadership roles is not without potential obstacles. Family members may encounter resistance or scepticism, either from within the family or the broader business community. The 'why not' encompasses these challenges, ranging from concerns about nepotism to doubts regarding the individual's capabilities. Overcoming these obstacles requires not only individual resilience but also a concerted effort from the family and the business to foster an environment that values merit and capability.

The 'who' in this equation involves identifying individuals who authentically embody the desire and commitment to leadership roles. It goes beyond familial hierarchies or preconceived notions, focusing on individuals who align with the values, vision and strategic needs of the business. Succession planners must actively identify and nurture these individuals, providing them with opportunities for skill development, mentorship and exposure to different facets of the business.

QUESTIONS TO ASK YOURSELF

1. Do all family members express a genuine desire to contribute to the family business's success?
2. What mechanisms are in place to understand the individual desires and career aspirations of family members?

3. How can personal desires and business aspirations be brought into alignment with the family's succession plan?
4. Is there a process for addressing conflicts arising from varying personal desires within the family?
5. In what ways can we foster an environment that encourages and supports individual desires while maintaining a collective commitment to the business?

E FOR EDUCATION

Continuous learning and education play a pivotal role in the strategic development of family scions, ensuring they are well-prepared to navigate the complexities of succession planning and assume leadership roles within the family business. Embracing a culture of such learning is not merely a trend but a timeless practice that underscores the enduring relevance of education in grooming future leaders. By offering formal education, specialized training and diverse business exposure, business families can empower their scions with the knowledge, skills and insights necessary to thrive in an ever-evolving business landscape.

Contrarily, without continual learning and a robust education framework, these future leaders may face significant risks that could compromise their effectiveness in succession planning and leadership roles. One such risk is the stagnation of skills and knowledge, which can hinder their ability to adapt to changing market dynamics and emerging business trends. At the same time, a lack of ongoing education may result in complacency and a reluctance to embrace innovation, leaving the family business vulnerable to competitive threats and disruptive forces in the industry.

Without access to quality education and learning opportunities, family business successors end up struggling to gain the necessary credibility and competence to earn the trust and respect of stakeholders, both within and outside the organization. Therefore, investing in continual learning and education is not just a prudent strategy but a critical imperative for ensuring the long-term success and sustainability of family businesses.

Neglecting education and skill development poses risks, leaving successors ill-prepared for business challenges. Inadequate learning opportunities hinder their readiness. Lack of mentorship and resistance to external resources further limit the family business's ability to adapt to modern practices and technologies.

Consider this case: a family business struggled to adapt to changing market trends because the next generation lacked exposure to modern business practices and technologies due to insufficient educational initiatives. The successors did not have adequate business knowledge and did not show interest in learning. They experimented with running the family business with old knowledge of their previous generation, and such a leadership style did not work. The lesson? Having outdated industry knowledge does not help anyone.

Therefore, in the context of succession planning, ongoing education is a strategic investment. It ensures that the next generation of leaders possesses the necessary knowledge and skills to navigate the intricate landscape of business leadership successfully. Formal education acts as a basic need, providing scions with a robust foundation of theoretical knowledge. Pursuing degrees in business administration, management or relevant fields not only imparts critical concepts but also instils a disciplined and analytical approach to problem-solving. This formal education provides a structured framework, enabling family scions to understand the broader business environment, industry dynamics and emerging trends.

Complementing formal education, specialized training becomes a dynamic conduit for honing specific skills and competencies required for leadership roles. Workshops, seminars and executive programmes tailored to the family business context offer targeted insights into areas such as strategic planning, financial management and innovative business practices. This targeted training enhances the practical acumen of family scions, aligning their skill sets with the evolving needs of the business.

Exposure to diverse aspects of the business is equally pivotal in the learning journey of the family successors. Rotation programmes and hands-on experiences across different departments foster a holistic understanding of organization. This exposure transcends siloed perspectives, providing future leaders with insights into operations, marketing, human resources and other critical functions. It nurtures a well-rounded skill set, preparing them to assume leadership roles with a comprehensive understanding of the business's intricacies.

Continuous learning goes beyond formal structures. It embodies a proactive commitment to staying abreast of industry trends, technological advancements and global market dynamics. Family heirs need to engage in continual learning through reading, attending industry conferences and participating in networking events. This self-driven approach ensures that they remain agile, adaptable and well-informed leaders in an ever-evolving business landscape.

Furthermore, the landscape of family businesses often demands an understanding of the delicate interplay between family dynamics and business operations. Education in areas such as family business governance, conflict resolution and succession planning itself becomes paramount. Equipping family scions with this specialized knowledge fosters a harmonious balance between familial relationships and professional responsibilities.

Higher education for scions is not just a formality but a strategic necessity, aligned with market expectations. In today's competitive business landscape, where stakeholders and investors increasingly emphasize on professionalism and expertise, engaging in higher education becomes a symbolic indicator of competence and commitment. Beyond the intrinsic value of knowledge acquisition, a formal education instils discipline, critical thinking and a structured approach to problem-solving.

Markets often perceive higher education as a testament to an individual's dedication to personal and professional development, bolstering their credibility as potential leaders. Therefore, it goes beyond a mere checkbox; it becomes a proactive step for family scions to align themselves with market expectations and position themselves as capable and well-prepared contributors to the family business and the broader business community. That's why business families invest in ensuring that their children attend renowned schools and colleges, not just for the education but also for the alumni network and the prestige associated with the school.

QUESTIONS TO ASK YOURSELF

1. What educational opportunities are available for family members to enhance their skills and knowledge?
2. How can we tailor educational programmes to address specific needs identified in the succession plan?

3. Are there mentorship programmes, on-the-job training and knowledge-sharing initiatives in place?
4. In what ways can we leverage external educational resources to supplement internal learning initiatives?
5. How can we measure the effectiveness of educational programmes in preparing the next generation for leadership roles?

F FOR FAMILY COUNCIL

Establishing a family council can be helpful for effective succession planning, especially for families with a larger number of members across generations. This is also useful when the number of businesses within the family increases. The family council serves as a forum for open communication, decision-making and conflict resolution. It plays a central role in ensuring that family members have a voice in the succession process and that decisions align with the family's collective values.

The transition from joint-family systems to nuclear families is a societal shift that has significantly impacted family businesses. In traditional joint families, decision-making was often collective and familial ties were tightly interwoven. However, with the emergence of nuclear families, the decision-making power and familial connections have undergone a transformation.

The evolution of societal norms, coupled with factors such as modern education, changing perspectives on marriage and individual lifestyle choices has led to a notable rise in nuclear families. This shift is particularly pronounced in the context of business families, where successive generations often pursue diverse career paths, live in different locations and prioritize individual aspirations.

The impact of this trend on business families is multifaceted. Traditional joint family structures, with their close-knit relationships and shared decision-making, are gradually making way for more autonomous nuclear family units. As family members explore varied opportunities and lifestyles, the need for a tailored approach to governance and decision-making becomes evident.

In this scenario, family councils emerge as a practical instrumental mechanism for navigating the complexities introduced by nuclear family dynamics. As individual family units become more geographically dispersed, pursuing individual interests, the family council serves as a centralized hub for fostering unity and alignment around common values and business goals.

Furthermore, the changing dynamics in the institution of marriage and the diverse preferences of each generation necessitate adaptive governance structures. Family councils become the vehicle through which wealth distribution, succession planning and other critical decisions are discussed and agreed upon. The autonomy of nuclear family units is acknowledged and integrated into the overarching governance framework, ensuring that the family business remains resilient in the face of evolving family structures.

In the context of business families, this shift necessitates a recalibration of governance structures. The personality-driven relationships that once facilitated informal communication and decision-making in joint families are replaced by a more dispersed and formalized framework. To adapt to this changing landscape, establishing a family council becomes paramount.

In the absence of a joint family setup, the family council plays a pivotal role in fostering unity and aligning family members with the shared values and goals of the business. It becomes the platform where the diverse perspectives of individual nuclear families converge, facilitating constructive dialogue and consensus-building.

❧

The pandemic has been an unyielding teacher, emphasizing the unpredictability and transience of life. Families that have weathered the storm have recognized the importance of preparedness, not just for the immediate future but for the perpetuity of their legacy. Succession planning, previously seen as an ominous subject, has now evolved into a strategic necessity, acknowledging the inherent uncertainty of life and the imperative to secure the future of the business.

Indian business families must overcome deep-seated inhibitions and biases that historically deterred open discussions about succession planning. The reluctance to broach the topic often stems from cultural taboos associated with the terms 'death' and 'successor'. Families need to recognize that framing succession planning discussions is not an acknowledgement of vulnerability but a demonstration of foresight and responsibility.

Overcoming these inhibitions requires a shift in mindset. Families need to view succession planning not as a morbid endeavour but as a proactive and empowering strategy. Family councils can help make this a priority. In these councils, routine inclusion of succession planning on the agenda becomes a catalyst for open dialogue. They provide a structured platform for navigating complex emotions, addressing concerns and aligning family members on a shared vision. The unpredictability highlighted by the pandemic serves as a stark reminder that postponing these discussions only amplifies the risks associated with leadership vacuums and unprepared successions. However, there are a few things to be mindful of when creating a family council:

Inadequate representation: Lack of adequate representation or exclusion of family members from the council can lead to dissatisfaction and conflicts.

Lack of conflict resolution guidelines: The absence of clear guidelines for conflict resolution within the family council structure can exacerbate tensions and hinder effective decision-making.

Decision-making without input: Making succession decisions without sufficient input from all family members within the family council can lead to internal strife and resistance.

Establishing a family council is a pivotal step in fostering effective succession planning within a family business. By providing a structured space for dialogue, the family council becomes instrumental in ensuring that each family member has a voice in the succession process, fostering inclusivity and transparency. Moreover, it serves as a mechanism to align decisions with the collective values and vision of the family, creating a shared understanding of the business's future direction.

To form a family council, key considerations include defining its constitution and governance structure. Further, respect for other stakeholders is paramount in the family council's functioning. Finally, confidentiality is a cornerstone of successful family councils.

QUESTIONS TO ASK YOURSELF

1. Do we have a family council in place to facilitate open communication and decision-making?
2. How often does the family council meet, and what topics are typically addressed?
3. Are there clear guidelines for conflict resolution within the family council structure?
4. How inclusive is the family council, and are all family members given an opportunity to voice their opinions?
5. What mechanisms are in place to ensure that decisions made by the family council align with the overall succession plan?

G FOR GOVERNANCE

Effective governance structures are important for managing the complexities of a family-owned business, especially in the context of succession planning. This involves establishing clear policies and procedures to guide decision-making, ownership transitions and overall business management. It is not just the business that needs governance, even how family involvement is managed needs to be governed. Here, a combination of regulations as well as family norms, both need to be taken into consideration equally.

Let us look at this example. A family business faced financial challenges and disputes among family members due to weak governance structures. There was infighting amongst family members, and the absence of external experts as well as an independent board exacerbated decision-making issues, all of which led to a lack of trust amongst external stakeholders about the business.

There are several pitfalls associated with weak governance practices. These include conflicts, mismanagement and a lack of transparency within the family business. Neglecting the need for independent advisors or a board of directors can exacerbate decision-making issues and lead to disputes among family members. Additionally, the lack of clear documentation and accessibility of governance policies and procedures can contribute to confusion and misunderstandings.

A robust governance framework goes beyond being a set of rules. It becomes a strategic approach that instils transparency, accountability and fairness in the processes governing the transfer of leadership and ownership within the family enterprise.

Central to this framework is the establishment of clear policies and procedures specifically tailored to guide succession planning. These policies serve as a compass, delineating the principles that govern crucial processes related to leadership transitions and overall business management. By articulating a set of well-defined procedures, family businesses can mitigate ambiguity, reduce conflicts and foster an environment where decisions align with the overarching goals and values of the family.

Clarity in ownership transitions is a key facet of effective governance in the context of succession planning. This involves specifying the criteria and mechanisms for transferring ownership stakes, be it through inheritance, buyouts or other agreed-upon methods. Clearly defined procedures provide a roadmap for navigating potentially sensitive issues, reducing the likelihood of disputes and ensuring a smooth transition of ownership from one generation to the next.

Moreover, a robust governance structure for succession planning extends beyond the immediate family circle to incorporate external perspectives. Involving external advisors, such as legal and financial experts, adds an objective dimension to this process. These advisors bring specialized knowledge and experience, offering valuable insights that contribute to a more comprehensive and well-informed succession plan.

~

Communication is essential for effective governance, particularly in the context of succession planning. Establishing mechanisms for regular and transparent communication among family members, stakeholders and relevant advisors fosters an environment of collaboration and shared understanding. This openness is vital in addressing concerns, managing expectations and ensuring that all parties are aligned with the overarching vision for the family business.

Furthermore, a governance structure for succession planning should anticipate and address potential conflicts. Establishing protocols for conflict resolution, whether through mediation or other agreed-upon mechanisms, provides a framework for resolving disputes amicably. This proactive approach helps to maintain family harmony while ensuring that the succession process remains on track.

~

Family governance in the context of succession planning is a comprehensive framework that addresses the intricate dynamics of a family-owned business, aiming to ensure a seamless transition of ownership and leadership across generations. The 'why' of family governance lies in its ability to mitigate conflicts, provide a structured decision-making process and uphold the values and vision that work as a foundation for the family business. It serves as a strategic mechanism to preserve the family legacy while adapting to the evolving needs of the business landscape.

The 'how' of family governance involves the establishment of clear policies, procedures and communication channels. This entails defining roles and responsibilities, articulating the criteria for leadership succession and ownership transfers, and instituting regular family meetings and family council meetings to facilitate open and transparent communication. Family governance mechanisms also include the creation of advisory boards comprising external experts who offer objective insights and strategic guidance.

The 'who' encompasses all family members involved in the business, as well as external advisors such as legal and financial experts. Family governance structures ensure that every member has a voice, irrespective of their position in the business hierarchy. Inclusivity is key to fostering a sense of shared responsibility and aligning the diverse perspectives of family members with the overarching goals of the business.

The 'what' of family governance includes the creation of a family constitution, codes of conduct and conflict resolution mechanisms. While the family constitution outlines the overarching principles, values and mission of the family business—serving as a guiding document for the functioning of the business—codes of conduct establish behavioural expectations, fostering a culture of respect and collaboration. Conflict resolution mechanisms provide a structured approach to managing disputes, ensuring that conflicts do not disrupt the succession planning process.

To understand the implementation of good governance, consider the case of a family-owned manufacturing business. The patriarch of the family recognizes the need for a structured succession plan and initiates the development of a family constitution, which outlines the criteria for leadership succession, defines the roles of family members within the business and establishes a family council to facilitate ongoing communication. External advisors, including a legal expert and a business consultant, contribute to the governance framework by providing legal insights and strategic guidance. This allows for clarity for each stakeholder on what to expect in their business roles, as well as offers grievance redressal mechanisms, which would, in turn, make them attractive to external investors.

However, there are potential challenges and resistances to implementing family governance. Family members may resist the formality of governance structures due to a perceived loss of autonomy or a fear of external interference. Overcoming this resistance requires a collective understanding of the long-term benefits and the creation of governance mechanisms that respect the unique identity and values of the family.

QUESTIONS TO ASK YOURSELF

1. How robust are our governance structures for managing the complexities of a family-owned business?
2. Are governance policies and procedures clearly documented and accessible to all family members?
3. How can governance mechanisms adapt to changes in family dynamics or business expansion?
4. Are there independent advisors or a board of directors to provide external perspectives on governance matters?
5. In what ways can governance practices enhance the long-term sustainability of the family business?

H FOR HARMONY

Maintaining harmony within the family is a key aspect of a successful succession plan. It can be challenging, especially as the family grows and encompasses diverse interests and perspectives. Each family member may have their own ideas, ambitions and priorities, which can lead to tensions and disagreements, particularly when it comes to matters as significant as succession planning. As the succession process unfolds, differing opinions and conflicting interests may come to the forefront, putting strain on familial relationships and potentially disrupting the unity that is essential for successful planning. Navigating these complexities requires open communication, mutual respect and a willingness to compromise, ensuring that the collective interests of the family remain at the forefront despite individual differences.

Maintaining harmony within the family is not just a desirable element but a foundational necessity for successful succession planning in family-owned businesses. Succession plans should closely consider its impact on family relationships, as it directly affects the environment of trust, open communication and collaboration. The intricate interplay between familial relationships and business dynamics underscores the need for a thoughtful approach that prioritizes family unity alongside business continuity. This holistic perspective recognizes that the success of a succession plan is not solely measured by financial gains but also by the preservation of familial bonds and shared values.

In practice, this involves cultivating an environment of trust where family members feel secure in expressing their opinions, concerns and aspirations. Open communication becomes a cornerstone, fostering a culture where dialogue is encouraged, and all family stakeholders have a voice in the succession process. For instance, regular family meetings can provide a structured platform for discussions, allowing family members to share their perspectives and collaboratively shape the future of the business.

Collaboration is essential to align family members on common goals and aspirations. This can manifest in shared decision-making processes, where consensus-building becomes a norm rather than an exception. An illustrative example is the establishment of a family council, comprising representatives from various genealogical branches of the family, to collectively deliberate on succession-related matters and ensure inclusivity in decision-making.

Furthermore, transparency plays a pivotal role in maintaining harmony during succession planning. Family members should have a clear understanding of the succession process, criteria for leadership roles and the implications for each member. This transparency reduces uncertainties and minimizes the potential for misunderstandings or conflicts. An example might involve the creation of a comprehensive family handbook outlining the succession plan, roles and responsibilities, ensuring that everyone is well-informed.

In numerous family businesses, the delicate balance between the enthusiasm of the emerging leaders in the next generation to assume control and the founder's hesitancy to relinquish authority often becomes the root cause of strained relationships and business failures. The founder may harbour doubts about the next generation's readiness to shoulder the business responsibilities, while the emerging leaders might feel a lack of empowerment. This deadlock leads to a costly impasse, jeopardizing both family harmony and the future trajectory of the business.

Addressing conflicts proactively is another crucial element. Conflict resolution mechanisms should be in place to manage disagreements constructively, preventing them from escalating and harming both family relationships and the business. One approach could involve engaging a family mediator or counsellor to facilitate discussions and guide the resolution process.

Successful succession planning transcends the mere transfer of business assets; it extends to the preservation of the family's emotional and relational wealth. Prioritizing harmony, trust, open communication and collaboration becomes paramount for family-owned businesses venturing into succession planning. In doing so, they navigate the complexities of succession with resilience, ensuring that the transition of leadership and ownership not only sustains the financial legacy but also nurtures the enduring strength of family bonds.

Pitfalls associated with neglecting the emotional aspects of succession planning include strained family relationships, conflicts and resistance to the succession plan. Overlooking the need for effective communication can result in misunderstandings and challenges in balancing business decisions with family relationships. Failure to address conflicts and foster harmony among family members may lead to a decline in overall family cohesion, highlighting the critical role of emotional intelligence in the success of succession planning.

QUESTIONS TO ASK YOURSELF

1. How well are interpersonal dynamics and relationships managed within the family?
2. Are there proactive measures to address conflicts and foster harmony among family members?
3. How can we ensure that business decisions do not negatively impact family relationships?
4. What role does effective communication play in maintaining harmony within the family business?
5. In what ways can we cultivate a supportive and collaborative environment that promotes overall family harmony?

I FOR INNOVATION

Incorporating innovation into succession planning is essential for the long-term sustainability of the family business. It is not merely an option but an existential need for family businesses aiming at enduring sustainability. This approach involves cultivating a culture that seamlessly integrates creativity, adaptability and forward-thinking into the intricate process of transitioning leadership across generations.

Fostering a culture of creativity within the family business is akin to nurturing an environment where novel ideas are not only welcomed but actively encouraged. For instance, envision a traditional family-owned manufacturing business that, under new leadership, introduces sustainable practices and eco-friendly production methods. This creative shift not only aligns the business with contemporary environmental consciousness but also opens avenues for market differentiation. This would happen only after much discussion on the cost–benefit analysis, as well as channelling money into financing such a production shift.

Innovation plays a crucial role in succession planning as it ensures the continued relevance and growth of the business across generations. Embracing innovation within the succession planning process allows the business to adapt to changing market dynamics, technological advancements and evolving customer preferences. By nurturing innovation, family businesses can stay ahead of the curve, remaining competitive in an ever-changing business landscape.

Moreover, incorporating innovative practices and technologies not only enhances the business's performance but also opens up new avenues for expansion and diversification, considering innovation drives efficiency, productivity and profitability, laying the foundation for long-term sustainability and success. Ultimately, innovation in succession planning ensures that the business remains agile, resilient and well-positioned to thrive in the future.

Adaptability is key to innovative succession planning. Family businesses must be agile in responding to the rapid evolution of market dynamics. Consider the case of a family-owned retail business adapting to changing consumer preferences and emerging online marketplaces. By incorporating e-commerce strategies and digital marketing, the business not only remains relevant but also expands its reach in the digital age. But this would also mean understanding what capex to allot for the business, what type of newer talent to onboard and how to move to digital marketing, amongst so many other business considerations.

Here comes the value of forward-thinking, an integral aspect of innovation that involves anticipating future challenges and proactively preparing for them. In succession planning, this could manifest in grooming successors with diverse skill sets, including digital literacy, global market awareness and the ability to navigate complex regulatory landscapes.

Moreover, innovation in succession planning extends beyond operational changes to encompass governance structures. Forward-thinking families might explore the establishment of family councils equipped with digital tools for efficient decision-making and communication. This innovative approach ensures that the governance framework adapts to the needs of the evolving business landscape.

However, potential pitfalls loom for those resistant to change or neglectful of innovation. Such attitudes can lead to stagnation and diminished competitiveness within the family business. Furthermore, a lack of emphasis on fostering a culture of creativity and adaptability may impede the business's ability to navigate the dynamic shifts in the market. Overemphasizing traditional practices, without due consideration for modern business trends, could similarly curtail the family business's potential for growth and success.

QUESTIONS TO ASK YOURSELF

1. Is there a culture of innovation within the family business, and how is it fostered?
2. How can innovation be integrated into the succession plan to ensure the business remains adaptable?
3. Are mechanisms in place for identifying and implementing new technologies or business practices?

4. How do we balance innovation with the preservation of core family values and traditions?
5. In what ways can family members contribute to a culture of continuous innovation within the business?

J FOR JOINT VENTURES

Exploring joint ventures or strategic partnerships can be a tactical aspect of succession planning. Joint ventures offer opportunities for diversification, collaboration and leveraging external expertise to strengthen the family business. Additionally, they can be strategically structured to provide financial exits as part of a timed succession plan for business families.

By strategically structuring joint ventures, families can not only enhance their business resilience but also create a pathway for financial exits. These ventures provide a unique avenue for diversification, collaboration and the infusion of external expertise. This innovative approach is instrumental in adapting to the evolving business landscape and ensuring the long-term sustainability and growth of the family enterprise.

Joint ventures offer family businesses a pathway to diversify their portfolio. For example, a family-owned manufacturing business specializing in traditional textiles might enter into a joint venture with a distribution company to explore innovative applications of textiles. This diversification not only opens up new revenue streams but also ensures the family business remains adaptable to changing market demands. Collaboration is a key element of joint ventures, providing family businesses with the chance to pool resources, share risks and access complementary skills.

Leveraging external expertise is a significant advantage of joint ventures. Family businesses may lack certain specialized skills or market knowledge that a strategic partner can bring to the table. Take another example: a family-owned agricultural business looking to enter the organic food market might form a joint venture with an established organic farming company, capitalizing on their partner's expertise.

Furthermore, joint ventures can be a softer way for family businesses to expand revenues without the need for significant capital investment. Instead of shouldering the entire financial burden of expansion, family businesses can share costs and risks with their joint venture partners. This collaborative approach ensures a more gradual and sustainable growth trajectory.

Building a business moat, or a competitive advantage, is another strategic benefit of joint ventures in the context of family businesses. By strategically aligning with partners who possess complementary strengths, family enterprises can create a fortified position in the market. An example is a family-owned logistics company forming a joint venture with a technology company to enhance its supply chain visibility, creating a distinctive advantage over competitors.

Potential pitfalls in joint ventures within the context of succession planning include inadequate due diligence and the absence of clear decision-making guidelines. When selecting partners, insufficient due diligence can lead to conflicts, financial setbacks and disputes, thereby posing a threat to the overall stability of the family business. Additionally, neglecting to establish clear guidelines for decision-making and risk-sharing in joint ventures may result in disagreements and operational challenges.

Furthermore, a critical stumbling block is the misalignment of joint ventures with the overarching succession goals. Failure to synchronize these ventures with the broader succession strategy can lead to diversification issues and impede the family business's long-term objectives. Real-life examples illustrate the potential consequences, such as a family business experiencing financial setbacks due to a poorly executed joint venture, leading to conflicts among family members and external partners.

QUESTIONS TO ASK YOURSELF

1. Have we explored the potential benefits of joint ventures or strategic partnerships for the family business?
2. What criteria do we use to evaluate potential partners in joint ventures?
3. How can joint ventures contribute to the diversification of family business interests?
4. Are there clear guidelines for decision-making and risk-sharing in joint ventures?
5. In what ways can joint ventures align with the overall succession plan and long-term goals of the family business?

K FOR KNOWLEDGE TRANSFER

Business families, through their enduring commitment to their companies, industries and nations, amass a reservoir of knowledge over the years. This wealth of experience, insights and industry-specific acumen is its resilient knowledge moat. Just as castles are fortified by robust structures, business families must fortify their enterprises with an impregnable knowledge moat. This moat serves as an invaluable asset, shielding successive generations and leaders from the turbulent tides of change. Knowledge here does not merely refer to a repository of information; it is a strategic advantage that propels family businesses forward, enabling them to navigate challenges, seize opportunities and leave an indelible mark on the ever-evolving business landscape. In an era defined by rapid transformations, building and reinforcing this knowledge moat becomes imperative for family enterprises aspiring not only to endure but to thrive across generations.

Successful succession planning hinges on a strategic and deliberate approach to knowledge transfer within family businesses. This multifaceted process encompasses the documentation and transmission of critical business knowledge, skills and insights from current leaders to the next generation, ensuring a seamless transition of leadership and the preservation of the family business legacy.

Business scions, as heirs to family enterprises, inherently possess a unique advantage. Having been immersed in business discussions and operations throughout their lives, they often absorb tacit knowledge that is integral to the family business. Growing up surrounded by business talk provides them with an intuitive understanding of the industry, market dynamics and the family's entrepreneurial journey. This early exposure serves as a foundation, positioning these future leaders with an insider's perspective and a nuanced understanding of the family's business landscape.

Additionally, the extensive business network cultivated by family connections becomes a ready-made asset for business successors. Leveraging existing relationships, partnerships and collaborations built over generations, scions have a head start in navigating the complex web of industry contacts. This network, intricately woven through family ties, provides valuable opportunities for collaboration, expansion and industry insights that can significantly benefit the next generation of leaders.

While this inherited knowledge offers a solid foundation, its successful transmission requires careful nurturing. Business scions must actively engage with current leaders by participating in decision-making processes and seeking mentorship to bridge the gap between theoretical understanding and practical application. Encouraging an open dialogue between generations fosters a culture of continuous learning, where both tacit and explicit knowledge is shared, refined and adapted to evolving business landscapes.

Moreover, the nurturing of knowledge involves creating structured mechanisms for learning, such as mentorship programmes, leadership development initiatives and knowledge-sharing platforms. These intentional efforts go beyond the day-to-day operations, encompassing broader aspects of business strategy, market trends and ethical considerations. An example could be the establishment of a mentorship programme where experienced family members guide younger members through real-world business challenges, imparting not only technical skills but also the wisdom gained from years of experience. External experts can also be brought in to impart additional knowledge and industry insights, and newer ideas can be brainstormed by the family members.

Neglecting a structured knowledge transfer process poses significant challenges for family businesses. The absence of a well-defined plan can result in the loss of essential business insights when key knowledge holders retire. Over-reliance on informal communication further hinders the comprehensive documentation and transfer of critical business processes. The pitfalls extend to the absence of evaluation mechanisms, as the failure to implement ongoing assessment and adjustment can lead to gaps and inefficiencies in the knowledge transfer process. Additionally, limited use of technology can hinder the family business's ability to leverage modern tools and platforms, impacting the efficiency of knowledge transfer. The lack of integration of knowledge transfer with overall succession planning further compounds these challenges, potentially leading to gaps in leadership development and preparedness among successors.

Real-life examples underscore the repercussions of these pitfalls, as a family business encountered operational challenges when key knowledge holders retired without a systematic knowledge transfer plan in place. Usually, the missing operational knowledge includes crisis management, customer insights and cost efficiencies, amongst other possibilities. This serves as a cautionary tale, highlighting the critical importance of addressing these pitfalls to ensure a seamless and effective knowledge transfer process within family businesses.

QUESTIONS TO ASK YOURSELF

1. What critical knowledge and skills need to be transferred to the next generation?
2. Is there a structured knowledge transfer plan that documents key business processes and insights?
3. How can mentorship programmes facilitate effective knowledge transfer between current and future leaders?
4. Are there mechanisms for ongoing evaluation and adjustment of the knowledge transfer process?
5. In what ways can technology be leveraged to enhance the efficiency of knowledge transfer within the family business?

L FOR LEADERSHIP DEVELOPMENT

Succession planning is a dynamic process that necessitates intentional and systematic leadership development, aiming to prepare the next generation to assume key roles within the family business. This multifaceted approach involves the identification of potential leaders, the provision of targeted training programmes and the facilitation of meaningful mentorship opportunities.

Identifying potential leaders within the family requires a nuanced understanding of each member's strengths, skills and aspirations. It goes beyond familial ties, focusing on competencies and attributes that align with the business's strategic goals. For instance, if a family-owned technology firm is considering leadership succession, identifying a family member with a strong background in innovation, adaptability to technological advancements and strategic vision becomes pivotal.

Once potential leaders are identified, providing targeted training becomes essential to equip them with the skills and knowledge required for leadership roles. This could involve specialized courses, workshops or executive education programmes tailored to the unique needs of the family business. As an illustration, a family-owned hospitality business would need to invest in training programmes that cover contemporary customer service trends, digital marketing strategies and sustainable business practices to prepare the next generation for leadership.

Mentorship plays a crucial role in the leadership development process, offering a personalized and experiential learning opportunity. Establishing mentorship programmes where emerging leaders work closely with seasoned family members provides invaluable insights, guidance and a transfer of tacit knowledge. Consider a scenario where a family member with extensive experience in supply chain management mentors the next-generation leader, offering practical insights into optimizing logistics, negotiating with suppliers and ensuring operational efficiency.

Moreover, leadership development involves exposure to real-world business scenarios. Encouraging potential leaders to actively participate in decision-making processes, take on challenging projects and assume responsibilities gradually builds their confidence and competence. This hands-on experience, coupled with mentorship, accelerates the development of leadership capabilities.

Effective leadership development is a cornerstone of successful succession planning within family businesses. Neglecting intentional leadership development can affect the business in more ways than one. Successors may be left ill-equipped to navigate the complexities of the business landscape, leading to operational challenges. A one-size-fits-all approach to leadership development can be equally detrimental, hindering personalized growth tailored to individual needs and strengths. The failure to adapt leadership programmes to changes in industry trends and business strategies may result in leaders lacking the agility needed to address modern challenges. Moreover, the absence of mentorship opportunities for emerging leaders limits their exposure to experienced family members or external advisors.

To foster a robust leadership pipeline, it is crucial to prioritize continuous learning and create a culture that embraces ongoing development within the family business. Leadership training within the context of succession planning encompasses a spectrum of essential areas designed to equip the next generation with the skills, knowledge and mindset necessary for effective leadership within the family business. Here are some of them.

Strategic Vision and Planning

Training programmes aim to develop the ability of family members to formulate and articulate a clear strategic vision for the business. For instance, a family member might undergo training in strategic management, gaining insights into aligning long-term business goals with dynamic market trends. This equips them with the skills to navigate strategic decision-making crucial for the sustained success of the family enterprise.

Financial Acumen

The focus of training is on gaining a comprehensive understanding of financial statements, budgeting and financial decision-making. An example involves a potential leader participating in financial literacy courses, delving into the interpretation of key financial indicators and acquiring the ability to make informed decisions. This financial acumen becomes a vital asset for effective leadership within the family business.

Operational Excellence

Training programmes centre on acquiring skills in optimizing operational processes for efficiency and effectiveness. An emerging leader, for instance, might engage in training programmes focused on lean management principles, contributing to the streamlined and effective operation of the family business. This operational excellence is fundamental for maintaining a competitive edge in the market.

Communication and Interpersonal Skills

The training focus here is on enhancing communication, negotiation and conflict resolution skills. For instance, a family member could participate in workshops on effective communication and learn techniques to foster a positive and collaborative work environment. These skills are integral to building strong internal relationships and external partnerships critical for the family business.

Innovation and Adaptability

Training programmes emphasize fostering a culture of innovation and adaptability to navigate evolving market dynamics. Leaders might undergo training on design thinking and innovation strategies, equipping them to embrace change and proactively respond to emerging market trends. This adaptability becomes a cornerstone for staying ahead in a rapidly changing business landscape.

Human Resource Management

Training focuses on understanding best practices in talent management, employee engagement and leadership development. An example could be a potential leader undergoing training on effective recruitment, performance appraisal and employee development strategies. This knowledge is essential for nurturing and retaining a skilled workforce within the family business.

Ethical Decision-making

The training focus is on developing ethical decision-making frameworks and navigating complex ethical dilemmas. This emphasis is crucial for maintaining integrity and trust in the business. Workshops on ethics guide family members in understanding the unique ethical considerations within the family business environment.

Risk Management

Training programmes centre on building skills in identifying, assessing and mitigating business risks. For instance, training in risk analysis and scenario planning prepares leaders to navigate uncertainties in the business landscape. This proactive approach to risk management is essential for safeguarding the family business against potential challenges.

Customer Relationship Management

Training focuses on understanding customer needs, building customer relationships and ensuring satisfaction. Courses in customer experience management equip leaders with strategies to enhance customer loyalty. This customer-centric approach is pivotal for maintaining a strong market presence and reputation.

Digital Literacy

Training programmes focus on navigating digital technologies, data analytics and emerging trends in the digital landscape. Family members might engage in training on digital transformation to stay abreast of technological advancements. This digital literacy is essential for leveraging technology to enhance business operations and stay competitive in the digital era.

These areas collectively form a comprehensive leadership training framework, ensuring that the next generation of leaders in a family business possesses a well-rounded skill set to address the multifaceted challenges of leading a successful enterprise.

QUESTIONS TO ASK YOURSELF

1. How do we identify and assess potential leaders within the family?
2. What leadership development programmes are in place to nurture the skills and qualities needed for succession?
3. Are there mentorship opportunities for emerging leaders to learn from experienced family members or external advisors?
4. How can leadership development adapt to changes in industry trends and business strategies?
5. In what ways can the family business foster a culture of continuous learning and leadership growth?

M FOR MERITOCRACY

Establishing a meritocratic culture is a crucial foundation for the equitable and efficient execution of succession planning. This approach entails appointing leaders based on their abilities, performance and potential, prioritizing merit over familial relationships.

Another way to understand its importance is to see how neglecting meritocracy affects businesses. A failure to prioritize merit can breed resentment and demotivation among family members. Transparent performance evaluations and objective criteria in leadership selection are essential components that are often overlooked, leading to perceived favouritism and internal conflicts.

Often there is a favourite child or successor in the family, or maybe a favourite individual of the patriarch within the wider family. Of course, many such situations bring awkwardness to the succession planning discussions. The manifestation of favouritism, driven by familial connections rather than merit, can sow discord and demotivate individuals within the family. When transparent evaluations and objective criteria are not emphasized, conflicts may arise, challenging the principles of meritocracy and fostering nepotism. Failure to address conflicts arising from perceived favouritism can strain family relationships, underscoring the importance of conflict resolution measures.

Moreover, the poor communication of merit values further exacerbates these challenges. Inadequate communication regarding the significance of meritocracy in the succession process can result in misunderstandings and resistance among family members. As such, embracing and effectively communicating the principles of meritocracy is integral to the success of fair and impactful succession planning within family businesses.

Establishing a meritocratic culture stands as a cornerstone for fair and effective succession planning within family businesses. This approach advocates for the selection of leaders based on their demonstrated abilities, consistent performance and untapped potential.

In a meritocratic culture, leadership positions are not predetermined by lineage; instead, they are earned through a transparent evaluation of an individual's capabilities and contributions. For instance, if a family-owned manufacturing business seeks a new CEO, the selection process might involve an assessment of candidates' track records, leadership skills and ability to drive innovation rather than defaulting to the eldest family member.

Meritocracy champions fairness and equal opportunities, creating an environment where individuals, regardless of their family ties, have an equal chance to ascend to leadership roles. An example could be a family-owned financial firm adopting a rigorous performance evaluation system, where promotions are linked to quantifiable achievements and not influenced by familial connections.

Effective succession planning, underpinned by meritocracy, recognizes and nurtures talent from diverse sources, ensuring that the most qualified individuals assume pivotal roles. This might involve implementing leadership development programmes that identify high-potential individuals within and outside the family, offering them opportunities to grow and contribute substantively. For instance, a family-owned hospitality business might think of sponsoring high-performing non-family executives to attend leadership courses to enhance their skills.

On the other hand, completely ignoring outside talent may land the business in trouble. For example, a family business faced internal conflicts when leadership positions were filled based on familial ties rather than individual capabilities. It created chaos with existing senior non-family leadership, who had built the business with the founder. It started with outcomes of their attrition from the group, as well as poaching teams in mid-management.

Meritocracy encourages healthy competition within the family business, motivating individuals to continuously strive for excellence. This could be exemplified by a family member working in the marketing department who, through consistently delivering successful campaigns and achieving measurable results, earns the opportunity to lead the marketing strategy for a new product line.

Moreover, a meritocratic culture extends beyond leadership appointments to encompass compensation, recognition and rewards.

Compensation structures are designed to reflect individual contributions and achievements rather than relying solely on family status. Recognition programmes celebrate excellence, irrespective of familial ties, fostering a culture where all members are inspired to excel.

QUESTIONS TO ASK YOURSELF

1. How do we ensure that leadership positions are awarded based on merit within the family business?
2. Are there transparent performance evaluation processes in place for potential successors?
3. How can the family balance the importance of familial relationships with the principles of meritocracy?
4. What measures are in place to address potential conflicts arising from perceived favouritism in leadership selection?
5. In what ways can the family business communicate the value of meritocracy to all family members involved in the succession process?

N FOR NEXT-GENERATION INVOLVEMENT

Active involvement of the next generation in decision-making and strategic planning is paramount for the successful transition of leadership within family businesses. This deliberate engagement serves multiple purposes, ensuring that potential successors not only gain exposure to the intricate workings of the business but also significantly contribute to their overall development.

By participating in decision-making processes, the next generation becomes acquainted with the complexities involved in steering the family business. For instance, if the business is considering a significant investment or diversification, younger family members may offer fresh perspectives, learn about risk assessments and understand the strategic considerations that underpin major business moves. This exposure fosters a sense of ownership and responsibility, preparing them for leadership roles. This is why many business families have their children intern or even work at global consulting firms or private equity (PE) firms abroad before joining their family business—to get exposure to these aspects of business.

Being involved in strategic planning alongside family leaders provides potential successors with a holistic understanding of the business landscape. This exposure allows them to grasp market dynamics, competitive forces and the long-term vision of the company. For example, family members participating in the formulation of a strategic plan contribute insights on market trends, innovation strategies and sustainability measures. This hands-on experience shapes their strategic thinking and positions them as contributors to the business's long-term vision.

While strategic planning is crucial, it is equally important for the next generation to understand and master the operational facets of the business before exclusively jumping into strategic considerations. Understanding day-to-day operations is foundational, as it equips future leaders with a practical grasp of workflows and all kinds of challenges including those within various departments. A family member aspiring to lead a manufacturing business might want to spend time working on the shop floor, learning about production processes, supply chain dynamics and quality control measures. This first-hand experience enhances their ability to make informed strategic decisions aligned with the business's operational capabilities.

Furthermore, gaining operational insights before transitioning to strategic roles facilitates a more gradual and comprehensive leadership development. This approach ensures that potential successors have a solid foundation and practical experience to complement their strategic vision. It cultivates leaders who balance strategic foresight with a grounded understanding of day-to-day business functioning.

Excluding the next generation from crucial business discussions poses significant problems for effective succession planning. This exclusion can result in disengagement and a lack of preparedness among potential successors. When the next generation is kept away from key decision-making processes, resistance and disengagement become prevalent issues that hinder a smooth transition. Neglecting mechanisms for diverse exposure to different facets of the business is another potential pitfall. Limited perspectives can emerge when successors are not provided with varied experiences within the business context. The failure to address this lack of diverse exposure may result in successors with restricted viewpoints, impacting their ability to navigate the complexities of leadership.

Moreover, resistance or disengagement within the next generation during the succession planning process can impede the seamless transition of leadership. Ineffectively gathering input and feedback from the next generation on strategic planning exacerbates the situation, leading to unmet expectations. Limited opportunities for potential successors to express their opinions and contribute to the family business's strategic vision can result in missed insights that are crucial for future success.

A straightforward way to avoid this is to involve the next generation today as much as possible to ensure a successful succession tomorrow. It ensures that potential successors gain exposure to the business, its network of stakeholders, and operational and financial dynamics, and contribute to their development.

QUESTIONS TO ASK YOURSELF

1. How actively are the next-generation members involved in key business discussions and decisions?
2. Are there mechanisms for gathering input and feedback from the next generation on strategic planning?
3. How can the family business ensure that the next generation receives diverse exposure to different aspects of the business?
4. In what ways can potential successors be encouraged to express their opinions and contribute to the family business's strategic vision?
5. What steps are in place to address any resistance or disengagement from the next generation during the succession planning process?

O FOR OWNERSHIP STRUCTURE

Succession planning encompasses a comprehensive evaluation of the ownership structure within a family business. This process involves meticulous consideration of how ownership is distributed among family members, a critical aspect that shapes the future trajectory of the enterprise. Family businesses often grapple with questions of equity, deciding how businesses or shares of their family business ownership should be divided among siblings, cousins or other relatives involved in the business. Striking a balance that aligns with each family member's contributions, skills and commitment becomes a delicate aspect of this endeavour.

One prominent example of this can be found in the case of a successful manufacturing business where the founding generation aims to transition ownership to their children. In this scenario, equitable distribution of shares becomes a central concern. Here, a fair assessment of each child's involvement, expertise and dedication to the business is crucial. However, if the family members decide not to hold any managerial roles in the businesses, then setting up leadership roles with external professionals is important.

Some family businesses opt for external professionals or investors to diversify ownership and infuse fresh perspectives. This strategic decision can be exemplified by a renowned retail business that, in its succession planning, decides to allocate a percentage of ownership to a seasoned executive from outside the family. This move not only injects new ideas into the business but also addresses the need for professional management skills, contributing to the sustained growth and competitiveness of the enterprise. However, the consideration of non-family ownership adds another layer of complexity.

Navigating the complexities of ownership distribution in succession planning requires a sensitive approach. Addressing potential conflicts and ensuring a fair and sustainable distribution model are fundamental to securing the longevity of the family business.

In another illustrative scenario, a well-established technology company faces the challenge of passing on ownership to the next generation while accommodating family members with varying degrees of involvement and interest in the business. Here, the family engages in candid discussions to assess the aspirations, capabilities and commitment levels of each member. Through open communication and a shared vision for the future, they tailor the ownership structure to align with each family member's preferences and contributions. This personalized approach helps avoid potential disputes and ensures that ownership is based on each family member's role within the company.

Considering the potential involvement of non-family members in ownership, a successful hospitality business chooses to collaborate with a PE firm during the succession planning process. This strategic partnership not only introduces external expertise but also diversifies the ownership structure. The family and the PE partner work collaboratively to define roles and responsibilities, fostering a harmonious co-ownership model that benefits from both familial insights and professional management practices.

Furthermore, a notable example in the retail sector showcases a family business that decides to establish a family office as part of its succession plan. The family office takes on the responsibility of managing the family's wealth and business interests, providing a centralized entity to oversee ownership matters. This approach allows family members to focus on their respective strengths within the business while ensuring a structured framework for ownership transitions and wealth management.

These diverse examples underscore the importance of tailoring the ownership structure to the unique goals of each family business. Succession planning, in this context, becomes not just a transfer of shares but a strategic alignment of ownership with the values, capabilities and aspirations of both family and non-family stakeholders. By navigating these complexities thoughtfully, family businesses can foster continuity, resilience and sustained success across generations.

Alternatively, neglecting the establishment of a clear ownership structure poses significant pitfalls for family businesses engaging in succession planning. It can lead to disputes, challenges in decision-making and overall confusion among family members involved in the business. The lack of a defined structure contributes to misunderstandings and conflicts, as there is a failure to communicate clear guidelines for the distribution of ownership among family members. Ineffectively addressing the distribution of ownership shares within the family business can lead to internal conflicts. This lack of mechanisms to manage potential disputes related to ownership shares can result in strained family relationships and hinder the overall succession process. The conflict may escalate, leading to legal disputes that further complicate the succession journey.

Moreover, failure to consult with legal and financial advisors to ensure a sound ownership structure is a snag that family businesses should avoid. Insufficient consultation can result in legal and financial challenges. Additionally, ignoring the need for the ownership structure to adapt to changes in family dynamics or business expansion can result in outdated practices that hinder the family business's ability to evolve effectively.

QUESTIONS TO ASK YOURSELF

1. How is the ownership structure of the family business currently defined, and does it align with the succession plan?
2. Are there clear guidelines for the distribution of ownership among family members, and have these been communicated effectively?
3. Have legal and financial advisors been consulted to ensure the ownership structure is legally sound and financially viable?
4. How can potential conflicts related to ownership shares be addressed and mitigated within the family?
5. In what ways can the ownership structure adapt to changes in family dynamics or business expansion?

P FOR PROFESSIONALIZATION

The phrase 'professionalizing the family business' often becomes ubiquitous, yet is misunderstood or overused in many family business conversations. While frequently uttered, its true essence is sometimes lost or oversimplified. It is crucial to recognize that professionalization involves a comprehensive transformation that goes beyond mere rhetoric, requiring a strategic and well-executed approach to modernize and optimize various facets of the family enterprise.

Professionalization transcends a mere shift in operations; it entails embracing sound business practices, erecting robust governance structures and engaging external professionals to elevate operational efficiency and decision-making capabilities. By instilling a culture of professionalism, family businesses position themselves to thrive in dynamic markets, fostering sustainable growth and resilience.

It is a transformative process that goes beyond familial ties, focusing on instilling a corporate mindset and adopting practices that ensure sustained growth and competitiveness. One exemplary case is that of a well-established manufacturing business that, in its journey of professionalization, decides to bring in a seasoned CEO from outside the family. This external leader brings a wealth of industry knowledge and a fresh perspective, steering the business towards greater operational efficiency and strategic innovation. At the same time, the family starts grooming the next generation, who actually begin to work under the professional CEO, so that they can become ready to take over the business leadership.

Professionalism in succession planning embodies a commitment to objective evaluation, meritocracy and strategic foresight. By adhering to professional standards and practices, organizations mitigate the risks associated with nepotism, favouritism and personal biases in leadership selection. Professionalism ensures that succession decisions are based on qualifications, experience and performance, rather than familial ties or personal relationships.

Moreover, professionalism in succession planning facilitates effective talent management and development, as it emphasizes the importance of identifying and nurturing individuals with the requisite skills and capabilities to lead the organization in the future. It ultimately impacts the quality of leadership, organizational stability and stakeholder confidence. Professionalism fosters a culture of accountability and transparency, where succession decisions are made with the best interests of the organization in mind, enhancing its resilience and long-term viability.

However, professionalism cannot be assumed as a given within family-owned businesses. While stakeholders expect professionalism in business enterprises, deliberate efforts are required to cultivate and maintain it. Professionalism encompasses not only technical competence and expertise but also ethical conduct, integrity and a commitment to continuous improvement. In the context of succession planning, it entails adherence to established processes and protocols, as well as a willingness to challenge assumptions, seek feedback and make decisions based on merit.

Even family members within family-owned businesses must undergo training and development to cultivate professionalism and acquire the necessary skills for leadership roles. While being part of the family may provide certain advantages, such as familiarity with the organization's history and values, it does not guarantee professionalism by birth. Family members need to demonstrate competence, commitment and a willingness to adhere to professional standards in their roles within the business. Training programmes, mentorship initiatives and exposure to external best practices can help them develop the leadership skills and professional acumen required to contribute effectively to the organization's success and ensure the continuity of its legacy.

Take these varied inspirational cases of effective professionalization for example. In the hospitality sector, a family-owned chain of hotels embraces professionalization by establishing a board of directors comprising both family and independent directors. This move injects a diverse range of skills and experiences into the decision-making process. The independent directors, often industry experts, contribute valuable insights, challenging conventional approaches and ensuring the business remains adaptive and resilient in a dynamic market.

Furthermore, a successful retail business transitions to a more professional model by implementing robust governance structures. They create dedicated committees, such as audit and compensation committees, comprising professionals with expertise in finance, legal matters and human resources. This systematic approach not only enhances transparency but also ensures that key decisions are informed by a broad arena of expertise.

In yet another case, a longstanding construction business recognizes the need for specialized project management expertise to handle large-scale infrastructure projects. In their pursuit of professionalization, they hire project managers with extensive experience in the field. These professionals introduce advanced project management methodologies, ensuring timely completion, cost-effectiveness and quality control in each construction project.

Additionally, a family-owned agricultural enterprise undergoes professionalization by investing in advanced technology and precision farming techniques. They enlist the expertise of agri-tech specialists to implement data-driven decision-making processes, optimize resource utilization and enhance overall agricultural productivity.

These examples illustrate that professionalizing a family business involves strategic decisions tailored to the specific needs and challenges of each industry. Whether through hiring external executives, establishing governance frameworks, or recruiting specialized talent, the goal is to cultivate a culture of professionalism, ensuring the family business is well-equipped for sustained success in a competitive business landscape.

Maintaining a dynamic relationship among family owners, the board and management is paramount for leaders of a family-owned business. This entails ensuring open lines of communication, where family members' ideas and opinions are respected, fostering a culture of trust and collaboration. It also involves aligning all stakeholders towards a common goal, with clarity on governance structures and roles and responsibilities across different groups.

Misunderstandings can quickly escalate into conflicts within family businesses, highlighting the critical importance of clear communication and mutual respect among stakeholders. While family owners bear the responsibility of providing a clear ownership strategy and family governance framework, including policies on family employment and succession planning, non-family professionals, comprising the board and management, play a pivotal role in supporting and implementing these policies.

For non-family leadership teams, establishing a personal connection with family members goes beyond business transactions; it entails investing time and effort and possibly making sacrifices to demonstrate genuine support for the family's vision and goals. Building this personal rapport fosters a sense of camaraderie and solidarity, reinforcing the family's trust in the leadership's commitment to their interests and the success of the business.

Moreover, fostering a dynamic relationship involves adapting to the evolving needs and aspirations of the family and the business. This requires leaders to remain receptive to feedback, flexible in their approach and proactive in addressing emerging challenges or opportunities. By prioritizing relationship-building and mutual understanding, leaders can cultivate a harmonious and resilient environment conducive to the long-term success of the family-owned enterprise.

Resisting the path of professionalization poses significant risks for a family business, potentially resulting in inefficiencies and impeding competitiveness in the market. The reluctance to embrace external expertise or implement changes to established practices can lead to missed opportunities and operational challenges. Beyond internal implications, the family business may encounter difficulties in attracting external investors and partners, hindering its growth trajectory. Striking a delicate balance between traditional values and the necessity for modern and professional business practices is essential to prevent internal conflicts. Challenges arising from resistance or obstacles in professionalizing specific aspects of the family business can detrimentally impact overall progress and success.

QUESTIONS TO ASK YOURSELF

1. To what extent has the family business embraced professional practices in its operations and management?

2. Are there mechanisms in place to attract and retain external professionals or advisors to enhance business performance?
3. How can professionalization contribute to the overall success of the succession plan and long-term sustainability?
4. In what ways can the family business balance traditional values with the need for modern and professional business practices?
5. What steps are in place to address potential resistance or challenges in professionalizing certain aspects of the family business?

Q FOR QUALITY OF LIFE

A pivotal consideration in the intricate web of succession planning for family businesses is the quality of life (QoL). Beyond the financial and operational aspects, this dimension acknowledges the holistic well-being of family members actively engaged in the business, which is a crucial aspect of sustainable family enterprises.

Succession planning should give serious consideration to the impact of the QoL of family members on the business, as neglecting it can have severe consequences, leading to burnout, stress and strained family relationships. Members immersed in the business may find themselves overwhelmed, facing not only the pressures of their roles but also the toll it takes on their personal lives.

The quest for success in the business realm should not come at the cost of one's overall happiness and fulfilment. Addressing conflicts between business interests and the QoL for family members is paramount. It involves balancing business responsibilities with personal well-being, emphasizing the importance of a healthy work–life balance. It also involves recognizing the pitfalls that may arise when personal well-being takes a back seat to professional demands. Failure to strike a balance can strain relationships within the family; we will soon see how.

It is entirely understandable for business family scions to prioritize the quality of their lives. Having witnessed the sacrifices and stresses endured by previous generations in building the family business, they may seek a different path that prioritizes personal fulfilment, well-being and work–life balance. With the financial security provided by their family's wealth, they have the opportunity to explore their passions, pursue diverse interests and contribute to society in ways that align with their values and aspirations. Emphasizing QoL allows them to lead fulfilling lives beyond the confines of business success, fostering a sense of happiness, fulfilment and holistic well-being.

On the flip side, failing to acknowledge the importance of QoL can pose significant risks to both the future of the business and the well-being of the family itself. Failure to strike a balance can strain relationships within the family, as conflicting priorities may result in excessive workloads and diminished satisfaction, and can create tension and hinder effective collaboration.

Furthermore, neglecting the quality-of-life considerations may hinder the next generation's engagement and commitment to the business, potentially resulting in succession challenges and a lack of continuity. It can, as a result, erode the family's cohesion and unity, as differing priorities and values may create tensions and conflicts. Many businesses have faced internal conflicts when family members experienced burnout due to excessive workloads and inadequate attention to their QoL. Ultimately, recognizing and prioritizing QoL is essential for the long-term sustainability and prosperity of both the business and the family.

Inadequate policies or initiatives to address the work–life balance of family members can lead to dissatisfaction and challenges in retention. Implementing clear policies that prioritize the well-being of individuals ensures a healthier and more sustainable work environment. Creating a supportive and healthy work environment is essential for attracting and retaining talent within the family business. Without sufficient mechanisms to promote well-being, the business may struggle to foster a culture that values the holistic development and happiness of its members.

As we have come to understand, succession planning transcends the mere transfer of business responsibilities; it extends its reach into the very fabric of the lives it touches. Considering the impact on the QoL for family members engaged in the business is not just a pragmatic approach but an ethical imperative. Balancing the scales between professional commitments and personal well-being is in a way recognizing that true success lies not only in the financial prosperity of the enterprise but also in the fulfilment and happiness of those steering its course. Wealth, when viewed as stewardship, entails responsibilities that stretch beyond the boardroom—responsibilities to oneself, to family and to society. A robust succession plan, mindful of the intricate interplay between professional and personal spheres, weaves a picture where prosperity is harmonized with well-being, and the legacy it shapes stands as a testament to the holistic values that guide the family and its enterprise.

Let us take a few examples. In the context of a manufacturing business, the founding generation initiates a succession plan that places a premium on QoL. Recognizing the toll that rigorous production schedules can take on familial relationships, the plan introduces flexible work arrangements. Family members are encouraged to embrace a healthy work–life balance, ensuring that business demands do not compromise the essential fabric of family bonds. This proactive approach not only enhances job satisfaction but also contributes to the overall QoL for those involved in the enterprise.

In the hospitality sector, a family-owned chain of resorts embeds QoL considerations into its succession strategy. The plan involves periodic sabbaticals for family members engaged in key managerial roles. These sabbaticals serve as opportunities for rejuvenation, allowing individuals to step away from the day-to-day pressures of the business and invest time in personal pursuits. This intentional break from routine contributes significantly to mental well-being, fostering a positive impact on the overall QoL.

Similarly, in the technology industry, a family business places emphasis on fostering a supportive work environment. The succession plan incorporates mentorship programmes, mental health resources and wellness initiatives. By prioritizing the mental and emotional health of family members, the business acknowledges that a positive QoL is not solely contingent on financial success but is intricately woven into the fabric of a supportive and empathetic workplace culture.

Another example is from the agricultural sector. A family-owned farm incorporates sustainability practices not only in farming methods but also in work practices. The succession plan encourages a shift towards regenerative agriculture while implementing rotational work schedules that allow family members to engage with the business without experiencing burnout. This approach not only contributes to the longevity of the farm but also enhances the QoL for those involved in its day-to-day operations.

These examples underscore that QoL considerations in succession planning extend far beyond material wealth. By nurturing an environment that respects personal well-being, family businesses can ensure that the transition of leadership does not come at the expense of the QoL for those intricately connected to the business's success.

QUESTIONS TO ASK YOURSELF

1. How does the family business prioritize the quality of life or QoL for family members involved in business operations?
2. Are there policies or initiatives in place to address the work–life balance of family members involved in the business?
3. How can succession planning ensure a balance between business responsibilities and personal well-being?
4. Are there mechanisms to address potential conflicts between business interests and the personal life of family members?
5. In what ways can the family business promote a supportive and healthy work environment that enhances the overall QoL for family members involved in the business?

R FOR RISK MANAGEMENT

Succession planning is often underestimated in terms of its relationship with risk management within family-owned businesses. It requires a comprehensive approach to risk management. While many organizations focus primarily on identifying and grooming successors, the broader context of risk management is often overlooked. This involves identifying potential risks to the business, developing strategies to mitigate these risks, and ensuring that the next generation is equipped to handle unforeseen challenges, which is why a cautious approach to succession planning is essential to future-proof the business against various uncertainties and ensure its long-term sustainability.

One key aspect of incorporating risk management into succession planning is the identification of potential risks to the business. These risks can range from internal factors such as leadership gaps and talent shortages to external factors such as economic downturns, technological disruptions and changes in regulatory environments. By conducting a thorough risk assessment, family businesses can proactively identify areas of vulnerability and develop strategies to mitigate these risks.

Moreover, effective succession planning involves not only selecting and grooming successors but also ensuring that they are prepared to navigate unforeseen challenges and disruptions. This requires equipping the next generation with the necessary skills, knowledge and experience to lead the business in an ever-changing landscape. Training programmes, mentorship initiatives and exposure to real-world business scenarios can help successors develop resilience, adaptability and strategic thinking skills to effectively manage risks and capitalize on opportunities.

Furthermore, succession planning should encompass contingency plans to address unexpected events or emergencies that may impact the business's continuity. This includes establishing protocols for interim leadership, outlining procedures for decision-making during times of crisis and ensuring that key stakeholders are aware of their roles and responsibilities in such situations. By preparing for contingencies and developing robust risk management strategies, family businesses can enhance their agility and resilience in the face of uncertainty.

⁂

In today's dynamic business environment, where disruptions are becoming increasingly common, the importance of integrating risk management into succession planning cannot be overstated. While succession planning is often viewed as a routine administrative task, it serves as a critical mechanism for safeguarding the future of the business and preserving its legacy for generations to come. By taking a cautious and proactive approach to risk management within the context of succession planning, family-owned businesses can position themselves to thrive in an ever-changing world. Let us look at the various risks associated with a business and how their management can be integrated into the succession plans.

The comprehensive succession planning strategy involves assessing the composition of family members holding key positions within the company. The risk of overconcentration arises when family members dominate these roles, potentially limiting diversity in perspectives and skill sets. To mitigate this, successful succession plans should strike a balance between family and non-family executives, ensuring a blend of expertise and fresh insights to propel the business forward.

Another dimension of risk in succession planning pertains to the actions of competitors. Aggressive moves by rivals can impact a family business's market share and profitability. To counteract this risk, it is essential to conduct regular market analyses and strategically plan within the succession framework. This proactive approach allows the business to respond effectively to competitive threats, ensuring its continued competitiveness.

Navigating the complex landscape of evolving regulations is a risk that family businesses must address within succession planning. Changes in regulatory frameworks can pose compliance challenges and impact established business models. Mitigating this risk involves staying informed about regulatory shifts, conducting regular legal assessments, and adapting succession plans accordingly to ensure compliance and minimize potential disruptions.

Tax implications represent another critical area of risk in succession planning. The transfer of ownership or changes in leadership may lead to unforeseen tax burdens, impacting the financial health of the business. To address this, succession plans should incorporate the expertise of tax professionals. Their insights can optimize structures and minimize tax burdens, ensuring a smooth transition that aligns with the family's financial objectives.

Identifying and fortifying competitive advantages, or 'business moats', is essential for mitigating risks associated with market vulnerability. Failing to do so may expose the business to increased competition. Consequently, succession plans should include strategies to strengthen and expand these moats, ensuring the business's long-term resilience and sustained success.

Succession plans also need to address the risk associated with capital allocation and financial management. Insufficient capital planning may jeopardize the successful execution of the succession plan. Robust financial forecasting aligned with the succession roadmap is crucial to ensuring the financial stability needed for a seamless transition.

Lastly, the emergence of unknown risks, such as technological disruptions or global events, represents a challenge for family businesses. To address this, succession planning should integrate scenario planning and risk simulations. This proactive approach enhances the business's adaptability, ensuring it can navigate unforeseen challenges in the dynamic business landscape. Overall, a comprehensive risk management approach within succession planning is integral to establishing a resilient foundation for the next generation.

❧

In navigating the turbulent waters of business, family enterprises face the inherent challenge of recognizing and mitigating potential risks. The cornerstone of effective risk management lies in the regular assessment and updating of strategies, ensuring they remain agile and aligned with the evolving business landscape. Failure to do so may lead to the adoption of outdated approaches, rendering the family business ill-prepared to handle emerging threats.

It is equally critical to integrate risk management seamlessly into leadership development programmes for the next generation, equipping them with the skills and foresight needed to navigate uncertainties. External expertise should not be overlooked, as insights from professionals can shed light on potential risks and effective mitigation strategies. Neglecting to prepare the next generation to handle these challenges can hinder their ability to adapt, making the integration of risk management an integral part of the family business's legacy of resilience.

Risk management emerges as a linchpin in the orchestration of effective succession planning for family businesses. Navigating the intricate landscape of familial transitions and business evolution demands a meticulous approach to identifying, assessing and mitigating risks. An adept succession plan, rich in risk management strategies, ensures the resilience and sustained success of the family enterprise.

For families overseeing operating companies within the realm of family business, the strategic dimensions of risk management assume paramount importance. While having established risk management infrastructure, policies and processes is foundational, the true measure of resilience lies in the family firm's adeptness at identifying and assessing an array of risks, both present and future. The crucial juncture emerges in mapping these risks onto the family business's risk appetite and, more significantly, onto its capacity to bear the consequences of the risks undertaken. In essence, the family's ability to align risk considerations with the unique dynamics of the family business profoundly influences its long-term survival and ultimate success. This nuanced approach ensures that risk management becomes an integral part of the family's strategic foresight, contributing to the legacy and sustainability of the family business.

Consider a family owned retail business where the succession plan integrates robust risk management protocols. In this case, the family conducts a thorough risk assessment, identifying potential market fluctuations, supply chain vulnerabilities and regulatory uncertainties. The succession plan then incorporates contingency measures, such as diversification of suppliers and proactive compliance strategies, to fortify the business against external pressures. By instilling risk awareness in the next generation, the family business not only shields itself from potential disruptions but also equips successors with the skills to navigate the complexities of the industry.

In the financial services sector, a family-owned investment firm tailors its succession plan to the intricacies of the market. Recognizing the volatility inherent in financial markets, the plan incorporates portfolio diversification strategies and hedges against potential economic downturns. This forward-thinking approach not only safeguards the family's wealth but also positions the business to adapt to changing financial landscapes, thereby mitigating risks associated with market fluctuations.

Similarly, in the technology industry, a family business emphasizes on cybersecurity as a critical component of its succession plan. With the increasing threat of cyber-attacks, the family recognizes the importance of safeguarding sensitive data and intellectual property. The succession plan allocates resources to train the next generation in cybersecurity measures, ensuring that the business remains resilient against evolving digital threats.

In the agricultural sector, a family-owned farm integrates climate risk management into its succession plan. Recognizing the impact of climate change on agricultural practices, the family invests in sustainable farming methods and explores crop diversification strategies. This proactive stance not only mitigates the risk of crop failures but also positions the farm for long-term sustainability in the face of changing environmental conditions.

These examples underscore that effective succession planning is inseparable from a robust risk management framework. By anticipating and addressing potential challenges, family businesses can fortify their foundations and empower the next generation to lead with resilience in the face of uncertainty.

QUESTIONS TO ASK YOURSELF

1. What are the key risks that could impact the family business, and how are they being addressed in the succession plan?
2. Are there mechanisms in place to regularly assess and update the risk management strategies of the family business?

3. How can the next generation be prepared to handle potential risks and uncertainties in the business environment?
4. Have external experts been consulted to provide insights into potential risks and risk mitigation strategies?
5. In what ways can risk management be integrated into leadership development programmes for potential successors?

S FOR SUCCESS METRICS

Defining success metrics is essential for evaluating the effectiveness of succession planning. These metrics should go beyond financial indicators and encompass factors such as family cohesion, employee satisfaction and the overall sustainability of the business. Recognition merely from peer families or markets (in the case of listed entities) or regulators is not sufficient. Succession planning needs to address all stakeholders impacted by the plan itself. Of course, it won't be able to satisfy everyone's every expectation. But if the process is fair and discussion-based, then no one can doubt its intent.

In family businesses, success in planning for the next generation goes beyond just looking at money. It is like creating a beautiful picture with different colours. Success is not only about making lots of profit but also about how well the family gets along, how happy the employees are and how the business keeps going strong. One may think of it like a good family story, where everyone works together and the leadership smoothly passes from one family member to another. Success is also about making sure the people working in the business feel good about their jobs. When they are happy, it is akin to planting seeds for the future success of the business.

And then there is sustainability—which means keeping the business strong not just for now but for a long time. It is about being ready for changes and making sure the family values continue through the years. So success is like a big storybook with happy families, satisfied workers and a business that lasts through generations. It is not just about money but about creating a legacy that everyone can be proud of.

Success variables for a business family succession plan encompass a range of factors that contribute to the long-term success and sustainability of the business. First, the seamless transition of leadership from one generation to the next is a critical success variable, ensuring continuity and stability within the organization. Second, the development and empowerment of the next generation of leaders, including family members and non-family professionals, play a vital role in driving innovation and growth. Additionally, fostering a culture of transparency, open communication and trust within the family and across the organization is essential for maintaining family cohesion and employee satisfaction. Furthermore, the successful implementation of succession planning should result in the preservation of the family's legacy and values while adapting to changing market dynamics and stakeholder expectations.

However, despite the importance of success metrics, there are inherent risks involved in their measurement and evaluation. One risk is the potential for subjective biases to influence the assessment of success, particularly when evaluating factors such as family cohesion and employee satisfaction. Additionally, focusing solely on quantitative metrics may overlook qualitative aspects of succession planning, such as the intangible impact on family relationships and organizational culture. Moreover, there is a risk of setting unrealistic or unattainable targets, leading to dissatisfaction and disengagement among stakeholders. Therefore, it is crucial to establish clear and objective criteria for measuring success and to have robust governance mechanisms in place to ensure accountability and fairness in the evaluation process.

Furthermore, it is easy to get carried away because of plenty of data, various metrics and attempts to solve the issues of succession planning. While individual metrics provide valuable insights into specific aspects of the plan's effectiveness, it is essential to avoid getting bogged down in micromanaging each metric. Instead, the focus should be on achieving the overarching goals of succession planning, such as ensuring the long-term viability of the business, preserving family unity and fostering a positive organizational culture. By adopting a balanced approach to measurement and governance, family-owned businesses can effectively assess the impact of succession planning on all stakeholders and drive sustainable growth and prosperity for generations to come.

Success metrics serve as the compass guiding the evaluation of succession planning effectiveness within family businesses. These metrics extend beyond mere financial indicators, offering a nuanced perspective that encapsulates the holistic health and sustainability of the business. The robustness of succession plans is, therefore, measured not just in monetary gains but in the synergy of family dynamics, employee satisfaction and the business's enduring resilience.

Consider a family-owned manufacturing business where success metrics extend beyond profit margins. The effectiveness of the succession plan is gauged by the level of family cohesion achieved during the transition. Harmonious relationships among family members actively engaged in the business become a qualitative success metric, emphasizing the importance of familial bonds beyond the boardroom.

In the service industry, a family business incorporates employee satisfaction as a pivotal success metric. Beyond financial growth, the succession plan aims to create a workplace culture where employees feel valued and motivated. Employee retention rates, job satisfaction surveys and the overall organizational climate become integral components of success, contributing to the long-term prosperity of the business.

Similarly, in the technology sector, a family business focuses on innovation and adaptability as success metrics. The effectiveness of the succession plan is measured by the business's capacity to embrace technological advancements and navigate industry shifts. The ability to foster a culture of continuous learning and innovation becomes a qualitative benchmark, ensuring the family business remains agile in a rapidly evolving landscape.

Or take the case of an enterprise in the agricultural domain. Sustainability becomes a key success metric within the succession plan. Beyond financial gains, the family business evaluates its impact on the environment, community and future generations. Implementing eco-friendly farming practices, community engagement programmes and land conservation efforts contribute to the qualitative success of the succession plan, aligning the business with broader societal values.

In a nutshell, having success metrics to gauge the health of your business or understanding its future is having a map that shows more than just the financial journey. When we focus only on the money part, it is like looking through a tiny window and missing the bigger picture. So, having a variety of indicators is essential—not just financial ones—to see how well things are going.

However, it is not just about having these indicators but also about sharing them clearly with everyone involved. Imagine having a map with confusing symbols—it wouldn't help much. Similarly, if success metrics aren't communicated transparently, it can lead to confusion and disagreements.

Now, imagine if your map only showed old routes and didn't consider new ones. Success metrics need to keep up with changes in the business world—much as updating your map to find better paths. Also, it's tricky when short-term money goals clash with long-term success plans. Balancing these is like finding harmony between two tunes.

Lastly, think of communication channels as the way you share your map. If the channels are limited or unclear, it's like having a great map that reaches nobody. So, success in a family business is like having a clear map, with various indicators, updated routes, and effective ways to share it with everyone involved.

QUESTIONS TO ASK YOURSELF

1. How is success defined for the family business in the context of succession planning?
2. What metrics are being used in your business to measure the success of the succession plan beyond financial performance?
3. Are transparent communication mechanisms in place to share success metrics with family members and stakeholders?
4. How can success metrics be adapted to align with changing industry trends and business strategies?
5. In what ways can the family business balance short-term financial goals with the long-term success metrics defined in the succession plan?

T FOR TRANSPARENCY

Transparency is a foundational element of successful succession planning. It involves open communication, clear documentation of processes and sharing relevant information with family members, stakeholders and employees. Transparency could be an elusive value—foundational yet challenging to achieve.

Transparency not only fosters trust and accountability but also ensures that all family members are well-informed and involved in decision-making processes. However, beneath the surface, doubts and uncertainties may linger among family members, especially regarding sensitive issues such as succession, governance and financial matters. Therefore, it becomes essential to adopt a strategy of over-communication and address any doubts transparently. This approach helps dispel misconceptions, alleviates concerns and promotes clarity and alignment among family members. By openly discussing challenges, sharing information and engaging in transparent dialogue, families can strengthen their bonds, mitigate conflicts and steer the business towards long-term success.

Transparency in succession planning means laying bare the intricate details, aspirations and challenges that shape the future of the family business. It is about openly discussing who takes the reins, how decisions are made and what values guide the journey. This openness is the linchpin that holds the intricate succession machinery together. However, transparency, despite its foundational importance, often proves to be the most challenging aspect. Why?

Because it demands more than just revealing financial statements and organizational charts. It requires unveiling emotions, acknowledging insecurities and discussing the unsaid. It is about airing concerns about competence, addressing fears of favouritism and navigating the delicate balance between tradition and innovation.

The challenge lies in overcoming the resistance to unveil the vulnerabilities within the family. Succession planning isn't just a business transaction, it is a deeply personal, emotional and sometimes uncomfortable journey. It is about recognizing that the transition isn't just about assets and titles but the family legacy, relationships and the very fabric that binds the family together.

Moreover, transparency isn't a one-time act; it is an ongoing commitment, which involves regular, honest conversations that evolve as the business and family dynamics change. It is about adapting to unforeseen circumstances, acknowledging mistakes and collectively recalibrating the succession path.

Yet, despite its challenges, transparency remains non-negotiable for successful succession planning. It is the bridge that connects generations, aligns expectations and builds trust. In its absence, assumptions fester, misunderstandings deepen and the smooth transition of leadership becomes a hazardous tightrope walk.

One key variable that transparency in succession planning addresses is the alignment of expectations. When family members and key stakeholders have a clear understanding of the succession process, including criteria for leadership selection and timelines, it minimizes ambiguity and reduces the likelihood of conflicts or misunderstandings. Moreover, transparency facilitates the identification and development of potential successors, enabling organizations to nurture talent and ensure a smooth transition of leadership when the time comes.

Furthermore, transparency in succession planning mitigates risks associated with uncertainty and instability. By providing visibility into succession processes and decision-making criteria, organizations can enhance trust and confidence among family members, employees, investors and other stakeholders. This fosters a culture of accountability and fairness, where individuals feel valued and empowered to contribute to the organization's success.

Additionally, open and proactive communication about succession planning builds resilience, as it allows organizations to proactively address challenges and adapt to changing circumstances, ensuring continuity and longevity in leadership transitions, which plays a pivotal role in the success of the succession plan. Starting with each family member and extending to external stakeholders, a well-executed communication strategy fosters transparency, aligns expectations and mitigates potential conflicts. Addressing doubts and concerns, especially negative ones, is crucial, and allocating adequate time for each conversation is essential for building consensus and ensuring a smooth transition.

Initiating the communication process within the family requires a delicate approach. Personalized discussions with each family member allow for a thorough understanding of individual expectations, concerns and aspirations. These conversations should be initiated well in advance, providing ample time for family members to absorb the information, express their thoughts and participate in shaping the succession plan. Listening attentively to each family member's perspective is key to addressing doubts and concerns effectively.

Internal family discussions should be followed by collective meetings to discuss the overarching succession plan. This forum can serve as an opportunity to share the vision, clarify expectations and ensure everyone is on the same page. Transparent communication about the selection criteria for leadership roles and the timeline for transitions builds trust among family members.

External stakeholders, including key employees and business partners, also require proactive communication. Timely and transparent updates on the succession plan prevent uncertainty and maintain stability within the organization. These communications should outline how the succession will affect daily operations, assure stakeholders of continuity, and highlight the strengths of the incoming leadership. Providing a forum for external stakeholders to express their concerns ensures a more comprehensive understanding of potential challenges and enables the business to proactively address them.

Adequate time for each conversation is vital to allow for thorough discussions, clarification of doubts and the building of consensus. Rushed communication can lead to misunderstandings and resistance. Providing family members and stakeholders with the necessary information well in advance allows them to process the changes, ask questions and contribute to the refinement of the succession plan.

When it comes to negative doubts or concerns, they should not be dismissed but addressed head-on. Actively listening to concerns and acknowledging their validity demonstrates a commitment to inclusive decision-making. Every effort should be made to provide detailed explanations, share the rationale behind decisions and seek collaborative solutions where possible. Ignoring negative sentiments can lead to resentment and potential resistance in the execution of the succession plan.

Regular updates and ongoing communication channels should be established to keep all stakeholders informed throughout the succession process. This ensures that any emerging concerns or issues can be addressed promptly, fostering a culture of transparency and trust.

Transparency, as a foundational element of successful succession planning, is characterized by a commitment to open communication, explicit documentation of processes, and the sharing of pertinent information with family members, stakeholders and employees. This multifaceted approach serves as the bedrock for fostering trust, aligning expectations, and ensuring a seamless transition of leadership within family businesses.

Clear documentation of processes is equally crucial. Transparency demands that the succession plan be outlined in detail, encompassing the criteria for leadership roles, the timeline for transition and the evaluation parameters for potential successors. Documenting these processes provides a tangible roadmap that family members and stakeholders can refer to, reducing ambiguity and facilitating a smoother execution of the succession plan.

Sharing relevant information extends not only to family members directly involved in the business but also to key stakeholders and employees. Transparent communication about the succession plan with external partners, customers and employees helps maintain stability and continuity. It reinforces the credibility of the family business and assures stakeholders that the transition is a carefully planned and well-executed process. Furthermore, it fosters a culture of inclusivity.

Confidentiality, while important, can become a pitfall when overemphasized without the establishment of appropriate communication channels. This overemphasis can erode trust and collaboration, hindering the seamless transition of leadership. Moreover, potential misunderstandings or conflicts resulting from a lack of transparency may go unaddressed, posing a threat to overall family cohesion.

The absence of transparency in family business succession planning can set the stage for misunderstandings, distrust and conflicts, not only within the family but also within the broader business community. When succession plans and decisions are shrouded in secrecy or communicated inadequately, it creates an atmosphere of uncertainty and negative perceptions.

For transparency to be effective, it must be seamlessly integrated into the culture and values of the family business. Failure to do so may lead to external scrutiny and negative perceptions, as seen in instances where succession decisions were made with limited transparency, resulting in a decline in market trust. The pitfalls of insufficient transparency underscore the importance of open, honest communication as the cornerstone of successful family business succession planning.

QUESTIONS TO ASK YOURSELF

1. How transparent is the family business in communicating succession plans and decisions with family members?
2. Are there mechanisms in place to ensure transparency in key business operations and decision-making processes?
3. How can the family business balance the need for confidentiality with the importance of transparent communication?
4. What steps are taken to address potential misunderstandings or conflicts that may arise due to a lack of transparency?
5. In what ways can transparency be integrated into the overall culture and values of the family business?

U FOR UNITY

In the world of family businesses, staying together as a united family is like having a superpower. When families plan to pass on their businesses to the next generation, this superpower—unity—is what makes everything work smoothly. It is not just about getting along but also about everyone in the family working together for a common goal. Maintaining unity within the family is a fundamental aspect of successful succession planning. It involves fostering a sense of shared purpose, collaboration and a commitment to the overall well-being of the family and the business.

Imagine passing the responsibilities of running the family business to the next generation. In a united family, everyone works together to make sure this transition happens smoothly. It is not just one person taking over but a team effort. Each family member plays a part in steering the business in the right direction. Now, think about the legacy of the family business—the story it tells and the values it holds. Unity is what keeps this story alive. It is not about forgetting the past but ensuring that everyone in the family agrees on what the business stands for. Unity helps the family business grow and change while holding onto its important traditions.

A good reputation serves the business in several ways. It is like a super valuable treasure for a family business. When the family stays united, people see the business as trustworthy and reliable. Clients and others in the community believe in the family because they see that the latter work well together. Unity becomes a shield that protects the business from problems. Why is unity so crucial, especially when planning for the future of the business?

Well, unity goes beyond just the day-to-day stuff. It makes the family strong and adaptable. Unity turns challenges into chances for success and passing the business to the next generation becomes more like a continuation of an exciting journey. Unity is not just a nice thing to have but like the special power that keeps the family business going and growing for a long, long time.

While it is entirely acceptable for family members to harbour different interests, passions and career paths, the linchpin for cohesion lies in the shared values that bind them together. These shared values serve as the bedrock of the family's identity and are non-negotiable components that contribute to the overall success and sustainability of the family business.

Maintaining unity within the family is not just important but fundamental for successful succession planning. A cohesive and harmonious family dynamic lays the groundwork for smooth transitions of leadership and ensures the preservation of the family legacy and business continuity. Unity fosters trust, open communication and mutual respect among family members, which are essential for navigating the complexities of succession planning with shared goals and a collective vision for the future.

However, the risks of succession planning can strain family unity if not carefully managed. Disagreements over leadership roles, inheritance and business decisions can create rifts within the family, leading to conflicts, resentment and division. Additionally, unequal treatment or favouritism among family members can breed animosity and erode trust, undermining the cohesion necessary for successful succession. Moreover, external factors such as market volatility or unforeseen challenges may exacerbate tensions within the family, further threatening unity and jeopardizing the succession process.

To avoid these risks and maintain family unity during succession planning, proactive communication, transparency and fairness are paramount. Establishing clear channels for dialogue and decision-making allows family members to voice their concerns, express their aspirations and participate in the planning process. Moreover, fostering a culture of inclusivity and collaboration ensures that all family members feel valued and heard, mitigating feelings of resentment or exclusion. Implementing structured governance mechanisms, such as family councils or advisory boards, can facilitate discussions and consensus-building, promoting unity and alignment around shared objectives. Additionally, prioritizing trust-building activities, such as family retreats or team-building exercises, strengthens bonds and fosters a sense of solidarity among family members, reinforcing unity and resilience in the face of succession challenges. Ultimately, by nurturing unity and cohesion within the family, succession planning can become a collaborative and enriching journey that preserves the family legacy and paves the way for continued success across generations.

Divergent interests among family members are a natural occurrence and can even be viewed as a strength. Embracing diversity in individual pursuits brings richness to the family dynamic, injecting fresh perspectives and skill sets into the business. It allows family members to explore their unique passions and contribute to the family's legacy in varied ways.

However, amidst these differences, the foundation of shared values becomes the unifying force. These values, often deeply rooted in the family's history, culture and vision, provide a common ground that transcends individual interests. Whether it's a commitment to excellence, integrity or a dedication to community service, these shared values create a cohesive thread that binds the family together despite diverse pursuits.

In the context of succession planning, recognizing and appreciating these individual interests while upholding shared values is crucial. It allows for a more inclusive and flexible approach to leadership transition, where family members can contribute according to their strengths and interests, aligning with the overarching values that define the family legacy.

This nuanced balance acknowledges the uniqueness of each family member's journey while reinforcing the collective identity that the family business represents. It promotes a culture of mutual respect, understanding and collaboration, fostering an environment where diverse talents coalesce for the benefit of the family enterprise. Ultimately, the success of succession planning hinges not only on navigating individual interests but also on anchoring the family in shared values that stand as unwavering pillars of unity and continuity.

Neglecting efforts to foster unity within a family business can give rise to internal conflicts, competing interests and an overall weakened family structure. Building unity becomes essential in avoiding internal divisions that may arise from conflicting priorities and challenges in alignment. Overemphasizing individual goals at the expense of the collective vision can lead to a fragmentation of efforts, hindering the family's ability to work towards shared objectives.

Effective communication plays a pivotal role in promoting a sense of unity and shared purpose among family members. Inadequate communication channels may result in misunderstandings, further exacerbating internal divisions. Promoting collective decision-making is key and facing resistance or challenges in achieving this can impede overall family cohesion.

Addressing potential conflicts and differences in goals within the family is crucial for maintaining unity. Failure to do so can result in strained relationships and a decline in overall family unity. Real-life instances illustrate family businesses facing internal divisions when succession decisions were made without addressing differing perspectives and expectations, leading to a decline in family unity. These pitfalls underscore the significance of actively fostering unity and shared purpose within family businesses.

QUESTIONS TO ASK YOURSELF

1. How does the family business promote a sense of unity and shared purpose among family members?
2. Are there mechanisms in place to address potential conflicts and differences in goals within the family?
3. How can succession planning contribute to building and maintaining family unity?
4. In what ways can individual goals align with the collective vision of the family business?
5. What role does effective communication play in fostering unity and a sense of shared commitment within the family?

V FOR VALUES

Values serve as the compass guiding the trajectory of successful succession planning within family businesses. The process of leadership transition should be deeply rooted in the bedrock of values that define the family's business ethos. This commitment to identifying and preserving core values is not merely a ceremonial gesture; rather, it is an indispensable element that ensures continuity, fortifies a strong sense of identity and provides a steadfast foundation for decision-making.

The identification of core values is a reflective process that delves into the family business's history, philosophy and overarching purpose. These values, often forged through generations, encapsulate the principles that have shaped the family's journey and underpin its distinct character. Whether it is a commitment to integrity, innovation, customer service or social responsibility, these values become the guiding principles that transcend individual leadership tenures.

Preserving these core values is paramount for ensuring continuity across leadership transitions. When values are ingrained in the fabric of the family business, they act as a unifying force, providing a shared ethos that resonates with family members, employees and stakeholders alike. This shared understanding fosters a sense of belonging and purpose, contributing to a cohesive organizational culture that withstands the test of time.

Moreover, values serve as a foundation for decision-making during succession planning. When faced with intricate choices, adherence to core values becomes a compass that steers the course. It helps family members align their decisions with the principles that have defined the family business, ensuring that the transition not only maintains but enhances the legacy established by previous generations.

Succession planning should be rooted in the values that define the family business, serving as a guiding principle throughout the transition process. By aligning the succession plan with the core values and principles that have shaped the business's identity, leaders can ensure continuity and preserve the essence of what makes the family enterprise unique. Integrating these values into every aspect of succession planning—from leadership selection to decision-making criteria—reinforces the family's commitment to its heritage and legacy while paving the way for future growth and success.

The seniormost generation often harbours concerns that their family values might be diluted during or after succession planning, fearing that the next generation may not uphold the same traditions or principles. This apprehension stems from a deep-rooted desire to safeguard the legacy they've worked hard to build. However, it is essential to recognize that values evolve over time, and each generation brings its own perspectives and experiences to the table. Instead of resisting change, senior leaders can embrace the opportunity to pass down their values in a way that resonates with the next generation. By fostering open dialogue, mentoring future leaders and leading by example, they can instil a sense of purpose and responsibility that ensures the enduring relevance of the family values in guiding the business forward. A succession plan that honours the past while embracing the future can reassure senior leaders that their values will continue to shape the business's trajectory in a meaningful and sustainable manner.

Consider a family business in the hospitality sector where the core value is exceptional customer service. In the succession planning process, identifying successors who embody this commitment ensures that the business's reputation for outstanding service persists. This alignment with values not only sustains the business but also resonates with customers who recognize and appreciate the enduring commitment to excellence.

Succession planning is not just about passing the business to the next generation but also about passing on the family's values. Neglecting the importance of values in this process can lead to misunderstandings and conflicts within the family. Imagine the family business as a ship navigating the seas of change. If the values are not aligned, the ship might head in the wrong direction, causing internal conflicts and a loss of cultural identity.

Adapting values is crucial, like adjusting the sails of a ship to changing winds. If the values remain static, the business might struggle to stay relevant in the dynamic market. It is like using an old map in a new territory; conflicts can arise when the next generation's values evolve differently from the established ones. Communication plays a key role here—transparently discussing values and their role in succession decisions prevents misunderstandings and resistance.

When conflicts arise, it is essential to have mechanisms in place that are anchored in value recognition for conflict resolution. Picture it as a compass that helps the family navigate through differences and maintain cohesion. Succession planning, after all, is not just a business transition but also a journey of values that shapes the legacy of the family.

QUESTIONS TO ASK YOURSELF

1. What are the core values that define the family business, and how are they communicated within the family?
2. Are there mechanisms in place to ensure that succession decisions align with the established values of the family business?
3. How can the family adapt values to remain relevant in changing market dynamics while preserving the core identity?
4. In what ways do values contribute to the overall sustainability and success of the family business?
5. How can potential conflicts related to differing interpretations of values be addressed within the family?

W FOR WEALTH MANAGEMENT

Succession planning involves effective wealth management to ensure the sustainability and growth of family wealth across generations. This comprehensive strategy extends beyond the immediate transition of leadership and incorporates elements of strategic financial planning, discerning investment decisions and addressing potential tax implications.

Wealth management is integral to succession planning for business families, as it ensures the sustainability and growth of family wealth across generations. By strategically managing assets, investments and financial resources, families can safeguard their wealth and create opportunities for future growth and prosperity. Wealth management encompasses various aspects, including tax planning, asset allocation, risk management and estate planning, all of which play a crucial role in preserving and growing family wealth over time.

While business families often excel at generating wealth through their entrepreneurial endeavours, the challenge of protecting and preserving that wealth for future generations cannot be understated. Despite their success in wealth creation, many families recognize the need for robust strategies to safeguard their assets and prevent the erosion of wealth in subsequent generations. By acknowledging this need and taking proactive steps to implement effective wealth management practices, families can ensure that their hard-earned wealth endures and continues to benefit future generations. Through prudent financial planning, sound investment strategies and a commitment to preserving family values, business families can build a legacy of prosperity that withstands the test of time, providing security and opportunities for generations to come.

One of the primary benefits of wealth management as part of succession planning is the protection of family assets and financial security. Through prudent financial planning and investment strategies, families can mitigate risks, minimize tax liabilities and optimize returns on their investments, thereby safeguarding their wealth for future generations. Additionally, effective wealth management ensures that family members are adequately provided for and that their long-term financial goals are met, whether it be funding education, retirement or philanthropic endeavours.

Furthermore, wealth management helps business families maintain control and autonomy over their assets, reducing the risk of financial mismanagement or loss. By establishing clear governance structures and implementing sound financial practices, families can protect their wealth from external threats and internal conflicts, ensuring its longevity and resilience.

Neglecting wealth management can have serious consequences for business families. Without proper financial planning and oversight, family wealth may be at risk of erosion due to inadequate asset allocation, poor investment decisions or unforeseen financial challenges. Moreover, failure to address tax liabilities, estate planning issues or asset protection strategies can leave the family vulnerable to wealth depletion and legal disputes.

Ultimately, protecting family wealth and ensuring its prudent management is essential for preserving the family's legacy and providing future generations with opportunities for prosperity. Therefore, prioritizing wealth management as part of succession planning is critical to securing the family's financial future and maintaining its legacy for generations to come.

At the core of this endeavour lies strategic financial planning, a meticulous process that involves forecasting and allocating financial resources to meet the family's long-term objectives. This goes beyond day-to-day financial management and involves crafting a roadmap that aligns with the family's values, goals and aspirations. Succession planning necessitates a holistic understanding of the family's financial landscape, encompassing income streams, expenses, debt obligations and contingencies.

Equally pivotal is the discernment in investment decisions. Succession planning requires a judicious approach to deploying family assets, considering both risk and return. This involves evaluating various investment avenues, diversifying portfolios, and ensuring that the investment strategy aligns with the family's overall wealth preservation and growth objectives. Prudent investment decisions contribute towards not only the financial security of the family but also the ability to fund future ventures and maintain the family's economic standing.

Addressing potential tax implications is a critical component of effective wealth management within succession planning. The interplay between tax regulations and wealth transfer is intricate, and careful consideration must be given to optimizing tax efficiency. This involves leveraging tax planning strategies, such as trusts, gifting and other wealth transfer mechanisms, to minimize the tax burden on the family estate. Navigating complex tax landscapes requires a thorough understanding of applicable laws and a proactive approach to adapting strategies as tax codes evolve.

For certain business families, tax planning becomes a pivotal aspect of their succession planning strategy, and at times, it intersects with the lifestyle choices of the next generation. In some instances, members of the family may choose to relocate to different countries, driven by the allure of a more favourable lifestyle or tax environment.

This dynamic introduces complexities, particularly in regulated industries, where the residency of key executives is often a prerequisite for leadership roles. The tension arises when tax-driven decisions clash with the strategic leadership needs of the family business. This dual consideration—balancing personal aspirations with business requirements—becomes a nuanced challenge in effective succession planning.

To navigate these complexities, families must establish a robust governance framework that aligns with corporate governance rules. This ensures that data sharing, especially related to succession plans, adheres to regulatory standards while respecting the privacy and autonomy of individual family members. Striking this delicate balance becomes crucial for maintaining transparency and compliance, safeguarding the interests of both the family and the businesses they oversee.

Tax planning, often a critical component overlooked at one's peril, is vital to wealth management. Succession planning introduces a new dimension to tax considerations, requiring a comprehensive understanding of applicable laws and the foresight to structure financial affairs in a tax-efficient manner. This involves leveraging tools like trusts, gifting and other tax-advantaged strategies to minimize the tax impact on the family's estate.

Consulting with external financial advisors is equally important. Neglecting this valuable input can lead to missed opportunities and suboptimal financial decisions. Additionally, integrating wealth management seamlessly into the overall succession plan ensures a cohesive approach to long-term financial sustainability. Learning from the failures of others is often helpful; take, for example, the case of a family that faced challenges when wealth management was not adequately integrated into their succession plan. It resulted in gaps and difficulties in sustaining their financial legacy. Wealth management, after all, is not just about the numbers but also about nurturing the financial health of the family across generations.

~

Effectively managing family wealth is as much about financial prosperity as it is about securing the legacy for future generations. Ignoring wealth management strategies can lead to financial setbacks, disputes over inheritances and an overall decline in family wealth. It is akin to tending a garden—neglecting certain areas can result in weeds that hinder the healthy growth of the entire landscape.

Adapting wealth management strategies to changing economic conditions is crucial, much like adjusting the watering schedule based on the weather. Failure to do so can expose the family's wealth to significant losses. Fair distribution is paramount; envision it as ensuring that each plant in the garden receives the right amount of water. Without fair distribution among successors and heirs, conflicts and dissatisfaction may arise, jeopardizing the family's financial harmony.

Preserving family wealth requires a nuanced understanding of the various assets, their vulnerabilities and potential challenges that may arise during succession. This preservation imperative goes beyond safeguarding financial assets; it encompasses the protection of family values, the legacy of the business and the overall well-being of family members. Implementing protective measures, such as trusts or legal structures, becomes crucial to shield the family's wealth from external risks and internal disputes.

Growth, an inseparable companion to wealth, demands a strategic and diversified approach. Successful wealth management, therefore, also involves identifying multiple risk buckets that align with the family's risk tolerance and financial goals. Diversification not only shields against market volatility but also exploits opportunities for growth across various asset classes. The interplay of risk and growth is a delicate dance, requiring constant monitoring and adjustment to ensure that the family's financial landscape remains resilient.

Mitigating risks within the wealth management strategy involves anticipating potential challenges and implementing proactive measures. This includes having contingency plans for unforeseen events, establishing clear guidelines for financial decision-making and fostering a culture of financial literacy within the family.

QUESTIONS TO ASK YOURSELF

1. How does the family business approach wealth management as part of the succession plan?
2. Are there mechanisms in place to address potential tax implications and financial challenges in succession planning?
3. How can the family adapt wealth management strategies to changing economic conditions and market trends?
4. What steps are taken to ensure a fair distribution of family wealth among successors and heirs?
5. In what ways can external financial advisors contribute to effective wealth management within the family business?

X FOR XENODOCHIAL

Being xenodochial (Greek for 'friendly to strangers'), synonymous with being hospitable, becomes a unique and valuable attribute within the domain of succession planning for family businesses. This quality extends beyond mere courtesy; it embodies the ethos of creating an environment that warmly embraces new ideas, diverse perspectives and external expertise. In the context of succession planning, fostering a xenodochial culture becomes a strategic imperative for ensuring the adaptability of the family enterprise to evolving market dynamics.

Welcoming new ideas is akin to inviting fresh winds of innovation into the family business. Succession planning becomes an opportune moment to re-evaluate established norms and explore novel approaches to challenges. A xenodochial environment encourages family members, both incoming and established, to contribute their unique insights and perspectives, fostering a culture of continuous improvement and adaptability.

Diverse perspectives within the family contribute to a richer decision-making landscape. A xenodochial family business actively seeks out and values the varied experiences, skills and viewpoints that family members bring to the table. This diversity becomes a reservoir of collective intelligence, enhancing the family's capacity to navigate complex challenges and capitalize on emerging opportunities during succession transitions.

Furthermore, embracing external expertise becomes a hallmark of a xenodochial family business. Succession planning often benefits from insights and guidance beyond the family circle. Engaging with professionals, advisors and industry experts injects a fresh stream of knowledge into the decision-making process. This external perspective not only supplements the family's internal capabilities but also introduces a level of objectivity that can be invaluable during succession-related discussions.

A xenodochial approach also nurtures a culture of learning and development. Navigating the ever-changing business landscape requires a willingness to embrace external input and foster innovation. Therefore, family members are encouraged to seek knowledge from diverse sources, be it industry trends, best practices or emerging technologies. This commitment to continuous learning positions the family business to adapt to evolving market dynamics and stay ahead of the curve. On the other hand, resisting external expertise and diverse perspectives can lead to missed opportunities and reduced competitiveness, akin to steering a ship without adjusting its course based on changing winds.

It is essential to recognize that welcoming fresh ideas is like planting seeds for future growth—neglecting this can result in stagnation. Like in the case of a family business that encountered challenges when succession decisions favoured traditional practices over innovative approaches. From their story, one can learn that overemphasizing traditional practices without considering modern and innovative approaches can be compared to relying solely on old navigation charts in uncharted waters.

Cultivating a culture of openness and adaptability is crucial for sustained success. Failing to do so is akin to constructing barriers around the garden, hindering its ability to thrive in different seasons. Leveraging external collaborations, partnerships or joint ventures is like exploring uncharted territories. Facing challenges in this area can limit overall business success and expansion, much like restricting the garden to a small plot.

Accordingly, a hospitable environment in a family business invites external input, fosters innovation and cultivates adaptability. These are essential strategies for ensuring the business thrives amid evolving market dynamics.

QUESTIONS TO ASK YOURSELF

1. How hospitable is the family business to external expertise and diverse perspectives in decision-making?
2. Are there mechanisms in place to encourage the next generation to bring new ideas and innovations to the business?
3. How can the family balance traditional practices with the need for modern and innovative approaches in succession planning?

4. In what ways does the family business cultivate a culture of openness and adaptability to external influences?
5. How can succession planning benefit from external collaborations, partnerships, or joint ventures to enhance overall business success?

BONUS

X could also stand for the 'X factor'. This X factor refers to all the elements that remain unpredictable and beyond the scope of traditional planning. Successful succession strategies embrace adaptability, agility and a holistic understanding of the multifaceted variables that contribute to the unique fabric of each family's succession journey.

For example, the X factor can lie in the external market forces. Economic shifts, industry disruptions and global events can exert unexpected pressures on the family business. The evolving regulatory environment represents yet another X factor. Changes in tax laws, governance regulations or industry-specific compliance requirements can introduce unexpected complexities into the succession equation.

Succession planning must be attuned to these external dynamics. Families need to consider how emerging trends or geopolitical and regulatory shifts could influence the market landscape and subsequently impact the succession journey. They must proactively stay abreast of these changes, ensuring that the family business remains compliant and resilient in the face of evolving economic and legal landscapes.

Y FOR YOUTH ENGAGEMENT

Youth engagement, marked by the letter Y in the succession planning lexicon, represents a pivotal facet that infuses vitality and innovation into the fabric of family businesses. Recognizing the significance of involving the younger generation is paramount for injecting fresh perspectives, energy and innovation into the business and steering the family enterprise towards a future that aligns with contemporary market dynamics.

Succession planning should actively involve the younger generation to ensure a seamless transition and adaptation to evolving market trends. This involvement is not merely symbolic but serves as a catalyst for bringing fresh vitality into the family business, fostering a culture of adaptability and innovation essential for long-term sustainability.

As succession planning unfolds, actively involving the youth becomes a keystone for ensuring a seamless transition across generational lines. By providing a platform for the younger generation to contribute their insights and actively participate in decision-making processes, family businesses can bridge the generational gap. This inclusivity cultivates a sense of ownership and commitment among the youth, fostering a shared vision for the family business's future.

Moreover, the younger generation often brings a natural affinity for technological advancements and emerging trends. Integrating their perspectives into the succession planning process allows the family business to leverage cutting-edge technologies, navigate digital transformations and stay abreast of evolving market landscapes. This synergy between experience and youthful dynamism positions the family enterprise to thrive in an ever-changing business environment.

Youth engagement extends beyond formal roles and responsibilities; it encompasses mentorship and knowledge transfer. Establishing mentorship programmes allows the younger family members to benefit from the wisdom and experience of their predecessors. This intergenerational exchange not only enhances the professional development of the youth but also fortifies the institutional knowledge that forms the backbone of the family business.

Recognizing the valuable contributions of the younger generation is akin to harnessing a wellspring of innovation and relevance within the family business. In contrast, ignoring their perspectives in key decision-making processes can lead to stagnation. This is similar to a family business resisting the adoption of modern navigation tools, hindering overall progress.

The absence of mechanisms for youth input and feedback in succession planning is like navigating uncharted waters without a compass, resulting in potential pitfalls. Providing ample opportunities for the younger generation to contribute to innovation and technological advancements is comparable to navigating through dynamic market currents.

However, failing to understand the needs and aspirations of the youth in the business family can pose significant risks. Disregarding their interests may lead to feelings of alienation, resentment and disengagement among younger family members, ultimately jeopardizing family cohesion and harmony. Moreover, a lack of alignment between the aspirations of the youth and the direction of the family business may result in conflicts, power struggles and a loss of interest in the business altogether. This could potentially lead to the fragmentation of the family, with members pursuing divergent paths and interests, thereby undermining the unity and sustainability of the family enterprise.

Flexibility in succession planning is essential to accommodate the diverse interests and aspirations of younger family members. While some may have a genuine passion for leading the family business, others may prefer to pursue alternative careers or ventures outside the business realm. By offering flexible pathways and opportunities for personal and professional development, succession plans can empower younger family members to explore their passions, hone their skills and contribute meaningfully to the family enterprise in ways that align with their interests and strengths. Embracing flexibility in succession planning not only nurtures individual fulfilment and growth but also ensures the continued vitality and adaptability of the family business across generations.

Integrating youth engagement into leadership development programmes is another strategic move to ensure the family business adapts to modern challenges. Neglecting this integration is like expecting a ship's crew to navigate a storm without proper training.

Understanding the needs and aspirations of the youth within a business family is paramount for ensuring the continuity and prosperity of the family enterprise. By acknowledging and incorporating the aspirations of young family members, businesses can foster a sense of belonging, motivation and commitment among the next generation, thereby nurturing future leaders and preserving family legacies.

QUESTIONS TO ASK YOURSELF

1. How actively is the younger generation engaged in key decision-making processes within the family business?
2. Are there mechanisms in place to ensure that the perspectives and ideas of the youth are considered in succession planning?
3. How can the family business create opportunities for the younger generation to contribute to innovation and technological advancements?
4. In what ways can youth engagement be integrated into leadership development programmes for potential successors?
5. How does the family business balance the need for experience with the benefits of youth engagement in succession planning?

Z FOR ZEAL FOR LEARNING

Zeal for learning, encapsulated by the letter Z in the context of succession planning, represents a fundamental quality that propels family businesses towards continuous growth, adaptability and long-term success. This zeal serves as a driving force behind a culture of continual learning, fostering an environment where every member of the family enterprise, irrespective of generational boundaries, embraces education as a catalyst for innovation and resilience.

In succession planning, zeal for learning manifests as an unwavering commitment to acquiring knowledge, staying abreast of industry trends and honing the skills needed to navigate the complexities of business leadership. It is an acknowledgement that the business landscape is in constant flux, and a proactive pursuit of learning becomes an indispensable tool for staying ahead of the curve.

Family members who demonstrate a zeal for learning actively seek opportunities for professional development. Whether through formal education, specialized training programmes or continuous exposure to diverse aspects of the business, this commitment to learning becomes a cornerstone for cultivating the competencies required for effective leadership within the family enterprise. It transcends age, recognizing that both seasoned leaders and emerging talents benefit from a mindset of continuous learning.

Furthermore, zeal for learning encompasses a forward-thinking approach to technology and innovation. Family businesses that prioritize continuous learning leverage emerging technologies to enhance operational efficiency, identify new market opportunities and remain competitive. This looking-ahead mindset positions the family enterprise to not only adapt to current market trends but also anticipate and capitalize on future industry shifts.

This zeal is not confined to individual pursuits but extends to the collective mindset of the family business. Succession planning becomes an avenue for shared learning experiences, where family members collaboratively explore best practices, lessons learned from past challenges and innovative strategies for sustainable growth. It creates a learning ecosystem where insights are shared, and the collective intelligence of the family becomes a strategic asset.

Ensuring a continuous focus on learning initiatives is akin to keeping the sails of a family business well-adjusted for the ever-changing winds of the market. Neglecting this crucial aspect can leave family members with an outdated skill set. This stagnation hinders the family business's competitiveness, much like trying to win a race with a slow and outdated vehicle.

Failure to provide opportunities for ongoing education and skill development is like expecting a ship to reach its destination without ever adjusting its course. In the dynamic business landscape, adaptation is key. Without the right opportunities, the family business risks falling behind.

Resistance to external resources and partnerships is akin to a ship's crew refusing assistance from experienced navigators. Ignoring the potential benefits of external insights can result in missed opportunities for growth and development. Similarly, neglecting the role of mentorship in fostering a zeal for learning among potential successors is like sailing without a seasoned captain—there is a lack of guidance and preparedness for the journey ahead.

Facing challenges in adapting learning initiatives to align with changing industry trends and technologies can result in a stagnant skill set, hindering the family business's ability to navigate the complexities of the modern business landscape. Embracing a culture of continuous learning ensures that the family business stays equipped to chart a course for sustained growth and success.

The zeal for learning, particularly among potential successors of family businesses, is intricately connected to their overall attitude and life outlook. It transcends mere academic or skill-focused learning, embodying a proactive and positive mindset that significantly influences how individuals confront challenges, perceive opportunities and contribute to the holistic growth of the family enterprise.

Individuals with a robust zeal for learning exhibit notable adaptability and resilience. This mindset extends beyond embracing change; it empowers successors to navigate uncertainties and respond positively to the ever-evolving dynamics of the business environment. Such adaptability proves crucial in succession planning, where the capacity to pivot and innovate is fundamental for sustained success.

Curiosity and open-mindedness are hallmarks of those with a zeal for learning. Potential successors characterized by this mindset approach situations with an innate curiosity, seeking to understand the nuances of the business, industry trends and emerging technologies. This curiosity fosters a continual exploration of new ideas and perspectives, cultivating a culture of innovation within the family business.

Proactive problem-solving is another trait associated with zeal for learning. Individuals embodying this mindset view challenges not as obstacles but as opportunities for learning and growth. This proactive approach proves invaluable in succession planning, where unforeseen challenges may arise. A learning-oriented attitude empowers successors to address issues with creativity and resourcefulness.

A zeal for learning is often coupled with a long-term vision. Successors prioritizing continuous learning understand the dynamic nature of the business landscape. Their commitment to ongoing education positions them to contribute meaningfully to the family enterprise's long-term sustainability. This forward-thinking perspective aligns seamlessly with the strategic nature of succession planning.

The learning-oriented attitude also enhances collaboration within the family business. Potential successors who value continuous learning are more likely to seek input from diverse perspectives, collaborate with other family members and foster a collective approach to problem-solving. This collaborative spirit proves instrumental in ensuring smooth transitions during succession.

Finally, zeal for learning is synonymous with an enthusiasm for innovation. Successors with this mindset are eager to explore and adopt new technologies, business models and strategies. This innovation-centric outlook is vital in succession planning, where modernizing and future-proofing the family business are critical components of a successful transition.

QUESTIONS TO ASK YOURSELF

1. How does the family business promote a culture of continuous learning among family members?
2. Are there mechanisms in place to identify and address skill gaps through ongoing education and training?
3. How can the family business adapt learning initiatives to align with changing industry trends and technologies?
4. What role does mentorship play in fostering a zeal for learning among potential successors?
5. In what ways can the family business leverage external resources and partnerships to enhance learning opportunities for family members involved in succession planning?

Part Three

The A to Z of Skill Sets of Successors

Effective succession planning includes ensuring that the successors are well-trained, equipped with skills and competencies, and understand the context of what they are stepping into. In this comprehensive list of skills from A to Z, it is essential to recognize that a young scion may not possess every skill. The key, however, is to bring awareness to these skills, understanding that each family member has unique strengths and areas for growth. By acknowledging the diversity of skills needed for effective leadership, the family can tailor development plans to nurture and enhance the specific capabilities of each individual, fostering a well-rounded and resilient leadership team for the family business. Whether you are a business family scion or involved in the succession planning process, these skill sets articulated with Indian examples would resonate with you.

A FOR ADAPTIVE LEADERSHIP

Adaptive leadership is crucial for scions navigating the complexities of the modern business landscape. This skill involves being agile in response to rapidly changing environments. Successful scions understand the need to shift strategies, embrace new technologies and pivot business models when required. By staying flexible and open to innovation, they can lead their businesses through economic shifts, industry disruptions and evolving consumer demands.

Take, for example, an Indian retail business that had been family-owned for several generations, operating primarily through brick-and-mortar stores. The younger generation, observing the rapid rise of e-commerce, recognized the need for a significant strategic pivot. They implemented an adaptive leadership approach, embracing digital transformation by launching an online platform, integrating advanced logistics and employing data analytics to understand consumer behaviour.

Despite initial resistance from the older generation, who were wary of straying from the traditional business model, the scions' adaptive strategies proved successful. The business not only survived but thrived during the Covid-19 pandemic when physical stores faced severe limitations. By demonstrating agility and a willingness to innovate, the younger leaders were able to steer the company through a challenging period, ensuring its continued growth and relevance in a digital age. This example illustrates how adaptive leadership allows family businesses to remain competitive and resilient, even in the face of unforeseen challenges and market disruptions.

B FOR BUSINESS ACUMEN

Business acumen is the cornerstone of effective leadership. Scions with strong business acumen possess a comprehensive understanding of their industry, competitors and market trends. They analyse financial data to make informed decisions, identify growth opportunities and mitigate risks. A keen sense of business acumen enables scions to anticipate industry shifts, capitalize on emerging trends and position their businesses for sustainable success in dynamic markets.

Consider an Indian manufacturing family business that had traditionally focused on producing low-cost consumer goods. When the younger generation took the helm, they conducted a thorough market analysis and identified a growing demand for high-quality, eco-friendly products. Leveraging their business acumen, they decided to pivot the company's strategy. They invested in new technologies, adopted sustainable manufacturing practices and rebranded their products to appeal to environmentally conscious consumers. This strategic shift required a deep understanding of global sustainability trends, competitor positioning and financial implications. The scions meticulously evaluated the costs and potential returns, ensuring that the business could achieve a competitive advantage while maintaining profitability.

Their informed decisions paid off, as the company not only gained market share but also established a strong brand reputation for sustainability. This example underscores how business acumen equips young leaders to navigate complex market landscapes, identify lucrative opportunities and steer their family businesses towards long-term growth and resilience.

C FOR COMMUNICATION SKILLS

Effective communication is a cornerstone for successful leadership. Young successors need to convey their vision, goals and expectations clearly to internal teams, external stakeholders and family members involved in the business. Strong communication skills empower them to articulate complex ideas, build consensus and inspire confidence. Whether addressing employees, negotiating deals or representing the family business in public forums, adept communicators can influence outcomes and foster positive relationships.

Take, for example, a prominent Indian retail family business transitioning leadership to the younger generation. The new scion faced the challenge of communicating a digital transformation strategy to a workforce accustomed to traditional retail operations. Through a series of town hall meetings, the scion clearly outlined the strategic vision, the rationale behind the shift to e-commerce, and the benefits for the company and its employees. They used a variety of communication tools, including detailed presentations, interactive Q&A sessions and follow-up emails to ensure that every team member understood the plan and felt included in the process.

This transparent and inclusive approach not only eased anxieties about the change but also garnered enthusiastic support from the workforce. Similarly, when negotiating partnerships with technology vendors, the young leader's ability to articulate the company's needs and long-term goals facilitated favourable deals. This example illustrates how strong communication skills enable scions to effectively bridge gaps, build trust and drive transformative initiatives within their family businesses.

D FOR DECISION-MAKING

Decision-making is a core competency for effective leadership, requiring a blend of analytical thinking and sound judgement. Scions must assess situations, consider multiple perspectives and make decisions that align with the family business's long-term objectives. Decisive leaders demonstrate confidence in their choices while remaining open to feedback and adapting strategies as circumstances evolve. This skill empowers scions to navigate uncertainties, ensuring the family business's resilience in the face of challenges.

Consider an Indian family business in the manufacturing sector facing a significant industry downturn. The younger scion groomed to take over the leadership was at a crossroads—continue with the existing business model or pivot to a new strategy. After thorough market analysis and consultations with industry experts, the scion decided to diversify the company's product line to include eco-friendly alternatives, anticipating the growing demand for sustainable products.

This decision involved considerable risk, as it required retooling production processes and investing in new technology. However, the scion's analytical approach—examining market trends, potential returns and long-term sustainability—helped in crafting a well-informed strategy. By involving senior family members and key stakeholders in the decision-making process, the scion ensured that diverse perspectives were considered, fostering a sense of collective ownership.

The scion's decisiveness and willingness to adapt to feedback were evident when initial prototypes did not meet quality expectations. Instead of pushing through with a flawed product, the young leader incorporated feedback from both internal teams and external focus groups to refine the offerings. This adaptability not only improved the final products but also demonstrated their commitment to excellence and responsiveness to market needs.

Ultimately, the shift paid off as the company carved out a niche in the burgeoning market for sustainable goods, securing its position in an evolving industry landscape. This example underscores how effective decision-making, rooted in thorough analysis and openness to feedback, can drive a family business towards sustained success and resilience amidst challenges.

E FOR EMOTIONAL INTELLIGENCE

Emotional intelligence (EI) plays a pivotal role in leadership success, especially for scions managing family dynamics within a business context. High EI enables scions to understand and regulate their emotions, fostering positive relationships with family members, employees and business partners. By empathizing with the perspectives of others and effectively managing conflicts, emotionally intelligent scions contribute to a harmonious business environment and a strong family bond.

Consider a prominent Indian family business in the hospitality industry. The young heir was poised to take over the reins but faced significant internal friction among family members over the direction of the business. Some favoured expansion into new markets, while others were more conservative, fearing the risks involved. The scion, possessing high EI, recognized the underlying concerns and emotions driving each family member's stance.

Instead of imposing a unilateral decision, the scion organized a series of family meetings aimed at fostering open communication. By actively listening and empathizing with each member's viewpoint, the family was able to address everyone's fears and build a consensus. The scion also employed conflict resolution techniques, facilitating discussions that allowed family members to voice their apprehensions and hopes without feeling dismissed.

This approach extended beyond family interactions. Within the business, the scion's high EI helped in understanding employee morale and motivation. For instance, during a period of restructuring, the scion's ability to communicate transparently about the changes and empathize with employees' anxieties led to a smoother transition. The scion ensured that employees felt valued and included, which mitigated resistance and preserved morale.

The EI of the scion was particularly evident when handling relationships with business partners. During negotiations for a significant joint venture, the scion's capacity to read the room, manage personal emotions and respond to the partners' concerns with empathy facilitated a deal that was beneficial for both parties. This not only strengthened the partnership but also built a reputation of trust and integrity for the family business.

Ultimately, it was the scion's high EI that contributed to a more cohesive and resilient family unit, a motivated workforce and strong, trust-based business relationships. By leveraging EI, the scion was able to navigate the complexities of family business dynamics, ensuring both familial harmony and business success. This example illustrates the critical role that EI plays in leadership, highlighting its impact on fostering a positive and productive business environment.

F FOR FINANCIAL LITERACY

Financial literacy is non-negotiable for scions involved in the family business. Understanding financial statements, budgeting and interpreting economic indicators are vital skills. Scions with financial literacy can make informed decisions about investments, acquisitions and resource allocation. This skill also enables them to communicate effectively with financial professionals, ensuring a comprehensive understanding of the family business's fiscal health and facilitating strategic financial planning.

Consider a well-established Indian family business in the manufacturing sector. The young successor, well-versed in financial literacy, demonstrated the critical importance of this skill when the company faced a financial downturn. Armed with the ability to thoroughly analyse the company's financials, the successor identified inefficiencies in the production process and overspending in certain departments. By implementing a more stringent budgeting process and reallocating resources, the successor managed to stabilize the company's finances.

Moreover, the successor's financial acumen proved invaluable during a potential acquisition. Understanding the nuances of financial statements allowed the successor to evaluate the target company's assets and liabilities accurately, deciding that the acquisition would not be a beneficial move for the family business. By conducting a thorough due diligence process, the successor was able to safeguard the family's interests and positioned the business for future growth without that acquisition.

Financial literacy also played a crucial role in communicating with stakeholders. The successor's ability to speak the language of finance enabled effective discussions with bankers, investors and auditors. For instance, when the family business sought additional funding for expansion, the successor could clearly present the company's financial health and future projections, instilling confidence in potential investors and securing the necessary capital.

In another instance, the successor's financial literacy facilitated strategic financial planning during an economic downturn. By closely monitoring economic indicators and understanding their impact on the business, the successor pre-emptively adjusted the business strategy to mitigate risks. This proactive approach not only protected the family business from severe financial strain but also allowed it to capitalize on emerging opportunities as the market conditions improved.

The importance of financial literacy for scions cannot be overstated. It equips them with the ability to make informed and strategic decisions, ensuring the long-term sustainability and growth of the family business. By understanding and managing the financial aspects of the business, scions can effectively navigate economic challenges, seize growth opportunities and communicate confidently with financial stakeholders. This skill set is essential for maintaining the fiscal health of the family business and securing its future success.

G FOR GLOBAL MINDSET

Cultivating a global mindset is essential for scions operating in an interconnected world. This skill involves an awareness and adaptability to diverse cultural and global business perspectives. Scions with a global mindset appreciate the nuances of conducting business internationally, fostering relationships with diverse stakeholders. This skill positions them to explore new markets, identify global trends, and navigate cross-cultural collaborations, ensuring the family business remains competitive on a global scale.

Consider an Indian family business in the chemicals industry. The young scion, having spent several years studying and working abroad, returned with a broad understanding of international markets and cultural dynamics. Recognizing the potential for growth beyond the Indian market, the scion initiated a strategic expansion into Europe. This move required not only knowledge of global trends but also an understanding of the regulatory environments, consumer preferences and regulatory norms and practices in different European countries. The scion's global mindset enabled the family business to adapt its product lines to meet the specific standards of various international markets.

In another example, the scion leveraged the company's global network to form strategic partnerships with suppliers and retailers in different regions. These partnerships were not just business transactions but culturally sensitive collaborations built on mutual respect and understanding. By appreciating the cultural nuances and business etiquettes of different regions, the young leader was able to build strong, long-lasting relationships that were beneficial for the family business.

Additionally, the scion's global mindset facilitated the identification and anticipation of global trends that could impact the business. For example, the rise of digital platforms and e-commerce was quickly integrated into the family business's strategy, allowing them to reach a wider audience and streamline operations. The scion also kept abreast of international trade policies and economic shifts, adjusting strategies accordingly to mitigate risks and capitalize on opportunities.

The impact of a global mindset is evident in the business's increased competitiveness and resilience. By being open to learning and adapting to global business practices, the scion ensured that the family business was not just surviving but thriving in a globalized economy. This approach also prepared the business to navigate the complexities of international trade, supply chain management and cultural differences, thereby securing its position in the global market.

For Indian family business scions, cultivating a global mindset is not merely an option but a necessity in today's interconnected world. It is the era of Indian businesses becoming global in operations, scale and even reach. It would involve continuous learning, cultural sensitivity and strategic adaptability. By embracing a global perspective, scions can drive innovation, explore new markets and build robust international networks, ultimately ensuring the family business's longevity and success on a global scale.

H FOR HUMILITY

Humility, often overlooked in the context of business success, is a crucial value system that business families should instil in their scions. Contrary to the misconception that humility implies being less ambitious or intense in pursuing goals, it is, in fact, a powerful force that enhances leadership and fosters long-term success. True humility involves recognizing one's strengths and achievements without arrogance, understanding the significance of collaboration and acknowledging that there is always room for growth and improvement. In the context of business families, humility acts as a catalyst for effective leadership transitions and harmonious family dynamics.

For scions to navigate the complexities of family businesses, they need the humility to appreciate the lessons of the past, respect the experiences of their predecessors and learn from both successes and failures. Humility encourages an openness to new ideas, perspectives and constructive feedback, fostering an environment conducive to innovation and adaptability. In a business landscape marked by constant change, humility enables scions to build strong relationships with employees, stakeholders and even competitors. It establishes a foundation of trust, as people are more likely to collaborate with and follow leaders who exhibit genuine humility.

Moreover, humility does not diminish the intensity or ambition of scions; instead, it channels these qualities in a more sustainable and inclusive direction. Ambition, when coupled with humility, becomes a force for positive change and ethical leadership, ensuring that success is not just measured in financial terms but also in the positive impact a business has on its employees and the wider community.

I FOR INNOVATION

Innovation is the lifeblood of enduring family businesses. Scions must foster a culture of creativity and adaptability to stay ahead in evolving markets. Innovative leaders encourage employees to think outside conventional boundaries, embrace technological advancements and explore novel approaches to problem-solving. By fostering innovation, scions can position their family businesses as industry leaders, driving growth and remaining resilient in the face of disruptive forces.

Consider an Indian family business in the manufacturing sector that had been operational for decades but was starting to face stiff competition from more agile and tech-savvy start-ups. The young scion, recognizing the need for innovation, initiated a transformation strategy that leveraged cutting-edge technologies such as automation and artificial intelligence to streamline production processes. By implementing IoT solutions, the business achieved real-time monitoring of manufacturing equipment, which reduced downtime and improved efficiency.

The scion also fostered a culture of innovation by encouraging employees at all levels to contribute ideas and solutions. Regular innovation workshops and hackathons were organized, providing a platform for employees to present their creative ideas. One notable initiative that emerged from these workshops was the development of a new product line and improved recycling methods to reduce costs.

Innovation was not limited to technology alone; another scion also focused on innovative business models. For example, the family business in the textile industry explored direct-to-consumer (DTC) channels, reducing dependency on traditional retail partners, which led to an increase in profit margins. By tying up with an e-commerce platform and leveraging social media marketing, the business reached a wider audience and built a strong brand presence online.

Scions must not only embrace technological advancements but also cultivate an organizational culture that encourages creativity and adaptability. By doing so, they can lead their businesses through market disruptions and position them as industry leaders.

Innovation, driven by a willingness to think beyond conventional boundaries and embrace new approaches, is crucial for the sustained growth and resilience of family businesses. Scions who prioritize innovation ensure that their businesses are not only able to navigate the complexities of the modern market but also thrive in it, securing a prosperous future for the generations to come.

J FOR (SOUND) JUDGEMENT

Exercising sound judgement is a critical leadership skill for scions. This entails making wise decisions based on a combination of analytical thinking and intuition. Leaders with strong judgement assess risks, weigh potential outcomes and consider the long-term implications of their choices. By developing a keen sense of judgement, scions can navigate complex business landscapes, mitigating risks and steering the family business towards sustainable success.

Take, for example, a prominent Indian family business in the retail sector facing a significant decision about expanding its footprint internationally. The young scion at the helm recognized the potential for growth in overseas markets but was also aware of the risks associated with such an expansion. Exercising sound judgement, the scion conducted a thorough market analysis, evaluating economic conditions, consumer behaviour and competitive landscapes in potential countries. Additionally, the scion considered the company's core competencies and brand reputation to ensure alignment with the new market's demands.

Intuition also played a role in this decision-making process. The scion leveraged insights gained from informal networks, industry peers and local experts to gauge the feasibility of the expansion. By blending this intuitive understanding with robust data analysis, the scion could anticipate potential challenges and opportunities, making a well-informed decision that balanced risk and reward. This thoughtful approach led to a successful international launch, which contributed to the company's growth and global presence.

In another instance, a family-owned conglomerate in the manufacturing sector faced a critical decision regarding investment in cutting-edge technology. The scion, exercising sound judgement, analysed the cost-benefit aspects of adopting advanced automation technologies. This involved not only evaluating the immediate financial outlay but also projecting the long-term benefits such as increased efficiency, reduced operational costs, taxation benefits with new capex and enhanced production quality. The scion also considered the workforce implications, recognizing the need for reskilling employees to operate the new technology effectively.

By weighing these factors, the scion made a judicious decision to proceed with the technology investment, coupled with a comprehensive training programme for employees. This decision proved to be a strategic move, enhancing the company's competitive edge and operational efficiency.

To put it in a nutshell, developing sound judgement enables scions to lead with confidence and foresight, fostering a culture of prudent decision-making within the family business. This skill is essential for maintaining the delicate balance between preserving the family legacy and driving innovation and growth, thereby securing a prosperous future for the enterprise.

K FOR KNOWLEDGE SHARING

Effective leaders recognize the importance of knowledge sharing within the organization. Scions should encourage an environment where insights and information flow freely among team members. By fostering a culture of open communication and collaboration, leaders ensure that valuable knowledge is disseminated across departments, empowering employees and family members alike. This not only enhances overall business intelligence but also contributes to a cohesive and informed decision-making process.

Consider the example of a well-known Indian conglomerate in the hospitality industry. The scion of this family business, understanding the value of knowledge sharing, implemented a series of initiatives aimed at breaking down silos within the organization. Regular cross-departmental meetings were introduced, where teams from marketing, operations, finance and customer service could share their experiences and insights. This open forum allowed for the free exchange of ideas and helped identify potential synergies between departments.

Additionally, the scion championed the creation of an internal knowledge portal, a digital platform where employees could upload and access valuable resources, case studies and best practices. This portal became a central repository of the organization's collective wisdom, making it easier for team members to find the information they needed to make informed decisions. By democratizing access to knowledge, the scion ensured that even the newest employees could benefit from the expertise of their more experienced colleagues.

In another example, a family-owned enterprise in the tyre sector faced the challenge of integrating new technologies into their manufacturing processes. Recognizing that the success of this transition depended on widespread understanding and acceptance, the scion facilitated a series of workshops and training sessions. These events brought together engineers, production workers and IT specialists to learn about the new technologies, discuss their implications and collaborate on implementation strategies. This approach not only disseminated critical knowledge but also built a sense of ownership and commitment among employees, easing the transition and enhancing overall productivity.

Moreover, the scion encouraged a mentorship programme where senior executives mentored younger family members and promising employees. This programme was designed not just to transfer technical skills but also to share strategic insights and the values that had driven the family business's success over generations. By fostering these close mentor–mentee relationships, the scion ensured that critical knowledge and the company's cultural ethos were preserved and propagated.

These initiatives highlight how fostering a culture of knowledge-sharing can significantly benefit a family business. When information flows freely, employees are better equipped to perform their roles, innovation is spurred and decision-making processes become more robust and inclusive. Furthermore, it helps in building a cohesive organizational culture where every member feels valued and empowered.

For Indian family businesses, embracing knowledge sharing is particularly vital. Given the complex interplay of family dynamics and business operations, ensuring that all members are well-informed and aligned with the company's goals is crucial for long-term success. By promoting open communication and collaboration, scions can harness the collective intelligence of their organization, driving sustained growth and maintaining a competitive edge in the market. Effective leaders understand that knowledge is a key asset and that sharing it freely within the organization is essential.

L FOR LEADERSHIP DEVELOPMENT

Commitment to leadership development is an ongoing journey for scions. Recognizing that growth is a continuous process, effective leaders invest in their own development and that of their team members. This involves participating in leadership programmes, seeking mentorship and providing opportunities for skill enhancement. By prioritizing leadership development, scions can ensure a pipeline of capable leaders within the family business, fostering a culture of continuous improvement and adaptability.

Consider the example of a prominent Indian conglomerate with diversified businesses. The scion of this family business, despite holding a senior leadership position, recognized the importance of honing his leadership skills continuously. He actively sought out opportunities to participate in executive education programmes, where he gained insights into the latest management practices and leadership techniques. Additionally, the scion engaged in mentorship relationships with seasoned industry veterans, both within and outside the family business. These mentors provided invaluable guidance, sharing their wisdom and experiences to help him navigate complex business challenges and develop his leadership acumen further. By learning from their successes and failures, the scion was able to accelerate his growth as a leader and gain a broader perspective on industry trends and best practices.

Moreover, the scion was proactive in identifying high-potential individuals within the organization and providing them with opportunities for leadership development. He established a leadership development programme that included workshops, seminars and experiential learning opportunities aimed at building essential leadership competencies. Through this programme, promising employees were given the chance to enhance their skills, broaden their perspectives and prepare for future leadership roles within the company.

In another example, the scion of a family-owned regional retail chain recognized the need to cultivate leadership capabilities across all levels of the organization. To achieve this, he implemented a tiered leadership development framework that catered to employees at different stages of their careers. Entry-level employees were encouraged to participate in foundational leadership courses, while mid-level managers had access to advanced training programmes focused on strategic thinking and decision-making. Furthermore, the scion leveraged technology to democratize leadership development within the organization. He introduced online learning platforms and virtual mentorship programmes that enabled employees to access educational resources and connect with mentors remotely. This approach not only made leadership development more accessible but also promoted a culture of continuous learning and collaboration across geographically dispersed teams.

These examples underscore the importance of ongoing commitment to leadership development for scions and their organizations. By investing in their own growth and that of their team members, scions can cultivate a cadre of capable leaders equipped to navigate the complexities of the business landscape. Moreover, fostering a culture of continuous improvement and adaptability ensures that the family business remains agile and resilient in the face of evolving challenges and opportunities.

M FOR MULTIGENERATIONAL COLLABORATION

Family businesses often span multiple generations, necessitating collaboration among individuals with diverse experiences and perspectives. Scions skilled in multigenerational collaboration create an inclusive environment where insights from various age groups are valued. This skill fosters a sense of unity and shared purpose, allowing the family business to draw upon the strengths of each generation. Successful collaboration across generations ensures the preservation of family values while embracing fresh ideas and approaches.

Consider the example of a leading Indian audit firm that has been passed down through multiple generations. The scion leading the business understands the significance of multigenerational collaboration in navigating the complexities of the industry. He actively seeks input and feedback from family members belonging to different age groups, including his parents, siblings and children, to gain a holistic understanding of the business landscape. Most of his extended family is also in the same profession.

Moreover, the scion encourages open dialogue and communication among family members, creating a platform where ideas can be freely exchanged and debated. He organizes regular family meetings and brainstorming sessions where individuals from different generations come together to discuss strategic initiatives, market trends and future plans for the business. By fostering an environment of collaboration and mutual respect, the scion ensures that all voices are heard and valued, regardless of age or seniority.

Additionally, the scion recognizes the importance of succession planning and talent development across generations. He actively involves younger family members in decision-making processes and provides them with opportunities to gain hands-on experience in various aspects of the business. Through mentorship programmes and internships, the scion empowers the next generation to learn from their predecessors while also bringing fresh perspectives and innovative ideas to the table.

Furthermore, the scion emphasizes the importance of continuity and evolution in family businesses. While respecting the traditions and values established by previous generations, he encourages adaptability and innovation to stay relevant in a rapidly changing market landscape. By embracing the strengths of each generation and fostering a culture of collaboration and innovation, the family business is able to navigate challenges and capitalize on opportunities with agility and resilience.

N FOR NEGOTIATION SKILLS

Negotiation skills are indispensable for young leaders engaged in business dealings, partnerships and internal discussions. Leaders proficient in negotiation can articulate their interests effectively, understand the needs of other parties and reach mutually beneficial agreements. Scions leverage negotiation skills not only in external business transactions but also in family discussions where aligning diverse perspectives is crucial. This skill ensures that the family business navigates challenges, forms strategic alliances and resolves conflicts with finesse.

Consider a prominent Indian family-owned conglomerate that has thrived through generations, largely due to the negotiation acumen of its leaders. The current successor, while relatively young, has already demonstrated a remarkable ability to negotiate favourable terms in various contexts. For instance, during a critical acquisition, the scion successfully articulated the strategic vision of the family business, addressing the concerns of potential partners and securing a deal that significantly enhanced the company's market position.

Internally, this scion also excels in negotiating family dynamics, ensuring that diverse viewpoints are heard and harmonized. In one notable instance, when the family faced a decision about expanding into a new market, the older generation took caution, valuing traditional approaches and risk aversion, while the younger members were eager to innovate and take bold steps. The scion facilitated discussions, acknowledging the wisdom of the elders while presenting data-driven arguments that highlighted the potential benefits and mitigated risks of the new venture. Through skilful negotiation, a consensus was reached that honoured the family's legacy while embracing future opportunities.

Such negotiation process is not limited to high-stakes business deals but extends to everyday interactions within the family business. Whether it's aligning on strategic priorities, addressing performance issues or resolving interpersonal conflicts, effective negotiation skills ensure smooth operations and a cohesive family unit. Scions who master this skill can balance empathy with assertiveness, creating outcomes that satisfy all parties involved and fortify the family's collective vision for the business.

O FOR ORGANIZATIONAL SKILLS

Efficient organizational skills are fundamental for scions managing multifaceted responsibilities within the family business. Leaders adept in organization can manage time effectively, set priorities and coordinate workflows seamlessly. This skill is crucial for overseeing diverse business operations, ensuring that resources are allocated optimally and projects progress smoothly. Well-organized scions contribute to the overall efficiency and productivity of the family business, creating a foundation for sustained success.

Take, for example, a renowned Indian family business that has successfully diversified into various sectors, including manufacturing, real estate and retail. The current scion, entrusted with leading the conglomerate, exemplifies exceptional organizational skills. When faced with the challenge of overseeing operations spread across different industries, the young leader implemented robust project management tools and processes to streamline workflows and enhance communication across departments.

In one instance, the scion spearheaded the launch of a new retail chain while simultaneously managing the expansion of the family's real estate ventures. By setting clear priorities and effectively delegating responsibilities, the young leader ensured that both projects received the necessary attention and resources. Regular progress reviews and meticulous planning allowed the scion to identify potential bottlenecks early and address them proactively, preventing delays and ensuring timely completion.

A good leader's organizational acumen must also extend to financial management. By instituting comprehensive budgeting and financial tracking systems, they ensure that each division operates within its means while contributing to the overall financial health of the conglomerate. This level of organization enables the family business to make informed decisions about investments, cost-saving measures and strategic growth opportunities.

An adept leader also places a strong emphasis on human resource management, recognizing that a well-organized workforce is critical to achieving business objectives. Through structured training programmes, clear job descriptions and performance metrics, such a leader fosters an environment where employees understand their roles and responsibilities, contributing to a cohesive and motivated team. This approach not only enhances operational efficiency but also promotes a culture of accountability and continuous improvement.

P FOR PROBLEM SOLVING

The ability to identify, analyse and solve complex challenges is a hallmark of effective leadership. The next-in-line who are skilled in problem-solving approach issues systematically, considering various solutions and potential outcomes. This skill is especially vital in dynamic business environments where unforeseen obstacles could arise. Leaders proficient in problem-solving guide the family business through uncertainties, fostering adaptability and resilience in the face of evolving market dynamics.

Consider an Indian family-owned manufacturing enterprise with global operations that faced a significant supply chain disruption due to geopolitical tensions. The heir apparent, known for their exceptional problem-solving abilities, took charge of navigating the crisis. Instead of reacting impulsively, the scion adopted a systematic approach, first gathering comprehensive data on the extent of the disruption and its impact on various aspects of the business.

The scion assembled a cross-functional team to brainstorm potential solutions, considering diverse perspectives and expertise. This collaborative approach enabled the identification of alternative suppliers, potential cost implications and logistical challenges. By conducting a thorough cost-benefit analysis, the scion was able to prioritize the most viable options, ensuring minimal disruption to production and maintaining the quality standards of the products.

Moreover, the scion's problem-solving prowess was evident in their ability to anticipate and mitigate potential risks associated with the chosen solutions. For instance, while shifting to a new supplier, the scion negotiated flexible contract terms to safeguard against future uncertainties, demonstrating foresight and strategic thinking.

The scion also leveraged technological advancements to streamline operations and enhance supply chain resilience. By implementing advanced supply chain management software, the family business could monitor real-time data, predict potential disruptions and respond proactively. This integration of technology not only resolved the immediate challenge but also fortified the business against future uncertainties.

Another example is a family-owned hospitality business that faced a drastic decline in bookings during an economic downturn. The scion leading the business showcased remarkable problem-solving skills by analysing market trends and consumer behaviour. Recognizing a shift towards experiential travel and staycations, the scion spearheaded the development of unique experience-based packages tailored to domestic tourists.

By transforming underutilized spaces into themed accommodations and promoting local cultural experiences, the business could be successfully revitalized. This strategic pivot not only addressed the immediate challenge of dwindling bookings but also positioned the family business as an innovative leader in the hospitality sector.

Q FOR QUALITY MANAGEMENT

Quality management is integral for scions committed to delivering excellence in products, services and business processes. Leaders with a focus on quality instil a culture of continuous improvement within the family business. They implement robust quality control measures, monitor performance metrics and seek opportunities for enhancement. Prioritizing quality ensures customer satisfaction, builds brand reputation and establishes the family business as a benchmark for industry standards.

For instance, consider the case of an Indian family-owned textile business that has been in operation for several decades. The heir apparent of this business recognized that maintaining high-quality standards was crucial for staying competitive in both domestic and international markets. To this end, the scion introduced comprehensive quality management systems that encompassed every stage of production, from raw material procurement to the final delivery of products.

One of the key initiatives was the implementation of a rigorous supplier evaluation process. The scion worked closely with suppliers to ensure that only the best raw materials were sourced. This also meant that the young leader had to take tough decisions around revisiting the terms of engagement with the people who had been supplying raw materials for decades and who were old friends of the family. This involved regular audits and assessments of suppliers' processes and quality standards. Additionally, the scion established an in-house quality control team responsible for continuous monitoring and testing throughout the manufacturing process. By leveraging advanced testing technologies and methodologies, the business could detect and rectify defects early, ensuring that only the highest quality products reached the market.

Furthermore, the scion fostered a culture of quality by empowering employees at all levels to take ownership of their roles in maintaining and improving standards. This was achieved through comprehensive training programmes focused on quality management principles and practices. Employees were encouraged to contribute ideas for process improvements and a reward system was implemented to recognize and incentivize those who demonstrated exceptional commitment to quality.

The scion also placed a strong emphasis on customer feedback. This proactive approach not only enhanced product quality but also built trust and loyalty among customers, reinforcing the brand's reputation for excellence.

Another example involves a family-owned restaurant chain known for its commitment to quality. The scion leading this business recognized that consistency in food quality and service was critical to maintaining customer satisfaction and loyalty. To achieve this, the scion implemented stringent quality control protocols in all restaurant locations. This included standardizing recipes and cooking procedures to ensure uniform taste and presentation across all outlets. The scion also introduced regular training programmes for kitchen and service staff, focusing on food safety, hygiene and customer service excellence. To maintain high standards, mystery diners were employed to evaluate the dining experience anonymously, providing valuable insights into areas needing improvement. Additionally, the scion invested in state-of-the-art kitchen equipment and technologies to enhance efficiency and quality in food preparation.

R FOR RESILIENCE

Resilience is a key attribute for inheritors facing the inevitable challenges of leadership. Leaders who embody resilience bounce back from setbacks, learn from failures and adapt to changing circumstances. This skill is particularly vital in industries prone to fluctuations and uncertainties. Resilient scions inspire confidence within the organization, fostering a culture that can weather challenges and emerge stronger in the aftermath of adversity.

For example, a family-owned niche manufacturing business in India faced a significant setback due to a sudden economic downturn. The scion leading the business demonstrated resilience by swiftly reassessing the company's strategies and operations. Instead of succumbing to panic or despair, the scion rallied the team, instilling confidence and determination to overcome the challenges.

The scion initiated cost-cutting measures without compromising on product quality or employee well-being. This involved renegotiating contracts with suppliers, streamlining production processes and optimizing resource allocation. Additionally, they explored new market opportunities and diversified the company's product offerings to reduce reliance on any single revenue stream.

Furthermore, the scion leveraged technology to enhance operational efficiency and adapt to changing market dynamics. Automation and digitization initiatives were implemented to improve productivity and agility, enabling the business to respond more effectively to fluctuating demand and supply chain disruptions.

Despite facing significant headwinds, the resilient leadership of the scion enabled the family business to navigate the crisis successfully. By remaining adaptable, resourceful and focused on long-term goals, the business emerged from the downturn stronger and more resilient than before.

S FOR STRATEGIC THINKING

Strategic thinking is the bedrock of visionary leadership. Scions adept in strategic thinking formulate and execute long-term plans aligned with the family business's vision. They analyse market trends, assess competitors and identify growth opportunities. This skill enables leaders to position the family business strategically, anticipating future challenges and capitalizing on emerging trends. Strategic thinkers guide the family business towards sustained success and relevance in a competitive landscape.

For instance, consider a boutique family-owned hospitality business in India that sought to expand its presence in the luxury travel segment. The heir apparent leading the business employed strategic thinking by conducting thorough market research and identifying key trends in the hospitality industry. Recognizing the growing demand for experiential luxury travel among affluent travellers, the scion devised a comprehensive growth strategy focused on offering unique and immersive experiences to guests.

The strategic plan involved investing in premium properties with luxe amenities, enhancing customer service standards and forging partnerships with local artisans and cultural experts to curate authentic experiences for guests. Additionally, the scion identified strategic locations for new hotel developments, leveraging market insights and demographic trends to maximize profitability and brand visibility.

Furthermore, the scion anticipated potential challenges such as regulatory hurdles, economic fluctuations and changing consumer preferences, incorporating contingency plans into the strategic framework. By proactively addressing risks and uncertainties, the family business could navigate obstacles more effectively and stay ahead of the competition.

Strategic thinking is a fundamental competency for scions leading family businesses in India. By analysing market dynamics, anticipating future trends and devising proactive strategies, they can lead and navigate complexities, seize opportunities and guide their organizations towards sustained success and relevance in a competitive environment.

T FOR TEAM BUILDING

Effective team building is a cornerstone of successful leadership. Scions skilled in team building create a collaborative and motivated workforce. They understand the strengths of individual team members, foster open communication and promote a shared sense of purpose. This skill ensures that the family business operates cohesively, with each member contributing their best towards common goals. Strong team building enhances productivity, innovation and overall workplace satisfaction.

There are a lot of examples where a young scion is tasked with leading a crucial project within the family business. Recognizing the importance of effective team building, the scion begins by assessing the strengths and talents of each team member. For instance, they identify a seasoned employee with extensive industry experience who can serve as a mentor to younger team members, fostering knowledge sharing and skill development.

Additionally, they recognize the creative flair of another team member and empower them to spearhead brainstorming sessions to generate innovative solutions. By leveraging the unique abilities of each team member, the scion cultivates an environment of collaboration and mutual respect. Through regular team meetings and open channels of communication, they ensure that everyone feels heard and valued, fostering a sense of camaraderie and shared purpose. As a result, the team operates cohesively, driving productivity, innovation and ultimately, the successful completion of the project. This example illustrates how effective team building can empower scions to harness the collective talents of their team members, driving success within the family business.

U FOR UNDERSTANDING TECHNOLOGY

Staying abreast of technological advancements is imperative for scions navigating modern business landscapes. Leaders who understand technology can leverage innovations to enhance operational efficiency, deliver cutting-edge products or services and gain a competitive edge. Whether implementing new software solutions or harnessing emerging technologies, tech-savvy scions position the family business for continued relevance in a tech-driven era.

Take, for instance, a traditional custom manufacturing business that has been operating for generations. Recognizing the need to adapt to changing market dynamics, the scion at the helm invested in the latest automation technologies to streamline production processes and improve efficiency, and brought in external talent, including design teams. By implementing robotics and artificial intelligence solutions, they not only reduced operational costs but also enhanced product quality and consistency.

Moreover, the tech-savvy scion leveraged data analytics tools to gain insights into consumer preferences and market trends, enabling the family business to tailor its offerings to meet evolving customer demands. Through their proactive embrace of technology, the scion ensured that their family business remains competitive and relevant in an increasingly digital world.

V FOR VISIONARY LEADERSHIP

Visionary leadership sets the course for the future. Scions with a visionary approach articulate a compelling vision for the family business, inspiring stakeholders and guiding strategic initiatives. Visionary leaders anticipate industry shifts, identify opportunities for growth and cultivate a sense of purpose within the organization. This skill ensures that the family business evolves with changing times while staying true to its core values and long-term objectives.

Consider the case of a legacy textile business facing stiff competition from fast-fashion brands and changing consumer preferences. The scion at the helm recognizes the need to diversify and innovate to stay relevant. Drawing upon their deep understanding of the industry and foresight into emerging trends, their initiatives to incorporate sustainable practices, introduce technologically advanced machinery for efficient production, and expand into new markets both domestically and internationally.

By envisioning a future where the family business is not just a manufacturer but a trendsetter in sustainable fashion, the visionary scion inspires stakeholders, including employees, suppliers and customers, to rally behind the shared vision. Their strategic foresight allows the family business to anticipate shifts in consumer behaviour towards eco-conscious products and high-end materials, positioning it as a leader in the evolving marketplace.

W FOR WORK-LIFE BALANCE

Maintaining a healthy work–life balance is crucial for leaders to sustain long-term success. Scions skilled in balancing professional and personal commitments create an environment that values well-being. They set boundaries, prioritize self-care and encourage a culture that respects an individual's personal lives. This skill fosters a positive workplace atmosphere, reduces burnout and ensures that leaders can bring their best selves to both their family and business responsibilities.

Take, for example, the scion of a prominent manufacturing conglomerate who juggles the demands of running the family business with the responsibilities of being a parent and spouse. Recognizing the importance of balance, they prioritize family time by setting aside dedicated hours for quality interactions with their loved ones, whether it's engaging in outdoor activities with their children or enjoying leisurely dinners with their spouse.

By demonstrating a commitment to both their family and business, the balanced leader sets a positive example for employees and family members alike. They emphasize the importance of taking breaks, delegating tasks, and seeking support when needed, fostering a culture that values holistic well-being. In doing so, they cultivate a workplace atmosphere where individuals feel empowered to prioritize self-care without fear of judgement or repercussions.

Maintaining a healthy work–life balance enables the leader to recharge and rejuvenate, thereby enhancing their productivity and decision-making abilities in the workplace. By honouring their personal commitments and investing in their well-being, the balanced leader ensures that they can sustain long-term success both professionally and personally. In the fast-paced world of Indian family businesses, where pressures can be immense, prioritizing work–life balance is not just beneficial but essential for the well-being and resilience of leaders and their organizations alike.

X FOR XENIAL APPROACH

Building positive relationships with external stakeholders defines successful leaders. Scions skilled in extending a xenial (Greek for hospitable) approach towards relations cultivate strong connections with clients, partners and the broader community. This skill involves effective networking, understanding diverse perspectives and fostering trust. Leaders with xenial relations contribute to the family business's reputation, opening doors to collaborations and opportunities.

Consider the scion of a renowned hospitality empire who actively engages with customers, suppliers and community leaders to foster strong connections beyond the confines of their business. By hosting regular networking events, participating in industry forums and supporting local initiatives, they demonstrate a genuine commitment to building meaningful relationships.

However, such examples extend to almost a large segment of Indian business families. Their xenial approach extends beyond transactional interactions, focusing on understanding the needs and perspectives of stakeholders and addressing them with empathy and integrity. A relational savvy not only enhances the family business's reputation but also paves the way for strategic collaborations and partnerships. For instance, by forging alliances with local artisans for sourcing authentic products or partnering with community organizations for corporate social responsibility initiatives, the leader strengthens the family business's ties with the broader ecosystem.

Furthermore, their xenial nature contributes to brand loyalty and customer satisfaction, as clients and partners appreciate the personal touch and genuine care demonstrated by such leaders. This goodwill translates into tangible benefits for the family business, including repeat business, positive word-of-mouth referrals and a resilient reputation in the marketplace.

In essence, having a xenial approach is more than just a business strategy; it is a testament to the leader's commitment to contributing positively to the community. In the interconnected landscape of Indian family businesses, leaders who excel in building positive external relationships are well-positioned to drive growth, innovation and long-term success.

Y FOR YIELD MANAGEMENT

Optimizing resource allocation and maximizing returns characterizes effective leaders. Scions with a focus on yield management ensure that the family business utilizes resources efficiently. This includes managing financial investments, human capital and operational processes to yield optimal outcomes. Leaders skilled in yield management contribute to the family business's financial sustainability and resilience.

Consider a scion leading a diversified conglomerate who meticulously analyses market trends, operational inefficiencies and investment opportunities to ensure optimal resource allocation across various business units.

Their focus on yield management extends beyond financial investments to encompass human capital and operational processes. For instance, they implement performance-driven incentive structures to motivate employees, thereby maximizing productivity and talent retention. Additionally, they leverage technological advancements to streamline operations, reduce wastage and enhance efficiency across the value chain.

By adopting a strategic approach to resource allocation, the leader ensures that the family business allocates its limited resources—whether financial, human or technological—in a manner that generates the highest possible returns. This disciplined approach not only enhances profitability but also fosters a culture of accountability and innovation within the organization.

Furthermore, their adeptness in yield management contributes to the family business's financial sustainability and resilience, enabling it to weather economic downturns and seize growth opportunities proactively. By optimizing resource allocation, the leader ensures that the family business remains agile and adaptive in a dynamic business environment, positioning it for continued success and relevance in the Indian market.

Z FOR ZEN LEADERSHIP

Zen leadership finds resonance in many Indian business families, where the ancient wisdom of mindfulness and compassion intertwines with modern leadership practices. In these families, leaders prioritize not only achieving business objectives but also fostering a harmonious work culture grounded in inner peace and emotional intelligence. They understand the significance of balancing ambition with empathy, ensuring that their actions reflect not just profitability but also ethical conduct and societal impact.

By embracing Zen principles, these leaders cultivate a sense of mindfulness in decision-making, fostering deeper connections with employees, stakeholders and the broader community. This approach to leadership transcends conventional metrics of success, emphasizing holistic well-being and sustainable growth for both the business and its stakeholders.

Consider the example of a prominent Indian business family that integrates mindfulness into their leadership ethos. The scion of this family emphasizes the importance of inner peace and clarity in decision-making processes. Through regular meditation and introspection sessions, the scion cultivates a sense of calm amidst the dynamic nature of business. By embracing Zen leadership principles, a work culture that values empathy, ethical conduct and holistic well-being is nurtured.

In this family business, leaders prioritize self-awareness and emotional intelligence, recognizing the impact of their actions on employees, stakeholders and the broader community.

Part Four

Smoothing the Rough Edges

Family businesses are built on bonds of trust, tradition and shared vision, but they are often tested by the complexities of human relationships and generational shifts. This section dives into the unspoken issues that can jeopardize both family harmony and business success—be it the allure of quick fixes, the pressures faced by young heirs, or sensitive topics like marital discord and unconventional heirs. Each chapter provides a candid exploration of these challenges, urging families to confront the uncomfortable, introspect deeply, and build frameworks that ensure both personal and professional growth. Because in the world of family businesses, the key to long-term success lies in addressing the rough edges that can't be ignored.

SAY NO TO JUGAAD

While the ease of *jugaad* or shortcuts in succession planning may be tempting, it poses significant risks for the long-term sustenance of the plan. Succumbing to quick fixes and shortcuts can undermine the strategic foundation essential for a seamless leadership transition within a family business. By bypassing crucial steps such as thorough talent assessment, leadership development and transparent communication, shortcuts can result in the appointment of inadequately prepared or unsuitable successors. This can lead to internal discord, lack of trust among family members and, ultimately, failure to sustain the business across generations. Moreover, shortcuts may neglect essential aspects of succession planning such as addressing family dynamics, aligning values and ensuring continuity in leadership, which are vital for fostering cohesion and resilience within the organization.

It is crucial to resist the temptation of expedient solutions and instead invest in a thorough, well-thought-out succession strategy. The complexity of family dynamics, business intricacies and external market forces requires a nuanced approach that prioritizes careful planning and strategic foresight. Resisting the urge for shortcuts ensures the development of a robust succession plan that aligns with the family's values, fosters organizational stability and sets the stage for sustained success across generations.

While shortcuts may offer apparent immediate benefits in terms of time and resources saved, they are often costly in the long run. By neglecting comprehensive planning and investing in the development of future leaders, organizations risk compromising business performance, innovation and strategic agility. Moreover, shortcuts in succession planning can erode family values and tarnish the company's reputation, leading to decreased stakeholder confidence and potential loss of competitive advantage.

Ultimately, the expenses incurred from rectifying the consequences of rushed decisions and inadequate preparation far outweigh the perceived benefits of taking shortcuts. Often viewed as an expedient way to navigate the complexities of family business succession, jugaad shortcuts might provide immediate relief, but they fall short in fostering sustainable and resilient successions. The pitfalls of jugaad in succession planning are evident in the long-term consequences that emerge when foundational aspects are neglected. Jugaad, while seemingly resourceful in the short run, can lead to conflicts, mismanagement and an overall lack of preparedness among successors. Let us take a close look at some of the pitfalls.

Lack of Long-term Vision

Jugaad, the art of improvisation and quick fixes, is inherently short-sighted. The lack of a long-term vision in jugaad-driven succession planning can be particularly detrimental to the sustained success of a family business. Jugaad, rooted in improvisation and quick fixes, tends to focus on immediate problem-solving without considering the broader, future-oriented aspects of succession. In family businesses, where the goal is often to ensure the enterprise thrives across generations, a myopic approach can lead to inadequacies in preparing successors for evolving market landscapes and emerging challenges. Succession planning, as a dynamic process, demands more than just short-term fixes; it requires a deliberate and forward-thinking strategy that aligns with the family's overarching goals. Neglecting this long-term perspective in favour of quick jugaad solutions may inadvertently sow the seeds of instability and unpreparedness in future leadership, hindering the family business's ability to adapt and thrive over time.

Adverse Impact on Organizational Culture

The adverse impact of jugaad on organizational culture within the context of succession planning cannot be overstated. Jugaad-driven solutions often prioritize expediency over alignment with core values and established cultural norms. In succession planning, this tendency can manifest in the hasty selection of successors without due consideration for their compatibility with the existing organizational ethos. The appointment of leaders who do not seamlessly integrate into the established culture can create a ripple effect of discord, as these successors may struggle to navigate the intricacies of the company's values and traditions. This misalignment poses a significant risk to the cohesive functioning of the organization, potentially eroding the collaborative spirit, employee morale and overall cultural harmony. In the long run, the adverse impact on organizational culture resulting from jugaad approaches in succession planning may undermine the very foundations that contribute to a company's enduring success.

Undermining Professionalism

The penchant for jugaad in the context of succession planning introduces a perilous element of undermining professionalism. Succession planning inherently demands a professional and structured approach. However, the improvisational nature of jugaad leans more towards quick fixes and ad-hoc measures than a systematic, well-thought-out strategy. This undermines the professional standards crucial for navigating the complexities of succession. The absence of a methodical plan can lead to a lack of clarity in roles and responsibilities, ultimately jeopardizing the overall stability of the business. The consequences may include leadership gaps, operational disruptions and a compromised ability to uphold the business's reputation and competitive edge in the market. In the realm of succession planning, eschewing professionalism in favour of jugaad poses a substantial risk to the long-term sustainability and success of the organization.

Ignoring Competency Assessment

One of the significant drawbacks of relying on jugaad in succession planning is the propensity to ignore competency assessment. While jugaad often seeks quick fixes, it may bypass the crucial step of conducting a rigorous evaluation of the competencies, skills and qualifications of potential successors. Succession planning extends beyond familial ties; it necessitates a thorough examination of individuals' capabilities to ensure that they are well-equipped to handle the responsibilities of leadership. Jugaad, by its very nature, tends to sideline this critical aspect, opening the door to the appointment of successors who may lack the necessary skills or qualifications. This oversight can result in leaders who are ill-equipped to navigate the complex challenges of the business landscape, potentially compromising the organization's long-term viability and success. The failure to assess competencies thoroughly is a fundamental flaw in the jugaad approach to succession planning, introducing risks that could have been mitigated otherwise.

Short-term Gains, Long-term Risks

Jugaad, with its focus on immediate relief and expedient solutions, introduces the risk of sacrificing long-term stability for fleeting advantages. Succession planning, as a critical process for the continuity and prosperity of a family business, demands thoughtful consideration and strategic foresight. Embracing quick fixes without a comprehensive, long-term vision can create ripple effects that resonate through generations. The decisions made hastily in the realm of succession planning can have enduring consequences, potentially destabilizing the very foundations that family businesses seek to build. The dichotomy between short-term gains and long-term risks underscores the need for a measured, deliberate approach to succession planning that prioritizes the enduring success and resilience of the family enterprise over immediate, makeshift solutions. The judicious balance of immediate needs and long-term vision is essential for sustained prosperity in the intricate world of family business succession.

Creating Ambiguity and Uncertainty

Jugaad's penchant for impromptu solutions in succession planning introduces a precarious element of ambiguity and uncertainty. Successful succession planning demands clarity and transparency to navigate the intricacies of leadership transition seamlessly. Unfortunately, jugaad's ad-hoc approach tends to cloud the succession process, leaving crucial aspects in a state of ambiguity. The lack of clear communication and transparent decision-making can sow seeds of tension within the family, create uncertainties among stakeholders, and cast shadows over the workforce. The potential for destabilization becomes pronounced as essential information becomes muddled or undisclosed, eroding the trust that underpins effective succession planning. In contrast, a structured and transparent approach ensures that everyone involved understands their roles, responsibilities and the overarching vision, fostering an environment of stability and confidence during the critical phase of the leadership transition.

Impact on Stakeholder Confidence

The impact of jugaad approaches on stakeholder confidence in the context of succession planning cannot be overstated. Succession planning is not merely an internal affair; it reverberates throughout the broader business ecosystem, affecting investors, employees and partners alike. Jugaad, with its improvisational nature, has the potential to erode confidence by introducing uncertainty into the equation. Stakeholders, particularly investors seeking stability and sustainable growth, may become apprehensive about the future direction of the business. Quick fixes devoid of a comprehensive and well-communicated strategy can leave stakeholders questioning the long-term viability of the organization. In contrast, a diligently planned and transparent succession strategy reinforces confidence by providing a clear roadmap for the future. Stakeholders are more likely to remain committed when they see a robust, well-thought-out succession plan that aligns with the business's values and long-term objectives.

Overlooking Systematic Talent Development

The oversight of systematic talent development is a critical pitfall associated with jugaad approaches in succession planning. Unlike well-structured strategies, jugaad tends to address immediate leadership gaps without a broader and more forward-looking perspective. Succession planning, at its core, involves cultivating a pool of capable talent across various levels of the organization. Jugaad, however, may prioritize quick fixes for existing vacancies, neglecting the essential aspect of nurturing a pipeline of skilled individuals for the future. This myopic approach can lead to a shortage of well-prepared successors, as there is insufficient investment in the continuous development and training of potential leaders. In contrast, systematic talent development ensures a steady flow of qualified individuals who are not only ready to fill current leadership roles but are also adequately equipped to navigate future challenges, contributing to the sustained success of the family business.

Family Dynamics and Conflict

The impact of jugaad on family dynamics and conflict in succession planning is profound. Jugaad's superficial nature may overlook the nuanced dynamics within a family business. Succession planning, particularly in a family context, is not only about selecting competent leaders but also about understanding and navigating intricate familial relationships. A quick-fix approach might neglect the emotional complexities and potential sources of conflict that can arise during the succession process. The lack of a thorough examination of family dynamics can lead to power struggles, disagreements and strained relationships, putting the success of the succession plan on the line. In contrast, a more structured and strategic approach to succession planning recognizes the importance of addressing familial dynamics, fostering open communication and implementing conflict resolution mechanisms. This ensures a smoother transition of leadership while preserving the family harmony essential for the long-term sustainability of the business.

Legal and Governance Risks

Jugaad poses substantial legal and governance risks for family businesses. The ad-hoc nature of jugaad might inadvertently sideline critical legal and governance requirements essential for a seamless transition. Succession planning, especially in family enterprises, involves adhering to legal frameworks, regulatory compliance and governance standards. Ignoring these aspects during jugaad can expose the business to legal challenges, regulatory scrutiny and governance lapses. It is crucial to recognize that a comprehensive succession plan requires a meticulous alignment with legal requirements to safeguard the business from potential legal complications in the future. A structured and legally sound succession strategy ensures not only a smooth leadership transition but also mitigates the risk of legal and governance issues that could impact the long-term stability of the family business.

Neglecting External Market Forces

Neglecting external market forces is a notable drawback of jugaad-driven succession plans. Jugaad lacks the strategic foresight needed to account for dynamic external factors and industry trends. Successful succession planning goes beyond immediate considerations; it involves positioning the business strategically in response to external market forces. Such unplanned approaches may overlook the importance of market intelligence, trend analysis and a proactive stance in adapting to changing industry dynamics. In contrast, a well-structured succession plan considers these external forces, ensuring that the family business remains resilient and competitive in the face of evolving market conditions. Recognizing and preparing for external market forces is integral to the long-term success and sustainability of the business.

Resistance to Cultural Shift

Resistance to change is a significant concern when employing jugaad in succession planning. Succession planning necessitates a cultural shift towards embracing formalized processes, strategic thinking and long-term planning. The rough and ready way of working may clash with the established culture of the organization, creating challenges in the adoption of new and better ways of doing business. Overcoming cultural resistance involves not just implementing a succession plan but fostering a mindset shift within the organization. It requires aligning the organizational culture with the principles of strategic succession, emphasizing the importance of foresight and planning for the long-term stability and success of the family business.

The appeal of jugaad as a band-aid solution is undeniable, offering a seemingly quick fix to immediate challenges. However, relying on jugaad shortcuts in succession planning is akin to putting a temporary patch on a leaky ship. While it may address the immediate issue, it leaves the underlying problems unattended, allowing them to fester and potentially cause more significant damage in the long run. Adequate succession planning measures, on the other hand, act as a comprehensive and strategic approach, addressing the root causes and providing a sturdy foundation for the family business's sustained success.

Strategic planning, careful consideration of various factors and a commitment to long-term goals are the cornerstones of a successful succession plan that stands the test of time.

WHEN YOUR CHILD ISN'T 'AMBITIOUS'

It is fair that every parent, especially in a business family, expects their child to be more intelligent than them. It is expected that their child would take their family business to greater heights. But what if the child is not as ambitious as anticipated? This question lingers in the minds of many business leaders, stirring up feelings of uncertainty and apprehension. However, it is essential to confront this reality with empathy and understanding. Not every individual is driven by the same aspirations or motivated by conventional measures of success. Recognizing and accepting each child's unique strengths, passions and ambitions is a crucial part of fostering a supportive and nurturing environment within the family enterprise. While it may require adjusting expectations and exploring alternative paths, embracing the reality of varying levels of ambition among children can ultimately lead to greater fulfilment and harmony within the family.

In the world of business, ambition is often hailed as a driving force behind success. Yet, in the quiet corners of family enterprises, there exists a concern that seldom sees the spotlight—the acknowledgement that not every child may harbour the same level of ambition as their predecessors. It is a conversation that many heads of business families grapple with behind closed doors. The worry, perhaps unspoken, revolves around the perceived lack of drive in the next generation. In a society that glorifies ambition and the pursuit of success, accepting a child's lack of ambition might seem like conceding defeat. However, it is time to unravel the layers of this concern and bring the human element to the forefront.

It can be a sobering realization for business families when they discover that one of their children lacks the drive and ambition typically associated with leadership roles in the family business. In a society that often equates success with professional achievement and ambition, it is natural for parents to feel a sense of disappointment or concern when their child deviates from this conventional path. However, embracing the reality that not every individual is wired for traditional career aspirations can be a liberating and unspoken comfort for families navigating succession planning.

First and foremost, parents need to recognize that ambition manifests in various forms, and traditional markers of success may not resonate with every individual. While one may not see their child spearheading corporate takeovers or venturing into new markets, it doesn't mean they lack ambition. While one child may excel in entrepreneurial ventures or executive leadership roles, another may find fulfilment and purpose in creative pursuits, community service or personal interests outside the business realm. Embracing this diversity of passions and talents within the family can foster a culture of acceptance, respect and support for each member's unique journey.

Second, not every individual is cut from the same cloth. The pressures of legacy and the weight of expectations can inadvertently overshadow the individuality of each family member. The lack of overt ambition might be a testament to a desire for a simpler, more meaningful life rather than a disinterest in contributing to the family legacy.

Rather than viewing lack of ambition as a failure or personal shortcoming, parents can celebrate their child's individuality and encourage them to pursue paths that align with their passions, values and strengths. By fostering an environment of unconditional love, acceptance and encouragement, families can empower their children to chart their own course and define success on their own terms.

Furthermore, recognizing and embracing the reality that not every child will follow in the footsteps of previous generations, that ambition doesn't always correlate with happiness, can be a source of liberation and opportunity for families. Instead of viewing divergent paths as a setback or disappointment, parents can embrace the richness and diversity that each family member brings to the table, leveraging their uniqueness to enrich the family enterprise. By embracing this reality with openness, empathy and flexibility, families can cultivate a culture of inclusivity that transcends traditional notions of ambition and success.

In the end, the heart of the matter lies in embracing the reality that not every family member needs to fit a predetermined mould of ambition. Human aspirations are diverse, and each family member contributes uniquely to the collective narrative. Rather than imposing expectations, there is a powerful beauty in allowing individuals to define their own paths, even if those paths don't align with conventional definitions of ambition.

So to the heads of business families grappling with this concern—it is okay if your child isn't ambitious in the way society expects. Celebrate the authenticity of their journey, recognizing that true success lies in happiness, fulfilment and the diverse ways each family member contributes to the legacy you have built together.

Navigating the terrain where a child might not be overly ambitious opens up opportunities for a thoughtful approach to succession planning. The concern is often accompanied by questions about what role such a child can play in the family enterprise. It is essential to recognize that not being ambitious in the traditional sense doesn't equate to a lack of capability or contribution potential.

One pragmatic avenue is to consider professional successors for key leadership roles within the enterprise. By doing so, the family can ensure that the business is steered by individuals with the necessary skills, drive and ambition while maintaining familial ownership. This approach bifurcates the responsibilities—the child, though not directly involved in the day-to-day operations, can continue to enjoy the financial dividends resulting from the enterprise's success.

Succession planning, in this context, becomes a strategic act of aligning individual strengths with business needs. It is about recognizing the unique qualities that each family member possesses and crafting roles that leverage those strengths effectively. The non-ambitious child might excel in areas such as relationship management, customer engagement or even maintaining the cultural ethos of the business, all of which are crucial for sustained success.

In essence, addressing the concern about a child's lack of ambition doesn't imply sidelining them from the family legacy. It is about redefining roles, acknowledging diverse strengths and embracing a more inclusive approach to succession planning. By doing so, the family enterprise not only secures a professional and capable leadership but also nurtures a familial bond that respects individual choices and aspirations. Success, in this context, transcends traditional definitions and encompasses the harmonious continuation of the family legacy.

SPOILT BRATS OF BUSINESS FAMILIES

Business families are not immune to the presence of spoilt brats and individuals who may exhibit undesirable behaviour within their ranks. Whether due to entitlement or lack of accountability, such individuals can pose significant challenges to the harmony and success of the family enterprise. Their actions and attitudes may undermine teamwork, erode trust and create tension among family members and employees alike.

Spoilt brats within business families pose a significant threat to the stability and longevity of the family enterprise. Their privileged upbringing often results in a lack of appreciation for the values that built the business. The absence of self-discipline can manifest in reckless decision-making, entitlement issues and an overall disregard for the hard work that went into creating the family wealth. These individuals, accustomed to instant gratification, might lack the resilience to navigate the challenges of running a business. Their unchecked behaviour can lead to internal conflicts, as family members witness a deviation from the core principles that define the family's success.

In the context of succession planning, the presence of spoilt brats can complicate matters. Their sense of entitlement might clash with the merit-based approach necessary for identifying competent successors. This dynamic introduces an element of favouritism and undermines the principles of fair leadership selection. Strengthening family values becomes imperative as a countermeasure. Instilling a sense of responsibility, work ethic and gratitude for the family legacy can mitigate the negative impact of the entitlement. A deliberate effort to cultivate humility and a deeper understanding of the family's journey is crucial for aligning these individuals with the values that sustain the business.

Spoilt brats within business families not only jeopardize the internal cohesion of the family unit but can also erode stakeholder confidence, causing tangible harm to the business. When family members exhibit entitled behaviour, engage in public scandals or make questionable decisions without accountability, stakeholders, including investors, employees and customers, can lose faith in the business's leadership.

Such publicized family conflicts can result in a loss of trust from stakeholders. Investors may become wary of potential disruptions to business operations, and customers may question the company's ethical standards. Employees, too, may feel uncertain about the company's future direction, impacting morale and productivity.

Spoilt brats who are perceived as taking undue advantage of their family's business can be a liability, causing reputational damage that goes beyond the confines of the family. Stakeholders value stability, transparency and ethical conduct in businesses, and any deviation from these principles can lead to a loss of confidence.

The grooming of the next generation within a business family is a critical responsibility that goes beyond providing financial privileges. While it may seem cute or endearing when children display confidence or assertiveness due to their family's wealth, the long-term implications of allowing wealth to shape behavioural arrogance can be detrimental to both the family and the business.

At an early age, the confidence displayed by affluent children may be perceived as harmless, even charming. However, if not tempered with a sense of humility, responsibility and empathy, this early display of entitlement can evolve into a pattern of arrogance as they mature. The danger lies in the fact that wealth-driven arrogance can manifest in entitlement, a lack of respect for others, and an assumption that success is guaranteed without the need for hard work or ethical conduct.

As these children grow older and assume roles within the family business, their behaviour can impact relationships with employees, partners and even family members. Arrogance can lead to a disconnect with the workforce, hinder effective collaboration and create a divisive atmosphere within the family. Moreover, stakeholders, including customers and investors, may distance themselves from a business perceived as being driven by arrogance rather than merit and competence.

In addition to the challenges of spoilt brat syndrome, there is a risk of the current generation and children in subsequent generations succumbing to vices, bad habits and undesirable company. As business families accumulate wealth over generations, the temptation of indulgence and excess can overshadow the values instilled by previous generations. This phenomenon poses a significant challenge for business families, as they must not only pass on their wealth and legacy but also ensure that their successors embody the values and principles that underpin their success.

Moreover, the proliferation of modern distractions and temptations, exacerbated by easy access to wealth, further complicates the task of steering successive generations towards a path of responsibility, integrity and purpose. Thus, business families face the daunting task of navigating these external influences while imparting the necessary values and discipline to their heirs, safeguarding both their family cohesion and the integrity of their business legacy.

One illustrative example is the case of a prominent business family whose scion, due to unchecked arrogance, publicly made derogatory remarks about employees. The incident not only caused internal turmoil but also led to a significant backlash from the public and damaged the family's reputation.

To avoid such pitfalls, the previous generation must instil values that prioritize humility, respect and a strong work ethic. While financial privilege can provide opportunities, it should not become a shield against the realities of life and business. Encouraging the next generation to understand the value of hard work, to appreciate the contributions of others, and to approach success with a sense of responsibility can prevent the emergence of toxic behaviours associated with wealth-driven arrogance.

However, addressing the issue requires a delicate balance. Heavy-handed tactics may exacerbate rebellion, while a laissez-faire approach risks an unchecked erosion of family wealth. This necessitates a nuanced strategy, blending discipline with empathy. Proactive intervention through mentorship programmes, exposure to the realities of the business and, if needed, external counselling can redirect the energy of spoilt brats towards constructive contributions. Encouraging them to forge their identity within the context of the family legacy rather than against it can harness their potential positively.

Families need to handle such situations with sensitivity and discretion, recognizing the potential impact on both the business and the family's reputation. Addressing issues related to spoilt brats and bad apples requires clear communication, setting boundaries and enforcing consequences for inappropriate behaviour. Family leaders must strive to uphold the values and principles of the business while fostering an environment of accountability and mutual respect.

Moreover, families may need to seek professional guidance or support from advisors experienced in family dynamics and conflict resolution to navigate these challenging situations effectively. By addressing issues promptly and decisively, families can mitigate the negative impact of spoilt brats and bad apples on their business and reputation, ensuring the long-term success and sustainability of the family enterprise.

In essence, grooming the next generation involves not only preparing them for the responsibilities of wealth management but also fostering a mindset that values collaboration, ethical conduct and a genuine respect for all stakeholders. By doing so, business families can ensure the continuity of a legacy built on principles that contribute to the success, sustainability and positive impact of both the family and the business.

Proactively addressing such behaviour becomes paramount not only for preserving family harmony but also for safeguarding the interests of stakeholders. By cultivating a culture of accountability, demonstrating ethical leadership and ensuring that family dynamics do not overshadow business priorities, business families can mitigate the risks associated with spoilt brats and reinforce stakeholder confidence in the long-term sustainability of the enterprise. The resolution lies not merely in addressing the symptoms but in fostering a generational mindset that values the collective strength of the family over individual indulgence.

CUTE OR CODDLED?

The interplay between wealth and behaviour within business families is a terrain rife with challenges. The notion that poor behaviour in affluent children is simply a passing phase, often dismissed as 'cute', can be a dangerous oversight as affluence tends to alter perceptions of misconduct. In reality, the unchecked display of poor behaviour in the formative years can evolve into ingrained habits, posing a threat to the family legacy.

Poor behaviour being mistaken as 'cute' often stems from the privilege and leniency afforded to children in affluent households. In some cases, behaviours considered inappropriate or disrespectful in other contexts are excused or overlooked due to the family's wealth and status. This dynamic can create a sense of entitlement and reinforce negative behaviour patterns, as children learn that their actions have minimal consequences.

However, it is crucial to address and correct such behaviour as soon as possible to ensure the stability of character and leadership qualities in the future. Wealth must be accompanied by a robust value system. While certain behaviours may be tolerated or even indulged during childhood, they can have significant repercussions as children grow into adulthood and assume leadership roles within the family business. Poor behaviour that is excused or ignored in childhood can manifest as entitlement, arrogance or a lack of accountability in professional settings, undermining effective management and damaging relationships with employees, colleagues and stakeholders.

This is not a mere phase that teenagers naturally outgrow; it is a manifestation of deeper issues that need parental guidance and intervention. Excusing poor behaviour as a part of adolescence can inadvertently become a tacit endorsement of actions that might not align with the family's core values. The impact of such behaviour isn't confined to the individual but has far-reaching consequences for the family's reputation and, consequently, the business. Let us delve into the ways in which such behaviour can prove detrimental.

Impact on Corporate Governance

Erosion of professionalism: Poor behaviour, especially if it involves a lack of professionalism, can seep into the corporate culture. In a family business, this may lead to a decline in the standards of governance and operational discipline.

Impaired decision-making: Behavioural issues within the family can spill over into boardrooms, affecting decision-making processes. Personal biases and conflicts may hinder the objective assessment of business strategies.

Impact on Business Sustainability

Succession planning challenges: If poor behaviour is pervasive, it can complicate succession planning. Family members demonstrating irresponsibility or a lack of commitment may not be suitable successors, jeopardizing the continuity of the business.

Impact on Reputation Management

Media and social media impact: In an era dominated by media attention and social media, any hint of poor behaviour can swiftly become public knowledge. Negative stories or scandals involving family members can tarnish the family's and business's reputation.

Customer and investor perception: A family business relies heavily on the trust and confidence of customers and investors. Poor behaviour by family members can erode this trust, leading to a loss of clientele and potential financial backers.

Impact on Internal Dynamics

Employee morale and productivity: Poor behaviour within the family can create a toxic work environment. Employees may witness internal conflicts, impacting morale and productivity. This, in turn, can affect the overall health of the business.

Legal and Regulatory Consequences

Legal repercussions: Certain behaviours, if crossing legal or ethical boundaries, can lead to legal consequences. This not only affects individual family members but also exposes the family business to legal risks and regulatory scrutiny.

Strained Relationships

Stakeholder relationships: Poor behaviour can strain relationships with key stakeholders, such as suppliers, partners and clients. The interconnected nature of business relationships means that negative perceptions can have a cascading effect.

In essence, the consequences of poor behaviour within a business family ripple through various dimensions, threatening the long-term sustainability of the family enterprise. Addressing behavioural issues becomes crucial for the overall health and success of the business. Business families need to be vigilant in cultivating a culture of respect, professionalism, and responsibility to safeguard their legacy and standing in the business world.

Addressing this challenge requires a proactive stance from the parents. Rather than brushing off disrespectful or entitled behaviour as a passing stage, it is crucial to instil values that emphasize the responsibilities that come with privilege. A teenager's poor conduct shouldn't be dismissed but addressed with constructive conversations about respect, humility and the family's ethical foundations.

Parents play a pivotal role in regulating and guiding their children's behaviour, especially when wealth is part of the equation. It is about establishing boundaries, emphasizing the importance of hard work and ensuring that the privileges bestowed upon the younger generation are met with a sense of gratitude, not entitlement.

Delving into the intricacies of wealth and behaviour within affluent family dynamics uncovers a tapestry of nuanced challenges. Take, for instance, the scenario where a teenager's entitled behaviour is not curbed but rather tolerated as a passing phase. This tolerance, if unchecked, may manifest in adulthood as a sense of privilege that colours interactions both within and outside the family circle.

Consider the case of a business family scion growing up in an environment where displays of affluence are not tempered with humility.

If a child is showered with material possessions without an accompanying emphasis on the values that underpin the family's success, there is a risk of sowing the seeds of entitlement. The teenager who flaunts wealth without understanding its origins may struggle to grasp the responsibilities that come with affluence.

In such situations, the impact goes beyond individual behaviour. It becomes a question of how these behavioural traits influence the family's reputation in the business world. A child's seemingly harmless antics, when unchecked, can develop into a pattern of behaviour that tarnishes the family's image, potentially affecting business relationships and partnerships.

Parents must recognize the critical role they play in shaping their children's values. Take the example of a family that, rather than addressing disrespectful behaviour, rationalizes it as an inherent trait of adolescence. By doing so, they miss an opportunity to instil essential values like respect, integrity and gratitude.

&

Wealth can act as a double-edged sword. A child born into privilege may struggle to comprehend the struggles that led to the family's success. If parents fail to bridge this gap through open and honest conversations, the child may perceive wealth as an inherent right rather than a result of hard work and sacrifice.

The impact of wealth on behaviour extends beyond mere material possessions. It seeps into attitudes towards work, relationships and societal responsibilities. A teenager accustomed to financial abundance might struggle to comprehend the importance of diligence, perseverance and empathy if these values are not actively instilled.

In essence, the example parents set and the conversations they engage in become crucial components in shaping the behaviour of their children. It is not just about curbing undesirable traits but fostering a mindset that appreciates the privilege bestowed upon the family.

To navigate the complexities of wealth and behaviour, parents must be proactive in guiding their children towards a balanced perspective. This involves not only addressing poor behaviour when it arises but consistently instilling a value system that forms the bedrock of the family's legacy. The challenge is not merely to react to behavioural quirks but to actively shape a mindset that aligns with the principles that have propelled the family to success.

By addressing and correcting poor behaviour early on, parents can instil values of integrity, responsibility and respect in their children, laying the foundation for ethical leadership and effective management. Setting clear expectations, providing constructive feedback and implementing consequences for inappropriate behaviour can help children understand the importance of accountability and cultivate the interpersonal skills necessary for success in both personal and professional domains. Ultimately, by prioritizing character development and fostering a culture of respect and accountability within the family, parents can ensure that their children are prepared to navigate the complexities of leadership with grace, integrity and humility.

PRESSURES ON YOUNG SCIONS

Young scions in a succession planning process often face immense pressure and expectations, both from within the family and external stakeholders. As inheritors of a family business legacy, they may find themselves thrust into positions of leadership and responsibility before they feel adequately prepared or equipped to handle such roles. Undue and sometimes unfair expectations can weigh heavily on their shoulders, leading to feelings of stress, anxiety and self-doubt.

From a young age, these scions may be groomed and conditioned to believe that they are destined to take over the family business and carry on its legacy. This sense of obligation can create a sense of pressure to live up to perceived standards of success set by previous generations. Additionally, external stakeholders, including employees, investors and customers, may also harbour high expectations for the young scions, assuming that they will seamlessly step into leadership roles and continue the business's trajectory of growth and prosperity.

Furthermore, the complexities of modern business environments, rapid technological advancements and global economic uncertainties add additional pressure on young scions. They may feel overwhelmed by the weight of expectations to innovate, adapt and navigate increasingly competitive markets while simultaneously honouring the traditions and values of the family business.

In some cases, these pressures can lead to feelings of isolation, imposter syndrome or rebellion as young scions struggle to reconcile their own aspirations and identities with the roles and responsibilities thrust upon them. It is essential for family leaders and stakeholders to recognize and address these pressures sensitively, providing support, mentorship and opportunities for the young scions to develop their confidence. By fostering an environment of understanding and collaboration, families can help alleviate the undue burdens placed on young scions and ensure a smoother and more sustainable succession process.

After the completion of succession planning, young scions find themselves at the helm of familial enterprises, stepping into a role laden with challenges that extend far beyond the boardroom. The expectations placed upon them are multifaceted, stemming from a diverse array of stakeholders. They find themselves navigating a complex set of pressures, uniquely nuanced by the cultural, societal and familial expectations intrinsic to their position. Let us see how these pressures significantly impact their personal and professional lives.

Legacy Expectations

The expectation to seamlessly transition into leadership roles is a considerable pressure. Succession planning is not just about individual competence but involves managing relationships, inspiring trust and ensuring a smooth handover. The weight of carrying forward a family legacy is perhaps the most palpable pressure on young scions. The expectations to not just maintain but elevate the family business to new heights can be overwhelming. The scrutiny they face is not merely based on individual achievements but is intricately tied to the reputation and success built by preceding generations.

At the same time, the delicate balance between preserving tradition and embracing innovation is a perpetual challenge. Young scions are often tasked with infusing a modern perspective into established family businesses while respecting the values and practices that have defined the enterprise. Striking this equilibrium requires deft leadership and an acute understanding of evolving market dynamics.

Within the organization, employees look to the young scion for direction and inspiration. Bridging the generational gap becomes a nuanced challenge as the scion seeks to blend the wisdom of experienced team members with innovative approaches that resonate with younger talents. The burden of fostering a cohesive work culture and ensuring employee satisfaction rests squarely on their shoulders.

Public Scrutiny

Being part of a prominent business family often means constant public scrutiny. Every decision, personal or professional, is subject to analysis and commentary from various stakeholders, including the media, industry peers and the general public. This relentless scrutiny can create a sense of vulnerability and the need for meticulous decision-making.

The public eye also often fixates on their personal lives. The allure of late-night revelry might be tempting, but understanding the weight of your family's legacy and the impact of your actions on its reputation is paramount. After all, a business leader is under perpetual scrutiny by a multitude of stakeholders and needs to constantly maintain a balancing act between individual autonomy and the perceived responsibilities that come with this role. They must navigate public opinion with grace, understanding that personal choices can impact the broader perception of the business.

Family Dynamics

Navigating familial relationships within the business context adds another layer of complexity. Sibling rivalries, traditional hierarchies and the expectation to maintain familial unity while steering the business forward require delicate handling. The scion becomes a mediator, a leader and a family member simultaneously, navigating a complex tapestry of emotions and expectations.

Regulatory Compliance

Regulatory compliance adds another layer of complexity, with regulators expecting the young leader to uphold ethical standards and adhere to legal frameworks. The media, known for its relentless scrutiny, demands transparency and communication finesse. The scion is tasked with managing the public image of the family business, navigating through potential crises and projecting a positive narrative.

Industry Competition

In the competitive landscape of business, especially in a globalized economy, young scions face the challenge of proving their mettle against industry rivals. The constant need to innovate, adapt to technological changes and lead in a fast-paced environment intensifies the pressures they experience.

Stakeholder Pressure

Investors, both internal and external, expect the scion to deliver financial results while demonstrating a clear vision for sustained growth. Balancing short-term performance with long-term strategic initiatives becomes a high-stakes juggling act. Shareholders seek reassurance that the young scion can steer the ship with the same efficacy as their predecessors. On top of this, the board, often composed of seasoned industry professionals, anticipates not only effective leadership but also strategic vision. The challenge for the scion is to earn their respect by demonstrating acumen, decisiveness and the ability to navigate complex business landscapes.

Social Responsibilities

Beyond business, scions are often expected to play active roles in social and philanthropic initiatives. Balancing these social responsibilities with the demands of the business adds another layer of pressure, requiring them to be adept multitaskers and community leaders.

Personal Identity

Amidst the overwhelming influence of the family business, young scions may grapple with establishing their personal identity outside the familial context. At the same time, they may grapple with imposter syndrome or the fear of falling short of familial expectations. The pressure to live to everyone's expectations and be seen as an individual with unique skills and contributions at the same time adds a unique dimension of challenge related to the notion of 'self'. Self-discovery then becomes a crucial way to step forward.

One of the ways to manage these pressures is to seek external help. Guidance from a non-family professional coach as a strategic ally in this transitional phase can work wonders. Such a coach acts as a confidential guide, offering insights into the delicate balance between personal life and professional obligations. They bring an impartial perspective, untethered from familial dynamics, allowing you to navigate the challenges of both the social and business realms with a pragmatic and objective mindset. They can help you establish boundaries, offering strategies to manage stakeholder engagements without compromising your professional standing. They also provide a safe space for you to discuss challenges, seek advice on handling scrutiny and develop the leadership skills necessary to represent your family business with grace and authority.

ELEPHANT IN THE ROOM: DIFFERENCES AND DISPUTES

The proverbial elephant in the room within business families is often the unaddressed differences and disputes that lurk beneath the surface. Ignoring or tiptoeing around these issues during succession planning is akin to allowing a silent storm to gather strength. The unspoken tensions, unresolved conflicts and festering differences can and often do erupt at the most inopportune moments, jeopardizing the very fabric of the family business. Succession planning should not be a mere formality; it requires a courageous confrontation with the elephant, a willingness to delve into uncomfortable conversations and a commitment to resolving disputes. Failure to acknowledge and navigate these differences not only risks derailing the succession process but also endangers the legacy and sustainability of the business itself. It is a stark reminder that in family businesses, the unspoken can be the most potent force, and addressing the elephant is not just a choice but a prerequisite for a resilient and thriving future.

Recognizing that differences are a natural part of any family dynamic, embracing open communication and seeking professional mediation or counselling, when necessary, can help facilitate constructive dialogue and foster a sense of unity and understanding among family members. By tackling the 'elephant in the room' with courage and compassion, Indian business families can navigate challenges more effectively and safeguard the long-term success and harmony of both their family and their business.

Family disputes within business families carry multifaceted implications that permeate the family fabric and business dynamics. These disputes can stem from various sources, including differences in business ideologies, conflicts over wealth distribution or struggles for leadership positions.

The 'why' of family disputes often lies in the complex intertwining of personal relationships and business decisions. Sibling rivalries, generational gaps and divergent visions for the business's future can trigger tensions. For instance, disagreements on strategic directions or investment decisions may escalate into full-fledged disputes if not addressed promptly.

The 'who' involved in these disputes can range from senior family members to younger generations, each with their own perspectives and stakes in the business. Disputes might manifest among siblings vying for control or influence, potentially jeopardizing the cohesion essential for a successful family enterprise.

Geographically, family disputes can unfold anywhere—within the confines of the family home, during business meetings or in public forums. The 'where' is not limited to a specific location but permeates both personal and professional spaces, affecting interactions across various contexts.

The 'how' of family disputes often involves a nuanced interplay of communication breakdowns, differing expectations and unresolved conflicts. Mismanagement of succession planning, unclear governance structures or inadequate conflict resolution mechanisms can exacerbate tensions. For example, a lack of open communication may lead to misunderstandings that fester into deep-seated disputes.

'What' a dispute does to a business family extends beyond the immediate conflict. It can fracture familial bonds, erode trust and hamper collaborative decision-making. In the long term, these disputes may have detrimental effects on the business's performance, reputation and overall sustainability.

One illustrative example involves a family-owned manufacturing business where disagreements among siblings regarding business expansion led to a protracted legal battle. The dispute not only drained financial resources but also tarnished the family's public image and jeopardized relationships with key stakeholders.

❧

While business discussions typically revolve around strategy and financial matters, the human element, including emotions and relationships, plays a crucial role in the dynamics of family-run enterprises. Instances where familial relationships extend beyond the professional world may introduce complexities that need careful consideration.

Jealousy and personal differences within a family can indeed become potent catalysts for disputes. Sibling rivalries over perceived favouritism, unequal distribution of responsibilities or assets and varying levels of success among family members can sow seeds of resentment. These personal differences, if left unaddressed, may fester into deep-seated conflicts that jeopardize both familial bonds and the stability of the business.

For example, consider a scenario where one family member's entrepreneurial venture achieves significant success, while another's struggles to gain traction. The disparities in individual achievements, coupled with unresolved feelings of competition or inadequacy, can fuel jealousy and contribute to family disputes.

Understanding human emotions and behavioural traits is paramount for impactful succession planning in family businesses. Emotions such as greed, jealousy, hatred, lust and anger, if not addressed and understood, can potentially disrupt families and derail any succession plan.

Greed, when unchecked, can lead to internal conflicts over wealth distribution, causing fractures within the family. Jealousy, often fuelled by perceptions of favouritism or unequal treatment, can breed resentment among family members, negatively affecting collaboration and cooperation. Hatred, if harboured within the family, can escalate into irreparable damage, leading to legal battles or complete breakdowns in communication. Lust for power or control can create power struggles among family members, hindering the smooth transition of leadership. Anger, if unmanaged, can escalate disputes, impair decision-making, and create a toxic family environment. Among the spectrum of emotions, even those associated with personal relationships, such as romantic entanglements or lust, can potentially introduce challenges in the context of succession planning.

It is crucial to recognize that these emotions are inherent to human nature and can influence interpersonal dynamics within a family business. For instance, a succession plan might face challenges when a family member's greed for a larger share of the business conflicts with the agreed-upon distribution. Jealousy could arise if one successor is perceived to be favoured over others, leading to resentment and rivalry.

Hatred among family members may result in legal battles that can jeopardize the stability of the business. Unaddressed anger can lead to confrontations that have the potential to damage relationships and, subsequently, the business.

Examining ancient history across various cultures and religions reveals the same theme—families often break apart due to fundamental human emotions. Whether in Greek mythology, Hindu epics or biblical tales, the narratives echo familial discord caused by these elemental forces. From the Greek House of Atreus to the Hindu *Mahabharata* and biblical stories like Cain and Abel, the consequences of family strife are evident. Similar instances occur in Roman history, Chinese folklore and Egyptian dynasties. This historical pattern underscores the enduring challenge of navigating human emotions within families. Thus, proactive succession planning and strengthening family values emerge not merely as practical needs but as crucial commitments to shaping a resilient legacy.

Maintaining a professional boundary and ensuring a focus on business-related decisions becomes paramount in addressing such nuanced issues. Balancing personal relationships with the professional requirements of succession planning is essential for preserving the integrity and functionality of the family business.

Family disputes in business families can be influenced by not only internal dynamics but also external factors, adding layers of complexity to the already intricate web of relationships. External influences such as economic downturns, changes in industry regulations or shifts in market dynamics can significantly impact family businesses, potentially giving rise to disagreements on how to navigate these challenges.

Addressing these external and internal influences requires a proactive approach. Establishing clear communication channels and fostering a culture of openness within the family can help mitigate misunderstandings. Additionally, seeking external expertise, such as family business consultants or mediators, can provide impartial insights and facilitate constructive dialogue.

However, one must keep in mind that external advisors, such as legal professionals or consultants, may unintentionally exacerbate disputes if not chosen carefully. Conflicting advice or biased opinions can intensify existing tensions. Moreover, disputes arising from external influences can impact the family's reputation, leading to potential challenges in attracting investors, retaining key employees or sustaining customer trust. Therefore, utmost caution must be exercised when choosing who to consult.

Dispute resolution within business families is a delicate balancing act that involves navigating intricate relationships, preserving trust and safeguarding the future of both the family and the business. The unique blend of personal and professional ties makes resolving disputes in business families especially challenging.

Confronting family differences does not necessarily imply a hostile confrontation. Instead, it involves acknowledging the existence of differences, fostering open communication and seeking mediation or professional advice when needed. Proactive family meetings, facilitated discussions and the establishment of clear governance structures are essential steps in mitigating disputes.

Moreover, adopting a mindset of collaboration rather than competition within the family can help alleviate jealousy and personal differences. Implementing fair and transparent governance structures, including mechanisms for conflict resolution, can create a foundation for navigating disputes effectively.

Trust, a cornerstone in any family, takes centre stage during dispute resolution. The rupture of trust can have long-lasting implications, potentially jeopardizing the foundation on which the family business rests. Rebuilding trust requires open communication, transparency and a commitment to addressing underlying issues. Family heads play a crucial role in facilitating this process by fostering an environment where trust can be restored, recognizing that it is a gradual and delicate endeavour.

The future of the business family hangs in the balance during disputes. Decisions made during resolution processes can significantly impact the trajectory of the business, succession plans and overall sustainability. Family heads must carefully consider the implications of their actions on the long-term health of the family business. This may involve making tough choices that align with the overarching goals and values of the family.

For example, if there is a dispute over succession, family heads might need to impartially evaluate the capabilities of potential successors, keeping the best interests of the business at the forefront. In cases of financial disagreements, finding compromises that balance individual interests with the financial health of the business becomes paramount.

All in all, mutual respect and trust form the bedrock of any successful family business. When disputes arise and these foundational elements erode, the repercussions are felt throughout the organization. The collaborative spirit that fuels innovation and growth is replaced by an atmosphere of discord, hindering the effective functioning of the business.

For example, when it comes to valuation, the perception of stability and unity is a key factor influencing how external stakeholders, investors and the market at large perceive a family business. A business tarnished by internal disputes loses its lustre, leading to a decline in overall valuation. Investors and partners become wary of involvement in a venture plagued by familial discord, as the associated risks loom larger than potential returns.

The destructive impact extends to the operational aspects of the business. Efficiency dwindles as attention shifts from strategic initiatives to internal conflict resolution. This diversion of energy and resources hampers the business's ability to adapt to market dynamics, innovate and stay competitive.

Furthermore, family disputes often escalate into legal battles, draining both financial and emotional resources. Legal proceedings can result in substantial financial losses, impacting the bottom line and further diminishing the business's valuation. The protracted nature of legal disputes adds an additional layer of uncertainty, creating an undesirable environment for potential investors or partners.

Thus, to safeguard the value of a family business, it is important to prioritize mutual respect and trust. Family heads must recognize that nurturing a culture of open communication, conflict resolution and shared values is an investment in the longevity and prosperity of the business. By addressing disputes promptly, transparently and with a commitment to rebuilding trust, family businesses can mitigate the destructive forces that threaten their valuation.

SKIPPING A GENERATION

Navigating the path of succession planning in family businesses often involves complex decisions, and among them is the consideration of skipping a generation. This strategic choice can be influenced by a multitude of factors, including the perceived capabilities, qualifications and readiness of the chosen successors. On the professional front, the desire to inject fresh perspectives and expertise into leadership roles might prompt a family head to leapfrog to the next generation. Simultaneously, personal relationships, trust dynamics and the ability of the surprise successor to align with the family's values can be critical variables in this decision.

Navigating succession planning in a family business is often fraught with complexities and emotional nuances. One such strategy that can spark both admiration and contention is the decision to skip a generation. While this approach may seem strategic from a business standpoint, it carries inherent risks of discord and strained relationships within the family. The emotional ramifications of such a decision can be profound, potentially giving rise to feelings of resentment and exclusion among family members who may feel overlooked.

Skipping a generation might be viewed as disruptive, challenging established norms and disrupting the anticipated order of ascension. However, the path to a resilient family business is seldom a straightforward one, and sometimes, challenging the expected trajectory is exactly what is needed for innovation, growth and the safeguarding of the family legacy. It is a decision that demands strategic foresight, a willingness to weather discontent and a firm belief that sometimes, the road less travelled leads to unforeseen prosperity.

Open and honest conversations become imperative in mitigating these challenges. Transparent communication can help manage expectations, address concerns and foster a shared understanding of the rationale behind the chosen succession strategy.

For instance, imagine a scenario where the head of a family business identifies a talented grandchild as the ideal successor, skipping over their own children. This decision might be rooted in the belief that the grandchild possesses a unique blend of skills and innovative thinking crucial for steering the business in a rapidly evolving market. However, such a move can trigger intense emotions within the immediate children, leading to feelings of inadequacy or neglect.

In another context, a family patriarch might choose a younger generation to foster a sense of continuity and adaptability in the face of technological advancements. The decision could be an acknowledgement that the younger family members are more in tune with contemporary business trends and possess the agility required for navigating a dynamic industry landscape.

In such scenarios, transparent and open communication becomes paramount in addressing concerns and managing expectations. By engaging in honest conversations, family members can gain insight into the rationale behind the chosen succession strategy and find common ground amidst differing perspectives.

Conversations around skipping a generation in succession planning are multifaceted. While the rationale might be clear from a strategic standpoint, the emotional fallout within the family is often underestimated. It is crucial for family leaders to anticipate these emotional responses and proactively engage in discussions that not only explain the decision but also emphasize the shared vision for the family's future. This includes addressing concerns, clarifying expectations and instilling a sense of unity even in the face of unconventional succession choices.

In such scenarios, family leaders must tread carefully, recognizing that their decisions have repercussions beyond the business realm. Successful navigation through this challenge requires a delicate balance between strategic foresight and familial harmony. Transparent communication becomes the linchpin in maintaining family cohesion while ushering in the next generation of leadership. The goal is to build an inclusive environment where every family member feels valued, even when succession decisions deviate from traditional expectations.

Succession planning, especially when it involves bypassing a generation, requires a thoughtful approach that balances the strategic needs of the business with the emotional well-being of the family.

OUT-OF-WEDLOCK CHILDREN IN SUCCESSION PLANNING

Navigating succession planning in a family business often involves addressing sensitive and complex issues, including those related to unacknowledged or out-of-wedlock children. The topic poses a sensitive challenge for business families, intertwining personal and professional space. The touchiness arises from the complex interplay of social norms, cultural expectations and legal considerations.

Acknowledging children born out of wedlock involves navigating a myriad of emotional, ethical and reputational factors, adding layers of intricacy to the already delicate fabric of family dynamics. Beyond the legal and regulatory hurdles, it demands a profound level of family acceptance and candid conversations. Tackling this sensitive topic head-on is no easy feat, but it is not uncharted territory for Indian business families.

In Indian society, scenarios involving unacknowledged or out-of-wedlock children are not uncommon, spanning across various social segments and family structures. It is not unusual for affluent individuals to have 'second' families outside of marriage, a situation that requires delicate handling with personal care and seriousness.

While these matters may have been kept under wraps or overlooked in the past, they merit careful consideration and equal accountability in succession discussions. It is essential to approach these situations with empathy, sensitivity and a commitment to fairness for all family members, regardless of their background or circumstances.

Incorporating unacknowledged or out-of-wedlock children into succession planning requires first and foremost acknowledging their existence and ensuring they are afforded the same opportunities and rights as other family members. This approach fosters a culture of inclusivity and respect within the family, honouring each individual's contribution and heritage. By addressing these matters with sensitivity, families can strengthen bonds, uphold integrity and pave the way for a more harmonious succession process.

In conservative social contexts, acknowledging such children can be met with societal judgement, potentially impacting the family's reputation and standing. Business families, often operating under public scrutiny, must carefully weigh the potential impact on their image and legacy. Moreover, the inherent privacy surrounding family matters intensifies the challenge, making it a deeply personal and guarded subject.

In succession planning, accepting children born out of wedlock introduces variables such as questions about legitimacy, fair distribution of wealth and concerns about competency. Sensitive discussions surrounding these issues can potentially lead to family disputes, especially when there are divergent views among family members or between generations.

The touchiness of this topic necessitates a delicate, empathetic approach that considers the emotional well-being of all parties involved. Open and honest communication, supported by professional guidance, becomes crucial in addressing these complex matters. Resolving such challenges requires a careful balance between family values, societal expectations and the imperative to ensure fairness and inclusivity in the succession planning process.

∾

The treatment of the topic of out-of-wedlock or unacknowledged children in business families is usually dictated by societal notions of morality. In many cultures, there exists a historical tendency to associate legitimacy with moral values, making discussions on these matters highly sensitive. Business families, often held to elevated societal standards, may choose to avoid open conversations on such topics to prevent potential erosion of trust and to maintain their esteemed social standing.

Addressing issues related to children born out of wedlock can inadvertently expose the family to moral judgements, potentially affecting their reputation and the perception of family values. The avoidance of these discussions is, in part, a protective measure aimed at shielding the family from undue scrutiny and ensuring that their public image remains untarnished. As a result, these matters are frequently treated with a degree of discretion, with families opting for a private and confidential approach to preserve the delicate balance between personal and public spheres.

In the domain of publicly listed companies, where adherence to corporate governance standards is paramount, the integration of out-of-wedlock offspring into succession planning necessitates a delicate equilibrium between legal conformity and the assurance of capable leadership. First, legal and regulatory compliance frameworks must be meticulously adhered to, ensuring seamless transitions and minimizing any disruptions to business operations. Second, proactive measures to foster transparency and accountability within the succession process are vital to instilling investor confidence and upholding the company's reputation in the market.

However, navigating the inclusion of out-of-wedlock children in succession planning demands a nuanced approach that goes even beyond legal frameworks. While legal provisions may delineate financial rights, the intricacies of family dynamics, competency evaluations and governance considerations necessitate comprehensive internal discussions.

Succession strategies must meticulously evaluate the successor's competencies, preparedness and alignment with the family's values and business ethos. The intricate nature of succession planning in the context of listed entities mandates comprehensive assessments of potential successor's qualifications, aptitude and strategic vision. Such evaluations not only safeguard the company's corporate governance integrity but also mitigate risks associated with familial dynamics and ownership structures.

The key lies in fostering open communication within the family to address emotional concerns, competencies and the long-term vision for the business. Successful succession planning acknowledges the multifaceted nature of family relationships and strives for a balanced, fair and transparent approach to accommodate the diverse dynamics associated with out-of-wedlock children.

We must not forget—addressing the presence of out-of-wedlock or unacknowledged children in the context of family businesses is not only about navigating legal intricacies; it is fundamentally tied to issues of dignity, self-respect, fairness and fostering a sense of belonging. Every individual, irrespective of their circumstances of birth, deserves to be treated with dignity and fairness. What is required is a careful balance between upholding family values, respecting the rights and dignity of every family member, and ensuring a sense of belonging for all. Navigating this terrain involves crafting solutions that honour the inherent worth of each family member, fostering an environment where everyone feels respected, valued and integral to the family's collective journey.

THE ISSUE OF FAILED MARRIAGES

The significance of marriage within business families extends beyond personal relationships; it is intricately intertwined with the very fabric of the business. Much like equity capital or social capital, the stability and success of marriages among family members are pivotal components contributing to the overall health of the business. A harmonious and supportive marital environment fosters a positive atmosphere, enhancing collaboration and focus within the family business.

Conversely, the challenges or failures in marital relationships can introduce complexities that resonate throughout the professional, financial and operational dimensions of the business. Recognizing marriage as a critical element akin to their capital assets emphasizes the need for careful consideration and strategic planning to ensure the well-being of both familial and business spheres.

Familial relationships, particularly marriages within business families, are subjected to dual scrutiny—both as individual, personal bonds and as matters of public scrutiny by a larger audience. The nature of business families, especially those listed, exposes them to heightened public interest and market scrutiny. Consequently, the personal lives of family members, including marital relationships, become linked with the public image of the family and its businesses. The perception of stability, harmony and success within the family unit contributes to the overall reputation and market confidence in the business.

As a result, the private dynamics of familial relationships are not only individual matters but also critical components influencing the broader perception of the family and its businesses in the public eye. Striking a balance between personal privacy and the public image becomes a delicate yet imperative consideration for business families.

Marriage breakups or strained marriages within a business family can significantly impact the fabric of succession planning. The complexities introduced by divorce or troubled marriages create ripple effects, influencing not only personal relationships but also the dynamics of leadership and ownership transitions within the family business.

In instances where family members undergo divorce, questions related to ownership stakes, financial settlements and potential shifts in loyalty arise. These situations can amplify existing family disputes, potentially jeopardizing the unity and coherence required for effective succession planning.

For instance, divorced family members may choose to sell their ownership stakes or advocate for specific successors, introducing an additional layer of intricacy into the succession process. Navigating these challenges requires a delicate balance of addressing personal matters with the broader business continuity goals, emphasizing the need for clear communication, fair resolutions and well-defined governance structures.

Marriage breakups or strained marriages within a business family can introduce multifaceted challenges to the already intricate realm of succession planning. Consider a scenario where a family member undergoing a divorce seeks a substantial financial settlement that involves liquidating a portion of their ownership in the family business. This financial restructuring could affect the overall valuation and financial stability of the business, disrupting carefully crafted succession plans.

Furthermore, the emotional fallout from a divorce might lead to fractured relationships within the family, potentially influencing the choice of successors or creating factions based on alliances and loyalties. In some instances, divorced family members may pursue independent business ventures, raising questions about non-compete clauses and the protection of the family business's interests.

Complications can escalate when there are disagreements over the involvement of divorced spouses in key decision-making processes or when stepfamilies become part of the broader succession landscape. The potential for disputes over inheritance, entitlements and the allocation of family assets adds additional layers of complexity.

Failed marriages within business families can introduce intricate complications that reverberate through various settings and scenarios. The ramifications extend beyond personal relationships, impacting professional, financial and operational dimensions of the family business, such as:

- **Wealth division and alimony:** In the aftermath of a failed marriage involving family members in business, the division of wealth becomes a critical consideration. Disentangling shared assets, including business stakes, can lead to financial complexities. Additionally, potential alimony and support obligations may strain the financial resources of the family and the business.
- **Boardroom tensions:** If divorcing spouses hold positions on the board or in executive roles, tensions may arise during board meetings or strategic discussions. Divorced family members may find it challenging to set aside personal differences, potentially hindering effective decision-making and collaborative efforts within the business.
- **Succession planning revisions:** A failed marriage may necessitate revisions to existing succession plans. If divorcing family members were earmarked for key leadership roles, adjustments in the succession strategy become imperative. This can lead to uncertainties and debates about the future direction of the business.
- **Impact on business relationships:** The fallout from a failed marriage can extend to the business's external relationships. Clients, partners and stakeholders may become wary of potential disruptions or internal conflicts within the family business, affecting the trust and credibility the business has built.
- **Legal and regulatory challenges:** Legal complexities can arise when divorcing family members are shareholders or involved in decision-making processes. Compliance with legal requirements, especially in jurisdictions where marital property laws apply, becomes crucial. This includes navigating potential conflicts of interest and adhering to corporate governance standards.
- **Employee morale and culture:** Failed marriages can affect the internal dynamics of the business, impacting the morale of non-family employees. A strained family environment may permeate the company culture, leading to decreased job satisfaction, increased employee turnover and challenges in maintaining a positive workplace atmosphere.
- **Media and public scrutiny:** High-profile business families may face increased media and public scrutiny during divorce proceedings. The

potential for negative publicity can tarnish the family's reputation, influencing customer perception and stakeholder confidence in the business.

In the context of Indian business families, considering prenuptial agreements or their legal equivalent, depending on the legal frameworks applicable to marriages, is a prudent strategy that can help mitigate potential risks and uncertainties in succession planning. Indian laws, influenced by cultural and societal factors, often prioritize the sanctity of marriage and family, and prenuptial agreements have not been as widely acknowledged or enforced as in some other jurisdictions. However, with the globalization of families and individuals, many business families are spread across different countries, each with its own legal landscape.

Prenuptial agreements can serve as a proactive measure to address concerns related to asset division, inheritance and financial settlements in the unfortunate event of a marriage dissolution. These legal instruments can define the financial rights and responsibilities of each spouse, helping to safeguard family wealth and business assets.

Considering the complexity of business structures, including family-owned enterprises, having a clear agreement in place can contribute to the smooth functioning of the business in case of marital discord. It is essential to involve legal experts who understand the nuances of both family and business laws in the relevant jurisdictions.

However, introducing prenuptial agreements in Indian business families requires a sensible balance between legal provisions and cultural sensitivities. Open communication within the family and an emphasis on mutual understanding can facilitate the acceptance and implementation of such agreements. Ultimately, the decision to explore any such agreements should align with the family's values, legal considerations and the specific dynamics of each situation. It is a proactive step that can contribute to the long-term stability and continuity of family wealth and businesses.

Another area to look at when thinking of solutions to this issue is managing public perception. In the age of pervasive social media and gossip columns, public scrutiny has become an inescapable reality for business families. The private lives of family members, including marital relationships, can often become subjects of speculation and rumours.

However, a mature and proactive approach to handling such situations can help mitigate the impact of public scrutiny. Business families that prioritize transparent communication, address issues openly and share information responsibly can actively manage their public image. By taking control of the narrative and emphasizing the human aspect of their lives, they can navigate public curiosity and prevent unfounded rumours from affecting their reputation.

Furthermore, business families need to recognize that their private relationships, including marriages, are not solely individual matters but are closely intertwined with the public image of the family and its businesses. This interconnectedness arises due to the nature of business families, especially the ones that are listed or have significant public visibility. The success or failure of familial relationships can have repercussions beyond personal consequences, impacting the perception of the family in the eyes of stakeholders, investors and the wider public. Therefore, a conscientious approach to familial relationships becomes an integral part of managing the holistic reputation of the business family.

THE A TO Z GUIDE FOR INTROSPECTION

Here are a set of questions to ask yourself and your family members.

A for Adaptation

1. How has your family business adapted to changing market trends over the years?
2. Can you share an instance where adaptation played a crucial role in your family business's success?
3. What strategies do you employ to encourage a culture of adaptation within your business?

B for Balance of Business Legacy

1. What values or traditions from the past generations are still integral to your family business?
2. How do you balance preserving the legacy of your family business while embracing innovation?
3. Can you share a memorable story or lesson passed down through generations in your family?

C for Collaboration

1. How does your family foster collaboration among members involved in the business?
2. Can you share an example of a successful collaboration that has positively impacted your business?
3. What strategies do you employ to resolve conflicts and maintain harmony within the family business?

D for Diversification

1. How has your family business diversified its offerings over the years?
2. Can you share a key decision related to diversification that had a significant impact?
3. What advice do you have for other family businesses considering diversification?

E for Entrepreneurship

1. What does entrepreneurship mean to your family, and how has it shaped your business journey?
2. Can you share a moment where a family member displayed exceptional entrepreneurial spirit?
3. How do you foster an entrepreneurial mindset within the younger generation of your family?

F for Family

1. How do you strike a balance between family dynamics and business decisions?
2. Can you share a challenge related to family dynamics and how it was overcome for the sake of the business?
3. What rituals or practices help strengthen the family bond within the context of the business?

G for Governance

1. How does your family prioritize and implement corporate governance in the business?
2. Can you share a situation where adherence to governance principles led to a positive outcome?
3. What steps do you take to ensure transparency and accountability in your family business?

H for Human Capital

1. How does your family business invest in the development and retention of talented individuals across all levels?
2. In what ways do you cultivate a culture that values diversity, inclusion and collaboration among family and non-family employees?
3. How do you strike a balance between hiring family members and external professionals to ensure the long-term success of the business?

I for Innovation

1. How does your family business foster a culture of innovation?
2. Can you share a specific innovation that has set your business apart in the industry?

3. How do you encourage the younger generation to bring fresh ideas to the table?

I for Integrity

1. How has maintaining integrity been a guiding principle for your family business?
2. Can you recall an instance where upholding integrity was challenging but crucial?
3. What measures do you take to ensure ethical practices within your family business?

J for Journey

1. Can you reflect on the journey of your family business and highlight key milestones?
2. How has the journey of your family business shaped the values and principles you follow?
3. Can you share a personal anecdote that represents a significant point in your family business's journey?

K for Knowledge with Wisdom

1. How does your family business prioritize knowledge transfer across generations? Can you share a piece of wisdom passed down through generations that still resonates in your business today?
2. Can you share an example of how continuous learning has contributed to your business's success? Further, how does the wisdom gained from past experiences guide decision-making in your family business?
3. What initiatives do you have in place to stay ahead in terms of industry knowledge and trends? Moreover, how do you balance incorporating new ideas with the wisdom of tradition in your family business?

L for Leadership

1. How do you define effective leadership within the context of your family business?
2. Can you share a challenge where strong leadership was pivotal in overcoming obstacles?

3. What leadership qualities do you believe are essential for the next generation of family members in the business?

M for Mentorship

1. How does mentorship play a role in the personal and professional development of family members within the business?
2. Can you share a mentorship experience that had a significant impact on your career?
3. What advice do you have for fostering mentorship relationships within a family business?

N for Next Generation

1. How does your family prepare the next generation for leadership roles in the business?
2. Can you share a specific initiative aimed at developing the skills of the younger family members?
3. What challenges do you foresee in transitioning leadership to the next generation, and how do you plan to address them?

O for Opportunities

1. How does your family business identify and capitalize on new opportunities in the market?
2. Can you share a story where seizing an opportunity led to significant growth for your business?
3. What strategies do you employ to stay agile and adapt to emerging opportunities?

P for Philanthropy

1. How does your family business contribute to philanthropic initiatives?
2. Can you share a memorable experience related to a philanthropic endeavour supported by your family?
3. What values guide your family's approach to giving back to the community?

Q for Quality

1. How does your family business maintain a commitment to quality in its products or services?
2. Can you share a situation where ensuring quality was a top priority and yielded positive results?
3. What measures do you take to continuously improve and innovate in terms of quality standards?

R for Resilience

1. How has your family business demonstrated resilience in the face of challenges or crises?
2. Can you share a specific instance where resilience was crucial to overcoming adversity?
3. What practices or strategies contribute to building resilience within your family business?

S for Succession

1. How does your family plan for and navigate the succession process in the business?
2. Can you share a success story of a smooth transition between generations in your family business?
3. What lessons have you learned from succession experiences, and how do you share them with others in similar situations?

T for Technology

1. How does your family business embrace and leverage technology to stay competitive?
2. Can you share a transformative moment where adopting new technology had a significant impact?
3. What role does innovation in technology play in the long-term strategy of your family business?

U for Unity

1. How does your family business foster unity among its members, especially during challenging times?

2. Can you share a situation where unity within the family was critical for business success?
3. What rituals or practices contribute to maintaining a sense of unity within the family business?

V for Values

1. How do the core values of your family influence the decisions and actions within the business?
2. Can you share an instance when staying true to your values led to a difficult but important decision?
3. What steps do you take to ensure that the values of your family business are passed down through generations?

W for Women in Business

1. Has there been an active involvement of women in leadership roles in your family business, and how has it influenced the overall dynamics and its success?
2. Can you share specific initiatives or strategies your family business has implemented to support and empower women in various capacities within the organization?
3. In what ways do you ensure equal opportunities and recognition for women in your family business, and how has this contributed to a more inclusive and diverse work environment?

X for (E)Xcellence

1. How does your family business strive for excellence in its operations and offerings?
2. Can you share a success story where a commitment to excellence was a driving force?
3. What practices or initiatives contribute to a culture of continuous improvement and excellence within your family business?

Y for Yield

1. How does your family business approach risk and yield in decision-making?

2. Can you share a situation where taking calculated risks resulted in a positive yield for your business?
3. What factors do you consider when evaluating the potential yield of a new business opportunity?

Z for Zeal

1. How do passion and zeal contribute to the success and sustainability of your family business?
2. Can you share a story where unwavering zeal played a crucial role in overcoming obstacles?
3. What strategies do you employ to maintain enthusiasm and zeal within the family and the business?

Part Five

Family Council

A family council serves as the heart of a well-run family business, fostering communication, alignment and collective decision-making across generations. This section explores the structure, purpose and role of family councils in bridging the gap between familial relationships and business governance. From defining clear roles and responsibilities to addressing conflicts and setting long-term goals, these chapters offer a roadmap for creating a platform where every voice is heard and the family's legacy is preserved. In a world where personal dynamics can easily spill into boardroom decisions, a well-functioning family council can transform potential discord into a shared vision for the future.

THE THOUGHT BEHIND FAMILY COUNCIL

Conventional wisdom and anecdotal evidence assert that family businesses, with their unique structures and leadership styles, have a long-term orientation that is supposedly lacking in traditional public firms. However, the specifics distinguishing family businesses remain largely unexplored. Each family is unique, with some commonalities and entrepreneurial–cultural values that they share with business families around the world.

Entrepreneurship ingrained in the history of multi-generational organizations is all about their resilience—their will to grit it out and survive and scale, their aspiration to be relevant and exist in the industry. Amidst structural and cultural constraints, sustaining entrepreneurial spirit across the organization is essential for competitiveness.

Yet, this quality often diminishes when leadership becomes fixated on operational efficiencies. Successful family businesses exhibit unwavering commitment to entrepreneurship, distinguishing them from their peers. They have this streak of entrepreneurship that allows them to move ahead despite flaws and failures.

The failure of family businesses to transition across generations, and the disinterest of younger generations in assuming significant responsibility within family businesses, stem from multiple familial challenges. Younger members may lack the preparedness or inclination to lead, potentially due to inadequate training or reluctance to manage the business or report to other family shareholders. Sometimes they feel the business is not to their liking.

Long-term business success hinges not only on operational performance but also on familial and ownership cohesion. Neglecting family unity and ownership support jeopardizes sustained business performance.

Establishing firm family structures demands thorough introspection, consensus and foresight, which needs time and patience to navigate the difficult conversations among the family members. Anticipating and addressing sensitive topics requires statesmanship-like leadership or saint leadership, empathy to understand everyone's views, and wisdom to balance the differences and sift aside the dissent. Facilitating open discussions within the family, free from discord, is essential for effective governance.

Invariably, family businesses require a defined vision, governance framework and members capable of navigating it with transparency, fairness, respect and stewardship. Anticipating the breadth of topics to be addressed in governance structures, such as new business ventures, succession, dividend policy and role allocation, is crucial. Large multi-generational family enterprises embed a strong sense of purpose within their ownership ethos. They develop agreements, both oral and written, to govern board composition, key decisions, CEO appointments and family member involvement in the business. The ongoing interpretation of these agreements involves various family forums, such as a family council and assembly, to build consensus on significant issues. While long-term survivors often adopt a meritocratic management approach, policies are tailored based on family size, values, education and industry dynamics.

Good governance is essential for the smooth functioning of family businesses, with clarity on roles, rights and responsibilities being paramount. This clarity extends to all members across the three circles of family, business employees and owners, fostering a culture of responsibility and accountability. Furthermore, the appropriate inclusion of family and owners in business discussions is crucial for informed decision-making.

❧

Family governance typically comprises three components:

1. Family assemblies
2. Family council meetings
3. Family constitution

While assemblies provide a platform for all family members to convene and discuss business matters, family council meetings facilitate strategic planning, policy creation and communication enhancement. At the same time, the family constitution serves as a written document outlining the family's policies, vision and values, regulating their relationship with the business. Transitioning a family-owned business to the next generation involves navigating complex relationships and numerous challenges along the way, and these three help with that.

As the business, family and ownership groups evolve, it is imperative that the membership and functions of governance structures adapt accordingly. A first-generation family business might suffice with a small, informal advisory board, while a third-generation family may require a family assembly and council to accommodate a larger and more diverse group. It is evident that as ownership becomes more divided over generations, adjustments to the board composition and the role of the family council are necessary. One must take proactive steps to create or modify these structures to meet current needs and regularly discuss updates to ensure they align with evolving family involvement.

Another thing to note is the common misconception that the board of directors and the family council serve the same function. However, they have distinct roles: the family council formulates policies for the family and advises the board on family-related matters, such as family employment within the business, while the board of directors sets policies for the business and may offer recommendations to the family council on business-related issues.

The board and family council must synchronize their efforts and respect each other's boundaries. This coordination can take various forms, such as regular updates on objectives, annual joint planning sessions or having a board member sit on the council, and vice versa.

In family businesses, cultivating trust, pride and teamwork among members is essential for maintaining commitment and discipline in their relationship with the business. Emphasizing consensus decisions, openness to diverse viewpoints, and transparency in company operations and decision-making processes can foster a cohesive environment. If there is reluctance within the family to engage in necessary discussions due to concerns about conflict or lack of understanding, consider hiring a council convenor to facilitate meetings and ensure productive communication.

Family is a unique social institution bound together by emotional ties among its members. Unlike in a business setting, where relationships among employees are contractual, the quality of relationships in a family is shaped by shared values and purposes. This delicate system requires constant nurturing.

In a family business context, the bonding among family members generates positive energy and a collective pool of non-monetary resources. This enables family businesses to not only endure challenges but also to establish lasting legacies, contingent upon a strong alignment of goals and intentions.

While initially, treating the family in a more formal or structured manner may feel unfamiliar, the value of this approach becomes evident over time. Many families have found that introducing some level of structure enhances discussions on sensitive issues and fosters better communication.

❧

Let us get to the family assembly first. Typically, it is an annual event lasting one to two days and includes all adult family members, including spouses. Families may choose to involve younger generations in meetings starting from high school age. For younger children, organizing group activities can be an effective way to introduce them to the business and foster relationships with their relatives.

Family assembly activities encompass learning about the business through presentations by both family and non-family managers, engaging in discussions (without making decisions) regarding the company's direction, and acquiring knowledge about critical skills such as interpreting financial statements. Additionally, it serves as a platform to stay informed about family-related developments such as significant events, achievements and changes in ownership, including any shares changing hands or the involvement of strategic investors.

The family council, on the other hand, is a strategic forum where core members come together to discuss and plan for the future of both the family and the business. The establishment of a family council reflects a forward-thinking approach to addressing the complex dynamics and challenges faced by family-owned businesses.

The overarching goal of the family council is to promote unity, transparency and effective governance within the family enterprise. By providing a structured platform for communication and decision-making, the council helps align the interests and aspirations of family members with the long-term vision and goals of the business.

One of the key considerations behind the formation of a family council is the recognition of the diverse perspectives, talents and experiences that exist within the family. By harnessing the collective wisdom and insights of multiple generations and branches of the family, the council can develop more robust strategies and policies that reflect the values and priorities of all stakeholders.

Moreover, the family council plays a vital role in fostering intergenerational dialogue and continuity. As younger family members prepare to assume leadership roles and responsibilities within the business, the council provides a platform for mentorship, knowledge transfer and succession planning. By engaging with younger generations early on, the council can ensure a smooth transition of leadership and preserve the family legacy for future generations.

Additionally, the family council serves as a mechanism for addressing complex family dynamics and resolving conflicts in a constructive manner. By providing a structured framework for communication and dispute resolution, the council can help mitigate tensions and strengthen relationships within the family, thereby safeguarding the cohesion and unity essential for long-term success.

Overall, the family council represents a proactive approach to family governance that recognizes the interconnectedness of family and business interests. By fostering collaboration, communication and shared decision-making, the council helps shape the future direction of the family enterprise, ensuring its continued prosperity and sustainability for generations to come.

A properly composed and managed family council can play a crucial role in this process by:

- establishing clarity on roles, rights and responsibilities for family members;

- encouraging responsible behaviour from family members, family employees and owners towards both the business and the family; and
- facilitating appropriate family and owner participation in business discussions.

The family council may also formulate policies on various aspects, such as employment standards for the next generation, career development, family compensation, succession planning, ownership agreements and dividend distribution. While these topics primarily concern business policies, the family council would typically consult with the board and obtain its endorsement before formalizing these policies.

❦

Responsible ownership is indispensable for the long-term viability of family businesses. Unity in ownership and clarity regarding rewards are pivotal for establishing enduring family enterprises. To safeguard ownership integrity, it is imperative to eliminate ambiguity concerning ownership rights by documenting ownership norms, rights and privileges through legally valid shareholder agreements. Such agreements precisely delineate ownership details, rules for transfer, inheritance, sale or exit, ensuring clarity among family members and minimising conflicts.

The Family Council can play a pivotal role in maintaining harmony and alignment within family-owned businesses, ensuring that the entrepreneurial spirit that propelled the business's inception continues to thrive. In addition to promoting innovation, the Family Council can ensure clarity on financial matters and other key issues, helping the family avoid misunderstandings and conflict. It nurtures intergenerational collaboration, providing younger members with an opportunity to learn from their predecessors while actively contributing to shaping the future of the business. Through structured discussions and decision-making processes, the council ensures that all family members are on the same page, protecting both the emotional and financial investments in the business. Ultimately, a well-functioning Family Council is essential for balancing tradition with innovation, allowing the business to evolve while safeguarding its legacy for future generations.

FORMATION OF THE FAMILY COUNCIL

Establishing a family council within a business family is a strategic imperative, serving as a crucial forum for open communication, decision-making and conflict resolution. The need for such a council arises from the multifaceted dynamics inherent in business families, where individual interests, diverse perspectives and potential conflicts must be navigated effectively.

The formation of a family council necessitates a thoughtful and inclusive approach. First and foremost, there should be a clear definition of its purpose and objectives. This involves outlining the specific goals the council aims to achieve, whether it be enhancing communication, facilitating succession planning or addressing disputes.

Constituting a family council involves identifying key family members who will be part of this governing body. Typically, this includes both active participants in the business and those with a stake in its success. Striking a balance between representation and efficiency is crucial to ensure that diverse voices are heard without impeding decision-making.

One of the challenges during the formation lies in aligning varying expectations and priorities. Family members may have divergent views on the council's role or approach its formation with scepticism. Overcoming these challenges requires proactive communication and a commitment to fostering an environment of trust and collaboration.

To develop a family council successfully, a robust governance structure is indispensable. This entails defining the council's powers and limitations to ensure that its decisions align with the broader family values and business goals. Establishing clear guidelines for decision-making processes and conflict-resolution mechanisms further contributes to the council's effectiveness.

Moreover, fostering an atmosphere of confidentiality is paramount. Family members must feel secure expressing their opinions without fear of repercussions. This trust-building process is incremental and requires continuous effort from all involved parties.

In essence, a family council serves as a linchpin for effective governance within business families, offering a platform for collective decision-making and conflict resolution. While challenges may arise during its formation, the long-term benefits of enhanced communication, shared values and strategic alignment make it an invaluable asset for the sustained success of the family business.

THE GUIDING PRINCIPLES

Forming a family council is a significant step in fostering cohesion, transparency and effective decision-making within a family-owned business. To ensure that the family council is engaging, effective and accountable, several key principles and practices should be considered.

First and foremost, the formation of the family council should be inclusive and participatory, involving representatives from various branches and generations of the family. This diversity ensures that a wide range of perspectives and interests are represented, fostering inclusivity and collective ownership of decisions.

Secondly, the family council should have clearly defined objectives, roles and responsibilities. This clarity helps members understand their purpose and contribution to the council's mission, enhancing engagement and accountability. Regular meetings should be scheduled to discuss important family and business matters, allowing for open dialogue, collaboration and consensus-building.

In addition, the family council should establish transparent communication channels to keep all members informed and engaged. This may include regular updates, newsletters or online platforms where information can be shared and discussed openly. Transparency builds trust and fosters a sense of accountability among council members.

Accountability mechanisms should also be put in place to ensure that decisions made by the family council are implemented effectively. This may include setting clear timelines, assigning responsibilities and monitoring progress towards established goals. Regular reviews and evaluations can help identify areas for improvement and ensure that the council remains focused and effective in its efforts.

Finally, the family council should prioritize ongoing education and development for its members, providing opportunities for skill-building, leadership development and knowledge-sharing. By investing in the growth and development of council members, the family can ensure that the council remains dynamic, forward-thinking and capable of addressing the evolving needs of the family and business.

Overall, by adhering to these principles and practices, a family council can become a highly engaging, effective and accountable body that plays a central role in the success and sustainability of the family-owned business.

❧

Based on these guiding principles, a set order of day-to-day conduct can be established keeping in mind the following:

- **Purpose and objectives:** Clearly articulate the purpose and objectives of the family council. Define its role in promoting communication, fostering unity, and addressing key family and business issues.
- **Membership criteria:** Establish clear criteria for membership, specifying who qualifies to be part of the family council. This may include active participants in the business, family members with ownership stakes, or other relevant criteria.
- **Decision-making processes:** Define the decision-making processes within the family council. Specify whether decisions are made by consensus, voting or through another established method. Clarify the authority and limitations of the family council in decision-making.
- **Confidentiality:** Emphasize the importance of confidentiality within the family council. Encourage open and honest communication while ensuring that sensitive family matters are treated with the utmost discretion.
- **Frequency and structure of meetings:** Outline how often the family council will meet and the structure of these meetings. Establish a regular schedule to facilitate consistent communication and collaboration among family members.
- **Agenda-setting:** Define how agendas for family council meetings are set. Encourage input from all members to ensure that relevant topics are addressed, and family concerns are heard.

- **Succession planning**: Incorporate succession planning as a key component of the family council's responsibilities. Specify how the council will contribute to the development and implementation of succession plans for family members in leadership roles.
- **Conflict resolution mechanisms:** Establish mechanisms for resolving conflicts within the family council. Define procedures for addressing disputes, ensuring fairness and maintaining a constructive environment for conflict resolution.
- **Educational initiatives:** Emphasize the importance of ongoing education for family members involved in the business. Encourage continuous learning and training and development to enhance the skills and knowledge of family members.
- **Communication protocols:** Define communication protocols within the family council. Specify how information will be shared, ensuring transparency while respecting the need for confidentiality in certain matters.
- **External advisors:** Address the role of external advisors, such as legal or financial professionals, within the family council. Define how and when external expertise will be sought to support decision-making.
- **Review and amendments:** Establish a process for regularly reviewing and amending the guiding principles. Recognize that family dynamics and business needs may evolve, requiring periodic adjustments to the family council's framework.

By carefully addressing these points, a family council can create a robust governance structure that contributes to the long-term success and sustainability of the business family.

STRUCTURE OF THE FAMILY COUNCIL

The structure and governance model of a family council are highly adaptable and contingent upon the specific needs, size and dynamics of each business family. There is no one-size-fits-all approach to establishing a family council, as the composition, responsibilities and decision-making processes must be tailored to accommodate the unique characteristics and objectives of the family enterprise.

Factors such as the number of family members involved, the complexity of the business operations, and the level of family unity and cohesion all play a significant role in shaping the structure and governance of the council. Considerations such as cultural norms, values and traditions within the family may influence the design and functioning of the council.

Furthermore, the evolution of a family council is an ongoing process that requires regular evaluation, assessment and refinement. As the family business grows and evolves over time, so too must the structure and governance model of the family council. A good family council will continuously measure its effectiveness, solicit feedback from members and adapt its composition, governance practices and impact to meet the changing needs and dynamics of the business family.

In essence, the structure and governance model of a family council are inherently unique to each family, reflecting the diversity and complexity of family-owned enterprises. By remaining flexible, responsive and committed to continuous improvement, a family council can serve as a valuable mechanism for promoting unity, communication and effective governance within the family enterprise. However, here's a typical framework:

1. **Chairperson:**
    - Responsible for leading and facilitating family council meetings
    - Acts as a liaison between family members and external advisors
    - Ensures that the council adheres to its purpose and objectives

2. **Council Members:**
    - Comprises family members actively involved in the business
    - May include members from both the senior and junior generations
    - Representatives from different branches of the family, if applicable

3. **Advisors/Consultants:**
    - External professionals, such as legal or financial advisors
    - Offer expertise on matters relevant to the family and business
    - Assist in decision-making processes

4. **Secretary/Coordinator**:
    - Manages administrative tasks related to meetings and communication
    - Keeps records of discussions, decisions and action items
    - Coordinates with members to ensure smooth functioning

5. **Committees:**
    - Subcommittees may be formed to address specific areas (e.g., succession planning, education, communication)
    - Comprise members with expertise or interest in the respective areas
    - Report findings and recommendations to the full family council

6. **Family Constitution:**
    - Outlines the purpose, objectives and structure of the family council
    - Defines the roles and responsibilities of council members
    - Specifies the decision-making processes and mechanisms

This structure provides a foundation for effective family governance, but it is crucial to customize it according to the family's specific context and objectives. The adaptability of the family council's structure allows it to evolve with changing circumstances and priorities.

HOW A FAMILY COUNCIL OPERATES

Beyond structure, the effectiveness of a Family Council lies in its functioning, which involves managing a wide range of responsibilities from decision-making processes to conflict resolution. While the earlier elements focus on setting up the council's framework, it is equally important to understand how it operates on a daily basis. The family council must handle sensitive family and business matters with transparency, efficiency and diplomacy. This list outlines key operational aspects such as regular meetings, communication channels, conflict resolution and succession planning. These elements ensure that the council is not just a formal structure but also a dynamic body actively shaping the family's business trajectory. The successful execution of these functions is critical for maintaining harmony, aligning interests and ensuring the long-term success of the business.

1. **Meetings:**
   - Regular meetings are scheduled to discuss various topics
   - Frequency may depend on the urgency of issues and the family's preferences
   - Special meetings may be called for critical decisions

2. **Decision-making Process:**
   - Consensus-building approach is often encouraged
   - Voting mechanisms may be established for certain decisions
   - Major decisions may require a higher level of agreement

3. **Communication Channels:**
   - Clear channels for communication among family members
   - Regular updates on family and business matters
   - Platforms for sharing ideas, concerns and feedback

4. **Training and Development:**
   - Initiatives to educate family members on business matters
   - Training programmes for potential successors
   - Continuous learning opportunities

5. **Conflict Resolution:**
   - Established mechanisms for addressing conflicts

- Mediation processes to resolve disputes amicably
- Focus on preserving family harmony

6. **Succession Planning:**
    - Plays a crucial role in identifying and preparing successors
    - Develops strategies for smooth transitions
    - Considers the interests and capabilities of potential leaders

7. **Review and Evaluation:**
    - Periodic reviews of the family council's effectiveness
    - Assessments of adherence to the family constitution
    - Adjustments and improvements based on feedback

8. **Inclusivity:**
    - Encourages the active participation of all eligible family members
    - Ensures that diverse perspectives are considered
    - Promotes a sense of belonging and shared responsibility

9. **Confidentiality:**
    - Establishes guidelines for maintaining confidentiality
    - Safeguards sensitive family and business information
    - Builds trust among council members

10. **Reporting to Stakeholders:**
    - Communicates with wider family members who may not be part of the council
    - Provides updates on key decisions and initiatives
    - Ensures transparency in governance

11. **External Relations:**
    - Represents the family in external forums
    - Engages with stakeholders, including investors and partners
    - Manages relationships with professional networks

12. **Emergency Protocols:**
    - Outlines procedures for handling emergencies or unforeseen events
    - Ensures a swift response to critical situations
    - Addresses business continuity concerns

An effective and well-functioning Family Council is not just a governance body—it is an effective engagement that ensures both the family and the business remain aligned and cohesive. By fostering open communication, promoting inclusivity and resolving conflicts, a robust Family Council creates a sense of shared purpose, bringing harmony among family members. It offers a structured platform where strategic decisions can be made with transparency and accountability, balancing family interests with business objectives. In doing so, the council safeguards the entrepreneurial spirit that built the business while steering it towards sustainable growth. Ultimately, a well-functioning Family Council is key to preserving family unity, driving business success and ensuring a legacy that endures for generations.

A TO Z QUESTIONS FOR THE FAMILY COUNCIL

A for Agenda-setting

- How is the agenda for family council meetings determined?
- Are family members encouraged to contribute topics for discussion?

B for Business Strategy

- How does the family council contribute to shaping the overall business strategy?
- What role does the family council play in long-term business planning?

C for Communication Protocols

- What are the established communication protocols within the family council?
- How is information shared among family members to ensure transparency?

D for Decision-making Processes

- What processes are in place for decision-making within the family council?
- Is there a defined method for reaching consensus or voting on key issues?

E for Education Initiatives

- How does the family council promote ongoing education for family members involved in the business?
- Are there specific initiatives to enhance skills and knowledge?

F for Frequency of Meetings

- How often does the family council convene for meetings?

- Is there a regular schedule, and are special sessions called when needed?

G for Governance Structure

- What governance structure does the family council follow?
- Are there specific roles and responsibilities assigned to family council members?

H for Harmony Preservation

- How does the family council address and preserve harmony within the family?
- Are there mechanisms in place to manage conflicts constructively?

I for Inclusivity

- How is inclusivity ensured in the family council?
- Are there criteria for family members to join or participate?

J for Joint Decision-making

- How does the family council handle joint decision-making between family members and external advisors?
- Is there a collaborative approach to important decisions?

K for Knowledge Transfer

- What steps does the family council take to facilitate knowledge transfer between generations?
- Is there a strategy for preserving institutional knowledge?

L for Legacy Preservation

- How is the family council involved in preserving the legacy of the business family?
- Are there initiatives to document and communicate the family's history and values?

M for Membership Criteria

- What criteria determine eligibility for membership in the family council?

- Are ownership stakes, active involvement or other factors considered?

N for Non-Family Professionals

- How does the family council manage collaboration between family and non-family professionals?
- Is there a strategy for fostering a positive working relationship?

O for Open Communication

- How does the family council encourage open communication among family members?
- Are there forums or channels for expressing concerns and ideas?

P for Purpose and Objectives

- What are the defined purpose and objectives of the family council?
- How are these aligned with the broader goals of the business family?

Q for Quality of Life Impact

- How does the family council consider the impact on the quality of life for family members involved in the business?
- Is there a balance between business responsibilities and personal well-being?

R for Review and Amendments

- Is there a process for regular review and potential amendments to the family council's structure and principles?
- How often is the framework assessed for relevance?

S for Succession Planning

- What role does the family council play in succession planning for leadership roles?
- How are successors identified, developed and prepared for their roles?

T for Transparency

- How does the family council ensure transparency in its processes and decision-making?

- Are there guidelines for sharing relevant information with stakeholders?

U for Unity Promotion

- What steps are taken to promote unity within the family through the family council?
- Is there a strategy for fostering collaboration among family members?

V for Values Alignment

- How is the family council aligned with the core values of the business family?
- Are there mechanisms for preserving and reinforcing these values?

W for Wealth Management

- How does the family council contribute to wealth management and financial planning?
- Is there a strategy for sustainable growth and distribution of wealth?

X for Xenodochial Atmosphere

- How does the family council foster a hospitable environment for diverse perspectives?
- Is there a welcoming approach to new ideas and external expertise?

Y for Youth Engagement

- How does the family council actively engage the younger generation in decision-making?
- What efforts are made to ensure a smooth transition and adaptation to evolving trends?

Z for Zeal for Learning

- How does the family council encourage a continuous zeal for learning among family members?
- Are there initiatives for ongoing education and personal development?

This comprehensive set of questions covers various dimensions that a family council should consider to ensure effective governance and collaboration within a business family.

Part Six

What's Next?

Preparing the next generation to lead while guiding the current one to step aside gracefully is one of the most delicate balancing acts in family businesses. This section delves into the twin challenges of grooming Gen Z for succession and helping retiring leaders redefine their purpose beyond the corner office. It also explores the critical role of choosing the right advisor—someone who can navigate both family dynamics and business strategy with wisdom and neutrality. Together, these chapters provide actionable insights for building a seamless transition of leadership and ensuring the family legacy thrives across generations.

GROOMING GEN Z FOR SUCCESSION

Grooming Generation Z (Gen Z) as part of succession planning poses unique challenges. It requires a sense of urgency due to several factors. First and foremost, Gen Z individuals, born roughly between the mid-1990s and early 2010s, have distinct characteristics and perspectives shaped by growing up in the digital age. Unlike previous generations, they are digital natives, accustomed to constant connectivity, rapid technological advancements and access to vast amounts of information at their fingertips. As a result, their approach to work, communication and problem-solving differs significantly from that of their predecessors.

One of the primary challenges in grooming Gen Z for succession planning is bridging the generation gap and understanding their worldview. Gen Z individuals tend to prioritize flexibility, autonomy and work–life balance, valuing experiences and meaningful contributions over traditional markers of success. They are also more inclined to seek purpose-driven work and expect organizations to align with their values and ethics. Therefore, family businesses must adapt their succession planning strategies to accommodate these preferences and engage Gen Z in ways that resonate with their priorities and aspirations.

Another challenge lies in addressing the information asymmetry that exists between generations. Unlike previous generations, Gen Z individuals have grown up in an era of unprecedented access to information, where knowledge is readily available and easily accessible online. As a result, they may not perceive information as a significant source of power or advantage, challenging traditional notions of expertise and hierarchy within family businesses. Therefore, grooming Gen Z for succession planning requires re-evaluating how knowledge is shared, valued and leveraged within the organization, emphasizing continuous learning, collaboration and innovation.

Furthermore, Gen Z individuals bring fresh perspectives and ideas to the table, but they may lack experience and exposure to the complexities of running a family business. As such, mentoring and leadership development programmes play a crucial role in grooming them for succession. These programmes should provide hands-on experience, exposure to different facets of the business, and opportunities for skill development and growth. Additionally, family businesses must create a supportive and inclusive culture that encourages open communication, experimentation and learning from failure.

The grooming of the next generation within a business family is a critical responsibility that goes beyond providing financial privileges, as we have already seen in Part IV.

The attributes of patience, the art of listening, humility and the ability to collaborate with diverse stakeholders are essential skills that contribute significantly to personal and professional growth. In the context of Gen Z, instilling these qualities through mentoring and guidance is particularly crucial.

Patience is a virtue that allows individuals to navigate challenges with resilience and composure, while impatience can lead to rushed judgements, hasty actions and a lack of thorough consideration for consequences. In a fast-paced world, cultivating patience becomes a valuable asset, enabling Gen Z to approach situations with a calm and thoughtful demeanour. Through mentorship, experienced individuals can share their own journeys of facing setbacks, emphasizing the importance of perseverance and patience in achieving long-term goals.

Now let's consider the art of listening. It is a skill that goes beyond hearing words; it involves understanding, empathizing and appreciating different perspectives. Effective mentors can guide the younger generation in developing active listening skills, fostering better communication and creating an environment of mutual respect. By honing this ability, Gen Z can build stronger relationships and contribute meaningfully in collaborative settings.

Humility is another important quality that encourages continuous learning and openness to diverse ideas. Mentors play a pivotal role in imparting the value of humility, sharing their experiences of growth and acknowledging that everyone, regardless of age or position, has room for improvement. This fosters a culture of humility, where Gen Z understands the significance of continuous self-reflection and learning.

The ability to work with multiple stakeholders, each with unique perspectives, is an essential aspect of today's interconnected world. Mentoring can provide practical insights into navigating complex relationships, resolving conflicts and finding common ground. Exposure to real-world scenarios allows Gen Z to develop adaptability and collaborative skills, preparing them for the multifaceted nature of professional environments.

Introducing coaching for the next generation, especially for Gen Z scions, can prove to be a valuable approach to usher them into the intricacies of the family business. Coaching provides a structured and personalized environment for learning, offering insights, guidance and skill development tailored to individual needs. This proactive strategy not only imparts practical business knowledge but also nurtures essential leadership qualities. It complements the foundational values instilled at home by providing targeted business knowledge, leadership development and strategies for navigating the complexities of the professional world. While family values and behaviour at home play a crucial role in shaping individuals, coaching remains a distinct and indispensable component in developing the skills and perspectives required for success in the family business.

A coach can help Gen Z scions understand the nuances of family dynamics, business operations and industry trends, fostering a well-rounded perspective. Coaching introduces an external, structured approach that goes beyond the familial environment, offering tailored guidance, insights and skill-building exercises. This intentional investment in coaching can contribute to their growth, instil confidence and equip them with the tools needed to navigate the unique challenges of the family business landscape.

∞

Having said all of the above, drawing comparisons between previous generations and Gen Z when it comes to their behaviour in their youth is a flawed approach. Each generation is shaped by unique societal, technological and cultural factors, resulting in distinct values, attitudes and behaviours. Therefore, it is important to recognize and appreciate the differences rather than imposing outdated expectations or standards on the new generations. Instead of comparing, it is more productive to understand and adapt to the evolving needs, preferences and characteristics of Gen Z individuals, fostering an environment that empowers them to thrive and contribute positively.

In succession planning, it is imperative to understand social and market shifts as well as disruptions in the business landscape. This requires a proactive approach to mapping the skill sets available within the family and identifying areas where additional expertise may be required. While family members bring unique insights, experiences and values to the table, blending their expertise with that of non-family professionals can enrich the succession planning process and enhance the overall capabilities of the organization. By leveraging a diverse talent pool and embracing collaboration across generations and backgrounds, family businesses can navigate complexities, seize opportunities and ensure sustainable growth and success for the future.

RE-PURPOSE: WHAT'S NEXT FOR A RETIRING LEADER

I often jest with clients from Indian business families, asking them how they spend their time outside the office if they don't indulge in common vices like smoking, drinking, affairs, golf or deep religious practices. It might seem light-hearted, but it points to a real challenge. For many business leaders, work is not just a facet of life but a core element, and sometimes a vice too.

Retiring from a leadership position is a monumental life transition, one that brings forth a myriad of emotions and uncertainties. The decision to step down from a leadership role can be both liberating and daunting. For many retiring leaders, the toughest question that looms large is how to repurpose their time, skills and identity in the next phase of their journey. They may find themselves at a crossroads, unsure of what lies ahead. It is a deeply personal and often lonely mental battle, as they grapple with questions of purpose, legacy and contribution to society.

For seasoned promoters, contemplating the daunting transition from leading their organizations to stepping down marks a profound and often lonely journey. Having dedicated decades to building reputable enterprises, they now face the enigmatic 'day zero' where their role transforms. These founders, who have given their all to their ventures, are confronted with a unique challenge as they navigate the uncharted waters of transitioning from the helm.

Each founder's journey through this transition is inherently distinctive, defying a one-size-fits-all approach. Advising a founder to simply 'relax and retire' is not just impractical, it is unrealistic. Many of these individuals lack non-work-related hobbies, leaving a significant void as they grapple with how to fill the 14 to 16 waking hours they once dedicated to their companies. The crucial question arises: what becomes their new purpose in life?

The crux of successful succession planning lies in uncovering this new purpose. While consulting firms may offer services rooted in analytical skills and competency mapping, the essence lies in delving into the founder's post-retirement purpose. This process demands trust-based, hierarchy-less conversations. The success of succession planning pivots on a fundamental starting point—intent. To shift from individual-led enterprises to institutionalizing businesses, the critical exploration of the 'why' behind succession becomes paramount.

It is not just about finding a replacement but about guiding these founders towards a new chapter in life that aligns with their values and aspirations beyond the business realm. The art of succession planning is, at its core, a nuanced understanding and fulfilment of the founder's post-leadership purpose.

Amidst the uncertainty of the shift, there is an opportunity for renewal and reinvention. Retiring leaders have the chance to explore new passions, pursue long-neglected interests, and redefine their sense of purpose beyond the confines of their professional roles. Whether dedicating time to family, pursuing hobbies or engaging in philanthropic endeavours, retirement offers the freedom to prioritize personal fulfilment and well-being.

Navigating this transition requires introspection, resilience and a willingness to embrace change. Retiring leaders may benefit from seeking support from peers, mentors or professional counsellors to navigate the emotional complexities of this transition. By reframing retirement as a new chapter filled with possibilities rather than an end to their career, they can embark on a journey of self-discovery and create a fulfilling and meaningful post-retirement life. To find out this purpose, ask yourself these questions:

1. What passions or interests, outside the realm of work, have always intrigued or fascinated me, and how can I integrate them into my post-retirement life?
2. In envisioning a day without work-related commitments, what activities bring me a genuine sense of joy and fulfilment?
3. If the primary focus shifts from running the business to contributing in a different capacity, what kind of legacy do I aspire to leave behind for the family and the enterprise?

4. How can I leverage my wealth of experience, skills and network to contribute meaningfully to areas or causes that align with my values and vision?
5. As I transition away from the daily operations, what personal goals and milestones do I wish to achieve, and how can I structure my time to make these aspirations a reality?

As the curtains draw on the illustrious careers of business family heads, it is a moment to bask in the glow of achievement, to reflect on the legacy woven through dedication and grit. The journey, marked by triumphs and challenges, has sculpted not just businesses but narratives of resilience and determination. For these stalwarts, the transition from the helm is an opportunity to witness their creations flourish in new hands.

Letting go is no surrender; it is an acknowledgement of triumphs and lessons learned. The baton passes to the next generation or capable non-family professionals not as a forfeiture but as an investment in the future. It is an act of generosity, sharing the wisdom and expertise garnered over years of hard-fought battles.

The retiring business heads should wear their achievements as a badge of honour, recognizing that they have achieved more than they might have imagined. The wealth they leave behind isn't merely financial; it's a treasure trove of experiences, values and a blueprint for overcoming adversity. As they contemplate the next chapter, it is an opportunity to lend their experience to new endeavours or philanthropic pursuits. The inner voice beckons with a myriad of possibilities, each resonating with the echoes of a lifetime of decisions, innovations and growth.

Retirement is not a conclusion but a prologue to new narratives waiting to unfold. Whether mentoring the next generation, immersing in passion projects or contributing to societal betterment, the retiring leaders stand at the threshold of reinvention. The canvas may change, but the colours of their legacy will continue to paint stories of inspiration and influence.

CHOOSING THE RIGHT ADVISOR

Choosing the right advisor for your succession planning is crucial for the long-term success and sustainability of your family business. This is so for several reasons. Firstly, they bring expertise and experience to the table, guiding the family through the complexities of succession planning with confidence and clarity. A skilled advisor can provide valuable insights, identify potential challenges and recommend effective strategies to ensure a smooth transition of leadership.

Additionally, a good advisor acts as a trusted confidant and mediator, fostering open communication and collaboration among family members. They understand the nuances of family dynamics and can navigate sensitive issues with empathy and diplomacy, ensuring that everyone feels heard and valued throughout the process.

Moreover, a qualified advisor can customize their approach to suit the unique needs and circumstances of the family business, ensuring that the succession plan aligns with the family's values, goals and vision for the future. They can also collaborate effectively with other professionals, such as lawyers and financial planners, to develop comprehensive plans that address all aspects of succession.

On the flip side, choosing the wrong advisor can have detrimental effects on the succession planning process. An inexperienced or ill-suited advisor may overlook critical factors, provide inadequate guidance or create unnecessary conflicts within the family. This can result in delays, inefficiencies and ultimately, a loss of faith in the idea of succession planning itself.

Unfortunately, there have been instances in India where families have experienced such negative outcomes due to poor advisory support. These examples serve as cautionary tales, highlighting the importance of selecting the right advisor for succession planning. By choosing a qualified and compatible advisor, families can navigate the complexities of succession planning with confidence and ensure a successful transition for future generations.

Here is a checklist that can help you ensure that you have on board the right advisor:

1. **Experience:** An advisor with extensive experience in succession planning brings valuable insights and proven strategies to the table. They understand the intricacies of different family businesses and can tailor their approach to suit your specific needs, ensuring a smoother transition.
2. **Expertise:** Succession planning involves complex legal and financial implications, requiring specialized knowledge and expertise. A knowledgeable advisor can navigate these intricacies effectively, offering strategic advice and recommending best practices to safeguard your family's legacy.
3. **Understanding of family dynamics:** Family dynamics play a significant role in succession planning. An advisor who understands these dynamics can navigate sensitive issues with empathy and diplomacy, fostering open communication and consensus-building among family members.
4. **Strategic vision:** A strategic advisor can offer insights and long-term planning strategies to align succession plans with your family's overall goals and vision. They can help you anticipate future challenges and opportunities, ensuring a smooth transition of leadership.
5. **Communication skills:** Effective communication is key to successful succession planning. An advisor with strong communication skills can facilitate open dialogue among family members, fostering collaboration and decision-making while ensuring everyone feels heard and valued.
6. **Holistic approach:** Succession planning should consider not only financial and legal aspects but also family values, culture and legacy. An advisor with a holistic approach can help you develop comprehensive plans that address all aspects of succession, ensuring continuity and alignment with your family's values.
7. **Understanding the aspirations of the younger generation:** As the next generation takes on leadership roles, it is essential to have an advisor who understands their aspirations and perspectives.

This ensures that succession plans incorporate modern context while respecting family values and heritage, bridging generational differences effectively.

8. **Collaborative approach:** Succession planning often involves collaboration with other professionals, such as lawyers, accountants and wealth managers. An advisor who can collaborate effectively with these professionals ensures that all aspects of your succession plans are well-coordinated and integrated.
9. **Customization:** Every family business is unique, with its own set of needs, goals and circumstances. A customized approach allows the advisor to tailor their recommendations and strategies to meet your specific requirements, ensuring a personalized and effective succession plan.
10. **Confidentiality and speed:** Confidentiality is paramount in succession planning, and an advisor who can maintain confidentiality while expediting the process ensures that sensitive information remains secure. Speed is also crucial to avoid delays and uncertainty, and a committed advisor can devote sufficient time and resources to ensure thoroughness and efficiency.
11. **Empathy:** Empathy is essential in navigating the emotions and concerns of family members during succession planning. An empathetic advisor can foster trust and collaboration, ensuring that everyone feels supported and valued throughout the process.
12. **Ethical standards:** An advisor who adheres to high ethical standards prioritizes the best interests of the family and business above all else. They ensure transparency, integrity and fairness in all their dealings, maintaining trust and credibility throughout the succession planning process.
13. **Commitment to education:** Succession planning requires ongoing education and staying updated on the latest trends, regulations and advancements. An advisor committed to continuous learning can provide informed guidance and recommendations, ensuring that your succession plans remain relevant and effective over time.

By considering these qualities when selecting an advisor for succession planning, you can ensure that you have a trusted partner to guide you through this critical process effectively. Remember, this checklist is not exhaustive but provides a good indicator of core essentials that your advisor should bring to the project.

INTROSPECTION FOR THE HEAD OF FAMILY

Succession planning is undeniably one of the toughest challenges for the head of a family business. While much of the attention in succession planning is rightfully directed towards the individual successors, whether they are children or other family members, the burden of ensuring the successful transition and future prosperity of the family lies squarely on the shoulders of the family head. As the leader and steward of the family's legacy, the family head carries the weight of not only their own aspirations and expectations but also those of past generations and future descendants.

The family head must navigate a complex web of familial dynamics, business considerations and personal emotions to develop a succession plan that balances the needs and desires of multiple stakeholders. They must grapple with the tension between preserving tradition and embracing change, ensuring continuity while fostering innovation and promoting unity while respecting individual aspirations. Moreover, the family head often faces the daunting task of grooming and preparing successors who may have differing levels of interest, aptitude or commitment to the family business.

At the heart of the challenge is the realization that the decisions made during succession planning will have far-reaching implications for the family's cohesion, prosperity and legacy. Every choice carries the weight of ensuring the family's continued relevance, resilience and growth in an ever-evolving business landscape. Thus, while the spotlight may shine on the individual successors, it is the family head who must bear the responsibility of steering the family through the complexities of succession with wisdom, foresight and unwavering dedication to the collective well-being of the family and its legacy.

'What-next' is a philosophical contemplation, an introspective exploration into the intertwining roles of a business leader, a family figurehead, and an individual seeking meaning beyond the boardroom. The head must grapple with questions of identity and purpose, recognizing that the legacy they built is evolving into a collective narrative carried forward by the next generation. This is to ensure that the legacy is not limited to financial success but extends to values, culture and impact on society. For the head of an Indian business family, 'what-next' becomes the poignant essence of succession planning, intertwining the threads of their personal and professional lives. This juncture transcends mere business decisions; it marks a transition where the legacy is entrusted to the next generation, blending familial values with strategic foresight.

In the professional sphere, 'what-next' necessitates a judicious selection of a successor, someone not merely capable but aligned with the ethos of the family business. The head must contemplate the future direction of the industry, embracing innovation without forsaking foundational principles. This involves meticulous planning, mentorship and a visionary approach to ensure that the business not only endures but thrives in dynamic landscapes.

On the personal front, 'what-next' encapsulates the head's aspirations beyond the boardroom. It prompts reflections on the legacy they wish to leave, the balance between familial bonds and individual pursuits, and the impact of their decisions on both personal fulfilment and the family's continued prosperity.

Succession planning is not a mere formality or a checklist item; it demands a genuine and profound intent from the heads of business families. Intent is the driving force that distinguishes a strategic succession plan from a mere legal document. It is the commitment to ensuring the continuity and prosperity of the family legacy, transcending financial structures.

When succession planning lacks sincere intent, it risks becoming a hollow exercise, akin to drafting a legal will without embodying the spirit of the family's values and aspirations. Intent brings life to the plan, aligning it with the overarching purpose of preserving the family's identity and values and impact on the business landscape.

Heads of business families must recognize that intent shapes the entire succession narrative. It is not just about passing on assets but about fostering a legacy built on principles, innovation and resilience. Without genuine intent, the plan risks becoming a mere transaction, detached from the emotional and strategic considerations that make succession planning truly effective.

❧

The head grapples with multifaceted roles—that of a business leader, a family figurehead and an individual seeking deeper meaning beyond the confines of the boardroom. This introspective exploration goes beyond the tangible aspects of wealth transfer; it encompasses the intangible elements that constitute the essence of a family legacy.

In the pursuit of answering the 'what-next' question, the head engages in a soul-searching journey. They navigate the delicate balance between ensuring the business's sustained success and safeguarding the principles that have defined the family's journey. This contemplation extends beyond immediate concerns, emphasizing the enduring impact of decisions on future generations and the broader societal context.

This introspective process is both personal and collective. It involves reconciling individual aspirations with the familial vision, understanding that the legacy goes beyond bricks and mortar. It is woven into the fabric of relationships, imbibed in the family's ethos and etched into the community it serves. As the head grapples with 'what-next,' they navigate not just the intricacies of succession planning but also the profound responsibility of steering a legacy that transcends time and space.

Succession planning, therefore, becomes a deeply personal and professional odyssey. It demands a delicate dance between tradition and innovation, family ties and corporate responsibilities. The head's vision, values and wisdom become guiding stars for the 'what-next' narrative, shaping not only the future of the family business but also the trajectory of familial relationships and the legacy etched into the annals of business history.

❧

In business families, it is imperative to recognize that past success does not guarantee future performance. The dynamism of markets, evolving consumer behaviours and the ever-changing global landscape demand a proactive and strategic approach to succession planning. Relying solely on historical achievements may inadvertently jeopardize the financial rewards for successive generations. The essence of wealth preservation lies not in resting on laurels but in anticipating, adapting and grooming leaders capable of navigating the uncertainties of the future. Proactive succession planning is not just a pragmatic choice, it is a fiduciary responsibility to ensure that the legacy endures and financial rewards continue to be reaped, resilient to the unpredictability that defines the business landscape. Failure to acknowledge this reality risks compromising the very foundation upon which the family's success was built. In this paradigm, foresight becomes the linchpin for sustained prosperity, transcending the illusion that past triumphs alone can secure the future.

In such circumstances, the role of the head is not just that of a leader but also a steward of a legacy, responsible for its preservation and continuity. As the custodian of the family's entrepreneurial journey, the head of the family business bears the weighty responsibility of ensuring a seamless transition to the next generation. The head of a business family shoulders a multifaceted array of roles, each demanding a nuanced understanding and a delicate balance. Professionally, they act as the chief architect of the family's economic engine, navigating the complexities of the business landscape. Their leadership is not confined to the boardroom; it extends to governance, where they are stewards of the family's values and principles.

The head is a guiding force for family members, providing mentorship and fostering an environment conducive to personal growth. They wear the hat of a familial figurehead, ensuring cohesion and unity while navigating the intricacies of interpersonal relationships within the family structure. Socially, the head is a representative of the family, contributing to the broader community and industry. Their decisions have implications not only for their immediate kin but also for the employees, partners and stakeholders connected to the business. In this context, they act as ambassadors, shaping the family's reputation and impact beyond the business.

The head serves as a strategic visionary, steering the enterprise through evolving market dynamics. They are not just a manager of profits and losses but an architect of sustainable growth, innovation and adaptability in an ever-changing business landscape. In the industry, their role extends to being a thought leader, influencing and shaping the sector's direction.

Regulatory and compliance responsibilities rest heavily on the shoulders of the family head. Ensuring that the business operates within the legal frameworks, adheres to ethical standards and contributes positively to societal welfare becomes part of their daily agenda.

This introspective journey becomes paramount as it sets the stage for a succession plan that is not merely a transfer of titles but a deliberate and thoughtful process guided by fairness, neutrality and merit. The questions in this chapter delve into the fundamental considerations that every family business leader should confront, aiming to lay the groundwork for a succession plan that not only reflects the family's values and aspirations but also ensures the sustained success of the business across generations.

The impending handover of leadership in a family business is a pivotal moment that demands introspection from its current head. Beyond the day-to-day operations, this introspection involves a deep dive into the core values, aspirations and potential pitfalls that may affect the seamless transition of the business to the next generation.

❧

Families often engage in discussions about succession planning with genuine intent, recognizing its significance for the long-term well-being of both the family and the business. However, the absence of a tangible deadline can lead to a lack of urgency in translating these discussions into actionable plans. To address this, it is imperative to instil a sense of commitment and accountability among family members by treating succession planning as a key performance indicator (KPI) for each individual involved.

When viewed through the lens of a KPI, succession becomes a measurable and trackable metric for family members. Each individual's contribution to the succession process is evaluated, emphasizing the importance of active participation. This approach shifts the mindset from considering succession planning as a distant task to an ongoing and integral aspect of family governance.

Integrating succession planning into regular family meetings or forums reinforces its status as important to the family. These discussions become a platform for evaluating the effectiveness of the plan, addressing challenges and adapting strategies as needed. These discussions would result in various inputs for introspection by the Head of the Family.

Family succession planning demands a delicate blend of heart-to-heart and hard conversations, intertwining emotions with strategic realities to navigate the intricacies of leadership transitions. The heart-to-heart talks delve into the emotional fabric of the family, addressing sentiments, aspirations and concerns that often lie beneath the surface. These conversations require an environment of trust and empathy, allowing family members to express their individual visions, fears and expectations openly. Discussing values, legacies and the emotional investment in the business lays the foundation for a succession plan deeply rooted in familial understanding.

Conversely, the hard talks plunge into the pragmatic and strategic aspects of succession. These discussions involve dissecting the business landscape objectively, evaluating the competencies of potential successors and aligning individual aspirations with the overarching goals of the enterprise.

An alignment of values and visions emerges as a crucial bridge between the sentimental and pragmatic dimensions of succession planning. For instance, understanding a family member's deep connection to a particular aspect of the business may lead to a strategic decision to preserve that element in the succession plan.

The questions presented here are not just prompts for consideration; they are invitations to embark on a reflective journey, setting the stage for a succession plan that not only passes the baton but also preserves and enhances the essence of the family's entrepreneurial spirit.

QUESTIONS TO ASK YOURSELF

1. What are the long-term goals and values that define our family business, and how can these be communicated effectively to the next generation to guide their involvement in the succession planning process?
2. Have we identified and nurtured the potential successors within the family who possess the requisite skills, knowledge and commitment to lead the business forward?
3. Is there a clear understanding of each family member's strengths, weaknesses and aspirations, ensuring that succession decisions are based on merit rather than favouritism or preconceived notions?
4. Have we established transparent criteria for evaluating potential successors, considering factors such as education, experience and alignment with the family's values and business vision?
5. What measures are in place to address potential conflicts or power struggles among family members during the succession planning process, and how can these be mitigated to foster a harmonious transition?
6. Are legal structures, such as trusts or family constitutions, in place to provide a clear governance framework for the succession plan, ensuring fairness and equity in decision-making?
7. How can we promote an open and inclusive culture within the family, encouraging honest communication and active participation in the succession planning discussions?
8. Have we considered external perspectives, such as seeking advice from impartial advisors or mentors, to bring objective insights and ensure that the succession plan aligns with industry best practices?
9. What educational initiatives are in place to prepare the next generation for leadership roles, providing them with the necessary skills, knowledge and exposure to effectively manage the business?
10. Are there contingency plans in case unforeseen circumstances impact the succession plan, and how can the family remain agile and adaptable to changes in the business landscape or family dynamics?

EPILOGUE

As we reflect on the landscape of family businesses in India, it is evident that they play a pivotal role, contributing significantly to the nation's GDP. With 79 per cent of the national GDP attributed to family businesses and the top 111 publicly-traded family-run companies valued at a staggering USD 839 billion, the impact of these enterprises cannot be overstated.* India stands as the third-largest home to family businesses globally, a testament to their enduring presence and influence in the economy.**

Yet, despite their prominence, Indian family businesses face a myriad of challenges that demand attention and proactive solutions. While many are micro or small enterprises, particularly prevalent in the service sector, the tradition of multi-generational involvement remains strong. However, issues surrounding succession planning and business continuity loom large, highlighting the need for strategic foresight and planning.

In particular, family businesses lag in the adoption of digital technologies, which should be a key priority, posing a significant hurdle for future growth and competitiveness. In addition, the absence of a written code of conduct or clearly defined values for family members, otherwise often passed down through oral instructions, underscores the need for greater clarity and alignment. The lack of clear job definitions and retirement plans for senior family members also perpetuates uncertainty and hampers effective governance.

Despite these challenges, there is optimism for the future. With an increasing trend of women's involvement in managerial roles and a growing awareness of the importance of succession planning, there is

---

*Sood, Sunil, 'Ushering India's Family Businesses into a New Era of Endless Possibilities', *The Economic Times*, 11 February 2022, https://tinyurl.com/yzdu5x9w. Accessed on 10 January 2025.

**'PwC's 11th India Family Business Survey', *PWC*, 15 December 2023, https://tinyurl.com/3eh22t2n. Accessed on 10 January 2025.

a sense of momentum towards positive change.

The path forward for Indian family businesses will require concerted efforts to address these challenges, embrace digital transformation and foster a culture of transparency, accountability and innovation. The winners in this journey will be those who dare to dream, but also proactively plan their succession, ensuring the continuity and success of their legacies for future generations. The best is yet to come for Indian family businesses, and with dedication and strategic foresight, they will continue to thrive and shape the future of the nation's economy.

As we conclude this book, it is essential to reflect on the myriad lessons learned, challenges faced and opportunities seized along the way. While the road to succession is fraught with complexities, emotions and uncertainties, it is also brimming with potential for growth, renewal and legacy-building. Throughout this book, we have covered the multifaceted aspects of succession planning, from the importance of clear communication and governance structures to the nuances of talent development and wealth preservation. We have witnessed the evolution of family businesses in the face of shifting market dynamics, technological disruptions and changing social norms. We have celebrated the triumphs of visionary leaders who have navigated succession transitions with grace and foresight, and we have mourned the missteps of those who faltered in the face of uncertainty.

At the heart of our exploration lies a profound understanding that succession planning is not merely a transactional process but a deeply human endeavour. It requires empathy, trust and collaboration among family members, stakeholders and external advisors. It demands a willingness to embrace change, adapt to new realities and envision a future that honours the legacy of the past while embracing the opportunities of the present. It underscores the importance of resilience, perseverance and humility in the face of adversity and uncertainty.

As we gaze into the horizon, we see a world teeming with possibilities for business families. The digital age has ushered in a new era of innovation, disruption and interconnectedness, reshaping the very fabric of commerce and society. In this rapidly evolving landscape, the imperative for succession planning has never been greater. Business families must rise to meet the demands of the times, leveraging technology, talent and tenacity to ensure continuity and relevance for generations to come.

In closing, let us remember that succession planning is not merely about passing the torch from one generation to the next; it is about stewardship, legacy-building and the enduring quest for excellence. It is about nurturing relationships, fostering talent and preserving values that transcend time and tide.

I cannot conclude this epilogue without extending my heartfelt wishes to you as you embark on your own succession-planning journey. May the wisdom you have gained and the lessons you have learned serve as guiding lights along the path ahead. Remember, the road to succession may be filled with twists and turns, but with courage, compassion and a steadfast commitment to your vision, you have the power to navigate through any challenge that comes your way.

Good luck! And may your journey be filled with abundance and prosperity!

QUESTIONS YOU MAY HAVE

This section is designed as a reiteration of key points discussed throughout the book, highlighting questions of prime importance that families must address when navigating the complexities of business and succession planning. While some of these have been covered earlier, this focused compilation serves as a quick reference guide to provoke thought, encourage dialogue and ensure no critical aspect is overlooked. These questions are meant to reinforce understanding, spark introspection and prioritize actionable steps.

1. How do I navigate the complexities of maintaining a balance between family dynamics and selecting the most competent leader for the business?
2. In the absence of a clear successor from within the family, what strategies can be employed to identify and groom external talent?
3. How can I ensure a fair and transparent succession process that minimizes conflicts and maintains family harmony?
4. What steps should be taken to prepare the next generation for leadership roles, both in terms of skill development and exposure to business operations?
5. If multiple family members express an interest in leadership, how do I manage potential rivalry and foster collaboration?
6. What role can professional advisors play in guiding the family through the complexities of succession planning, and how do I choose the right advisors?
7. How do I address the challenges of integrating diverse skills and perspectives when bringing in non-family professionals to lead the business?
8. What strategies can be employed to ensure a smooth transition and minimize disruption to ongoing business operations during the succession process?
9. How do I prepare for unforeseen circumstances such as sudden illnesses or unexpected events that may impact the succession plan?

10. In the context of evolving market trends and industry disruptions, how can the family business stay agile and innovative in its approach to succession planning?
11. What if you realize your child is not smart enough to run the business?
12. What if you think your grandkid is better to lead your group, instead of your son?
13. How should the family approach succession planning when faced with a significant age gap between potential successors, and what considerations come into play?
14. In the event of sudden wealth or financial windfalls, how can the family ensure responsible management of resources and prevent negative consequences on the succession plan?
15. When a family member leverages familial connections for networking and business opportunities, how does this factor into the succession plan and potential concerns from other stakeholders?
16. How can the family address the challenge of feuding siblings during the succession planning process, and what strategies promote unity rather than internal conflicts?
17. In cases where non-family employees view family members with scepticism, how can the family build trust and demonstrate competency to the broader professional team?
18. When family members are highly involved in social activities and events, how does this impact their perception within the business, and how can it be managed in the context of succession planning?
19. What steps can the family take to balance the preservation of historical legacy with the need to embrace contemporary trends and innovations during succession planning?
20. How should the family handle situations where external stakeholders view the business with scepticism due to perceived dynastic practices, and what measures can be taken to address these concerns?
21. How does the family navigate succession planning in the event of a divorce, and what impact does it have on the family business?
22. In cases of family splits or disputes, what strategies can be employed to ensure a fair distribution of business assets and responsibilities?
23. How should the family address poor behaviour or ethical lapses

among potential successors, and what implications does this have on the overall succession plan?

24. What considerations should be taken into account when dealing with the presence of illegitimate or unacknowledged children in the context of succession planning?
25. If there is a history of sibling rivalry or strained relationships within the family, how can these dynamics be managed during the succession process?
26. In the case of family members who may not be interested or committed to the business, how can their roles be redefined or addressed in the succession plan?
27. How does the family handle situations where the chosen successor lacks the necessary skills or qualifications for the role?
28. What role does gender play in succession planning, and how can the family address traditional gender roles and expectations?
29. In the face of generational divides and differing visions for the business, how can the family create a succession plan that accommodates diverse perspectives?
30. If a family member exhibits poor behaviour or ethical lapses, how can the family address these issues within the succession planning framework, and what implications might it have?
31. How should the family handle situations where a potential successor has a track record of strained relationships or conflicts with key stakeholders, and how might it affect the succession plan?
32. In cases where a family member faces mental health challenges or addiction issues, what role should these factors play in succession planning decisions, and how can support be provided?
33. How can the family navigate the complexities of splitting business assets in the case of sibling rivalries or disputes during succession planning?
34. When faced with a potential successor who lacks genuine interest or commitment to the business, how can the family address concerns about dedication and effectiveness in the role?
35. How can the family approach succession planning when a potential successor has a history of external relationships that might affect their reputation or standing within the family enterprise?

These questions are not just a checklist but a friendly handholding, guiding you to introspect deeply and navigate the complexities of succession planning. While some of these questions may seem difficult to answer quickly, they are an essential part of the journey, prompting you to reflect on all contours of your family dynamics and business aspirations. Addressing them thoughtfully is not about rushing to conclusions but about building clarity and intentionality, laying the groundwork for a legacy that endures across generations.

ACKNOWLEDGEMENTS

I am grateful for the input, advice and time that leading business leaders, board members and professionals shared with me. I bow in recognition of their commitment and wisdom. I also extend my gratitude to all the sources referenced throughout this book. If any source has inadvertently been omitted, I offer my sincerest apologies. I appreciate the efforts that every thinker takes to articulate their creative ideas, a task I discovered to be arduous and that requires tremendous discipline.

My heartfelt thanks go to the numerous stakeholders who generously shared their insights, experiences and knowledge. A special acknowledgement is reserved for the business families who graciously allowed me to be a part of their journey, sharing the intricacies of succession planning. Your openness and trust have been invaluable in shaping the narrative of this book.

I am indebted to family office leaders, tax experts, legal advisors, management advisors, consultants, heads of family philanthropy entities and knowledge partners whose extensive experience enriched this work and added layers of depth to the discussions. Your perspectives have been instrumental in creating a resource that transcends individual limitations.

To the operational leaders within family enterprises, thank you for offering real-world insights and practical perspectives. Your on-the-ground experiences have been essential in translating the theoretical concepts into the pragmatic realities of family businesses.

My *pranam* to my Guru, Swami Shekaranand, for his guidance and for teaching me to introspect everything but chase nothing.

A special thank you to Rupa Publications for giving wings to my project for its eventual flight—Dibakar Ghosh and Shatarupa Dhar, thank you for refining my ideas and words. And Rajesh Mahapatra, thank you for initiating the conversation between me and Dibakar. Serendipity works its magic through people.

I cannot express enough thanks to the few close friends who have been my rock in the past few years. You know who you are. A hearty gratitude.

And of course to all readers who picked up my book, a massive thank you for diving into the pages. In case you have any feedback, kindly send an e-mail to srinath75@gmail.com.

Finally, a special thanks to 'my dear girls' for their support and patience with my idiosyncrasies while writing this book, and otherwise! I reflect on the strength I had to muster to embark on this journey and realize that it is because you stand by me. This book is for you. Kalyani, Ninupta and Sannuta—you rock, and you are my rock.

BUSINESS FAMILY IDIOMS

There are several commonly used phrases or statements that can often be heard in business families, covering several aspects of discussions, succession planning and family dynamics. This is not to generalize the family discussions, but to bring familiarity around numerous topics or views or biases that do exist. Needless to say, the flavour of some of these phrases may have been lost in translation from various Indian languages to English. The hope, however, is that the essence has remained.

1. Tradition is non-negotiable; it is what built this empire.
2. In this family, we prioritize loyalty over competence.
3. Succession is a family matter; no need for external interference.
4. Our family legacy is at stake; we can't afford to experiment.
5. Business is in our blood; it is not a career choice, it is destiny.
6. We have always done it this way; no need for unnecessary changes.
7. Hard work alone builds character; book smarts don't guarantee success.
8. Business and family are inseparable; personal and professional lines blur.
9. We have faced tougher challenges before; we'll overcome this too.
10. Success is measured by the size of our empire, not individual happiness.
11. Wealth is a privilege, not a right; don't question the family fortune.
12. Outside perspectives are irrelevant; only the family truly understands.
13. Money speaks louder than words; success is seen, not discussed.
14. Conflict is a sign of weakness; we present a united front to the world.
15. In this family, we solve problems internally; no need to involve outsiders.
16. Growth means maintaining control; don't dilute our family authority.
17. External consultants won't understand our unique family dynamics.
18. Marriages should strengthen the family network, not introduce external influences.

19. Public image is everything; internal issues stay behind closed doors.
20. You inherit more than the business; you inherit the family's reputation.
21. Failure is not an option; we can't afford to tarnish the family name.
22. Innovation is overrated; stick to what has always worked for us.
23. Business decisions are not open for debate; the eldest makes the call.
24. You can't escape family responsibilities; it is your duty to carry the legacy.
25. Diversification is a distraction; focus on what we have always excelled in.
26. Succession planning is for outsiders; we know our family's natural leaders.
27. We don't air our internal conflicts; it is a sign of weakness.
28. We built this from the ground up; do not take it for granted.
29. Success is about maintaining the status quo, not rocking the boat.
30. The family business is not a democracy; it is a hierarchy.
31. Wealth is a tool for control; never let it slip out of family hands.
32. Outside education is supplemental; real learning happens in the family business.
33. You can't choose your family; loyalty is not optional.
34. Risk is for outsiders; we play it safe to protect the family fortune.
35. Delegation is a sign of weakness; true leaders are hands-on.
36. The family crest represents more than a business; it is our heritage.
37. You can't escape the family bubble; it defines who you are.
38. We don't apologize for success; it is our birthright.
39. You don't have a job; you have a role in the family enterprise.
40. Adaptation is overrated; we stick to our proven methods.
41. The family elders know best; their decisions are final.
42. Legacy preservation is your responsibility; don't let the family down.
43. We don't discuss personal issues in the boardroom; it is unprofessional.
44. Your success is the family's success; individual achievements are secondary.
45. Trust is reserved for family members; outsiders must earn it.
46. Elders lead; questioning their decisions is disrespectful.

47. Entitlement comes from birthright; never forget your position in the family.
48. Success means maintaining family unity at all costs.
49. In our family, wealth equates to influence; do not underestimate its power.
50. Family gatherings are not just social; they are strategic planning sessions.
51. The family business is a man's world; women have other roles to fulfil.
52. Inheritance is based on gender; sons carry the legacy, daughters find their place elsewhere.
53. Marriage outside the community is a threat to our family's purity and traditions.
54. We don't discuss mental health in our family; it is a sign of weakness.
55. Succession planning considers lineage, not competence; blood matters more than ability.
56. Wealth should stay within the family; outsiders dilute our financial power.
57. Adoption disrupts our bloodline; it is not a solution for succession.
58. We do not need diversity; our family values are strong enough.
59. Business acumen skips a generation; the young ones lack the wisdom to lead.
60. We don't trust external professionals; they don't understand our family dynamics.
61. Modern education is overrated; it doesn't prepare our youth for the family business.
62. Couples must stay together for the sake of the family image, regardless of personal happiness.
63. Family disagreements stay within the family; we don't seek external mediation.
64. Older generations set the rules; the youth should blindly follow them.
65. Mental health struggles are a private matter; don't air your problems in public.
66. Succession planning doesn't consider skills; it is predetermined by birth order.

67. Daughters should marry into wealth; sons are the providers in our family.
68. The family's reputation is more important than individual happiness.
69. Favouritism is natural; certain family members are more deserving of opportunities.
70. We don't invest in external ventures; our wealth is for family enterprises only.
71. Age comes before merit; elders' decisions are unquestionable.
72. Children are assets for the family business, not individuals with personal aspirations.
73. Divorce is a stain on the family name; unhappy marriages are sustained for appearances.
74. Family history determines leadership; individual achievements don't matter.
75. We don't recognize any other marriage except between a male and a female; it goes against our family values.
76. Failure is a disgrace to the family; it is better to hide mistakes.
77. Family gatherings are not for open discussions; stick to safe, superficial topics.
78. We don't need external training; our family culture imparts all the necessary skills.
79. Business and family are separate; personal problems don't affect professional decisions.
80. Success is predetermined; hard work alone won't change your fate in our family.
81. Family elders have veto power; their decisions override all objections.
82. Disability is a family secret; it is not discussed openly.
83. We don't entertain interfaith marriages; it disrupts our religious and cultural harmony.
84. Succession isn't open for debate; the eldest is the natural leader.
85. We don't embrace technological advancements; our traditional methods have always worked.
86. Political neutrality is crucial; we don't want external influences impacting our family.
87. Maternity leaves are discouraged; women should balance family and work seamlessly.

88. Education abroad is discouraged; it may expose our youth to conflicting values.
89. We don't recognize the accomplishments of non-family employees; they are not part of the legacy.
90. Social standing is tied to family standing; maintain our societal reputation at all costs.
91. Financial independence is secondary; reliance on family resources is expected.
92. Succession disputes are not for public knowledge; we handle them internally.
93. Marriage is a business alliance; emotions should not cloud the family's financial interests.
94. We don't believe in retirement; elders continue to guide the family until the end.
95. Wealth determines respect; family members with financial success are esteemed.
96. Failing in the family business is not an option; it is a betrayal of our legacy.
97. We don't recognize non-traditional family structures; adhere to the conventional model.
98. External friendships are discouraged; family members should be each other's primary allies.
99. Individual aspirations should align with family goals; personal dreams are secondary to the family's collective vision.
100. Family values are non-negotiable; they dictate our way of life and decision-making.